THE SOUTHERN WAY

CONTENTS

© Kevin Robertson (Noodle Books) and the various contributors 2014
ISBN 978-1-909328-17-4
First published in 2014 by Kevin Robertson
under the **NOODLE BOOKS** imprint
PO Box 279
Corhampton
SOUTHAMPTON
SO32 3ZX
www.noodlebooks.co.uk
editorial@thesouthernway.co.uk

Printed in England by
Berforts Information Press Ltd.

David Lindsell kindly submitted this image of former 4SUB unit No 4348 coupled to a motley collection of withdrawn stock 'resting' on the truncated remains of the Longparish branch. The coaches were destined to be stored for some time - the wooden chock will be noted and also the 'currant-bun' - condemned symbol. Little in the way of obvious vandalism is apparent, the cab window perhaps the only example, was this even removed officially? Hugh Abbinnett (retired Eastleigh driver), recalls having to collect stock from the branch after it had languished there for some considerable time. He commented that as it had not moved for so long it was almost seized, so much so that a hefty jolt was needed to makes the wheels revolve, at which point body flexing caused any number of the windows to break with showers of glass resulting.

Front cover - The 'electric' southern. I am sure like many this is the Clapham Junction we recall: electric units seemingly everywhere and of an infinite number of types. Approaching is a 4SUB, No 4356, which from the 'V' symbol is on a 'Waterloo circular' via Teddington.

Editorial

So where do we go from here? I will admit as each issue of 'SW' 'goes to bed' mild panic almost sets in '..have I got enough for the next issue and is it what the readership wants'? On the first count I will admit there is actually plenty in hand for several issues, a number of our regular contributors kind enough to supply a variety of pieces from which I can pick and choose. Then there are also the promises made - occasionally a gentle 'nudge' may be required but again the person concerned invariably comes up trumps. Finally there are the unsolicited submissions, again always welcome, and usually from those who already read 'SW', gentlemen (and the occasional lady), we thank you all. I should perhaps add I also have a number of items which have been purchased, passed / left to, acquired etc (it sounds more polite than 'beg, borrow and steal' although DO NOT take the last phase literally), and with these it is simply a question of finding the time to actually sit down and complete the necessary research / compilation. Hence in response to my own initial panic, we are actually in a strong position.

But, and this is the question, is it what people want? I worry that 'SW' and indeed every periodical has to appeal to two distinct markets, firstly that of the enthusiast-historian, and secondly the enthusiast-modeller. So putting it bluntly how much more is there to say on, 'Bulleid / Clapham Junction / signal boxes etc etc'? New original research is indeed welcome but I am also conscious we can only regurgitate the same history so many times using different words.

So to a question, and this IS over to all of you, 'Tell me what it is you would like to see'. I may know someone who has that information - but no guarantees.

Personally there is no end of subjects I would ideally wish to see covered but have so far failed to convince anyone to do, examples being SR turntables, signal box design, goods workings and so on. You will gather then, any takers?

I will now turn to the topic of books. Once upon a time producing a book on almost any subject was also almost a guarantee every High Street retailer would take copies in quantity. Print runs in the high four-figures were commonplace, I can assure you it is a very different situation today. The High Street book shops are but a shadow of what they once were.

I might then offer a piece of advice, if you have an idea for a book, try same with your preferred publisher, but if that does not work then why not have a go yourself. It is not as difficult as might at first seem, but with the key component not unit cost but distribution. You may have the best book in the world, and let us be fair every author will feel that about his particular subject, but several hundred or even thousand sat on a warehouse floor is not the ideal scenario. An accountant friend once said to be about business, 'never speculate what you are not prepared to lose', wise words indeed. Some may even recall the late photographer and author Geoff Gammell, he had his own publishing imprint 'GRQ' - not sure the intended initials (which stood for 'Get Rich Quick') ever really worked for him.

For those of you who have got this far fear not, this is not a dispirited or disillusioned editor 'going off on one' instead it is one who is genuinely concerned as to the future. I say this for two reasons, firstly the spectrum of our hobby is so vast: history old and new, motive power steam/diesel/ electric, signalling etc, add to that present day modelling, relics, preservation. I could go on. It seems to me that so many operate solely within their own little field and as if to prove this on the occasions when I have attended a railwayana auction it is with an almost totally different clientele to that seen at shows or when visiting a preserved railway. Trying to find a product that will appeal to all factions of a diverse hobby is not easy.

Finally on this topic I will add a perhaps sadder but poignant point. In 2013 I attended three funerals of former railwaymen, one a very senior man indeed. Listening to and discussing with his former colleagues it was immediately apparent that here was a group who have very often remained in the shadows so far as the enthusiast is concerned. If then you are involved in research, do not omit the managers, some of their revelations were indeed eye-opening.

So having gone around a number of topics where have we got to? Simply this, tell me what you would like to see in 'SW' but perhaps don't be surprised if I throw it back at you to have a go yourself. *IF* you have an idea for a book and no one seems interested then have a go yourself. And in the meanwhile we will keep filling Southern Way with articles on both mainstream and the obscure - and thank you all for both contributing to and reading the results.

Kevin Robertson

Pages 2/3 - N15 No 30805 'Sir Constantine' against a backdrop of the Ashford coal stage on 23 July 1953. Reported as 'new to traffic' in January 1927, it spent all but six months of its life on the Central and Eastern sections before finally coming to Eastleigh on 14 June 1959. Five months later it was withdrawn, being reported as having been cut-up before the end of the year. The official record (with thanks to 'The Book of the King Arthur 4-6-0s' from Irwell Press), reports to it having remained with tender number 922 throughout its life and having covered a total mileage of just over one million miles under steam. The engine spent seven years at Ashford from June 1950 onwards. Colour Rail 208812D / I Davidson
Rear cover - A dismal day for the 'Belle', Brighton 4 December 1971. Mark B Warburton courtesy Mrs Margaret Warburton

*The 'Cenotaph' coaling tower at **Exmouth Junction MPD** had a steel canopy with the motor house at the top and a steel balance weight on either side. The reinforced concrete bunker served two locomotive roads. The tower dates from the MPD rebuild of the late 1920s. The other 'Cenotaphs' on the Southern were at Stewarts Lane, Nine Elms, Feltham and Ramsgate. Although they improved coaling productivity, they tended to crush the softer coals into dust. AFP 1959.*

SOUTHERN COAL REVIEW

Alan Postlethwaite

Coal and the Firebox

Coal is decayed vegetable matter that has been laid down, buried and compressed in geological time to produce a solid substance that can be burnt. Burning releases the **solar energy** that was absorbed chemically by the plants in photosynthesis. The youngest coals are called peat and the oldest are anthracites. In between is a wide range of ligneous and bituminous grades.

Coal produces heat in the locomotive firebox by the combustion of carbon, hydrogen and sulphur to make carbon dioxide, water vapour and sulphur dioxide. When sulphur dioxide cools, it combines with water vapour to produce acids that corrode boiler parts. A **low sulphur** content is therefore desirable in locomotive coal.

A low **ash content** is desirable to minimise the work of coal and ash handling and to minimise the production of clinker on the grate. This is a hard deposit formed by the fusion of sulphur with ash. Clinker is difficult to break up and remove and reduces the output of the boiler if it is allowed to build up. The invention of rocking grates in the 1860s helped to resolve this problem.

The ideal **coal size** for a locomotive is about a fist. Larger lumps can be broken by the fireman's pick and hammer but dust can pass through the boiler incompletely burnt to become an environmental nuisance as grits or sparks. Dust can be minimised by using a hard coal which is mined by hand.

The ideal locomotive coal is therefore hard and low in sulphur, ash and suitable for mechanisation. Many anthracites meet this specification but pure anthracites can be difficult to ignite and keep alight on the grate because they are low in **volatiles**. These are the gaseous and liquid hydrocarbons which are released when coal is heated.

Anthracites also tend to be difficult and expensive to mine. Anthracite locomotives were nevertheless developed in the USA. The earliest designs had a thick bed, an oversize firebox and a centre cab. Their ungainly

*The shovel is the common tool of coal yards. Bunkers were commonly made of old railway sleepers, sometimes longer baulks of timber, but at **Shepton Mallet Charlton Road** they were concrete blocks. The grounded coach is a Midland clerestory with side corridor connections. The embankment beyond carries the GWR's East Somerset line. AFP 1962.*

appearance earned the name Camelback or Mother Hubbard.

To meet early environmental regulations to 'consume their own smoke', early British locomotives burned **coke**. This was made in coking ovens which drive off the volatiles. The porosity of coke makes it easier to burn than anthracite but coke is more expensive than coal. So there was an incentive to devise ways to burn coal economically without making dark smoke. Ideas evolved to introduce a **secondary chamber** to burn off the volatiles. Of the ten or so variations, the designs most relevant to the Southern were as follows:

In 1845, **Joseph Beattie** of the L&SWR developed a front-and-rear double firebox which was complicated and costly to make. His well tanks had this firebox until they were reboilered by Adams from about 1880.

In 1853, **Matthew Kirtley** of the Midland Railway, together with Charles Markham, developed the brick arch with secondary air. This was the simplest and cheapest of the designs and it became standard world-wide.

In 1857, **James Cudworth** developed a side-by-side double firebox with two fire doors. Although costly to maintain, the SER, LC&DR and LB&SCR persevered with it for several decades (Ref. 1).

Low-grade bituminous coals can be high in dust and ash. They are especially high in **slack** which is waste from coal processing. The railways had to use them at times, especially after 1939 when there were coal shortages, resulting in reduced locomotive performance. To compensate for this, designers such as Gresley, Stanier and Bulleid turned to a wide firebox whose extra weight was supported on a trailing pony truck. Only the Great Western had continuous access to high quality coals (from South Wales) which is why GWR kept to the narrow firebox with no need for a pony.

The **table** below shows some typical analyses of different types of British coal. Fixed carbon is the carbon content after volatiles have been removed. The best British locomotive coals were semi-anthracitic (or semi-bituminous) from South Wales.

Some **moisture** in coal is unavoidable. It is undesirable because the latent heat of evaporation reduces the heat output of the firebox. Moisture content is variable, occurring naturally and enhanced by the processes of mining, washing, storage and transport in all weathers. Locomotive crews may also dampen coal in order to reduce wind-blown dust.

Coal Handling at MPDs

Some large Southern depots had 'Cenotaph' towers with wagon hoists. Others had covered stages, either high-level with a wagon ramp or low-level with a crane and a bottom-opening skip. Early cranes were steam powered with a boiler behind the cab. Later cranes had an electric hoist on a transverse overhead gantry rail. At small MPDs and stations, coal stages were open to all weathers. Coal was sometimes shovelled direct from wagon to locomotive. Baskets and wheeled belt conveyors were also used.

Locomotive Fuel Sources

The **Canterbury & Whitstable** was the world's first public steam railway, opening to passengers and freight in 1830. Northumberland coal was one of the goods already

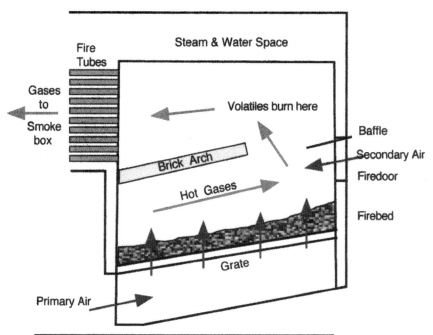

The Standard Firebox with Brick Arch and Secondary Air

Fuel Type	Peat	Lignite	Bituminous	Semi-anthracite	Anthracite	Coke
Fixed Carbon %	26	31	45 < 80	70	80 < 86	91
Volatiles %	52	25 < 36	9 < 19	9	3 < 9	1
Ash %	4	4 - 6	3 < 12	< 10	5 < 10	5
Sulphur %	< 1	< 1	1 < 5	0.5	< 1	< 1
Moisture %	< 75	25 < 55	18 < 38	7 < 10	7 < 10	2

being carted by road to Canterbury from a primitive wharf at Whitstable. Coal had been shipped to the Thames from NE England from around 1200 and before that by the Romans. The C&W sought to take over and expand all goods traffic by building a more substantial harbour at Whitstable. This opened in 1832.

Shunting at **Whitstable Harbour** was primarily by horse, a practice that continued until the C&W closed in 1953. Until cranes were introduced in the early 20th century, the coal was unloaded at Whitstable by a process called 'whipping'. Men would jump from a quayside trestle holding a rope which raised a basket from the ship through pulleys. This was repeated until the basket could be tipped into a wagon (Ref. 2).

The C&W's first locomotives burned coke shipped from the North-east. When the SER took over the C&W in 1844, it built its own **coking ovens** at Whitstable Harbour. The ovens opened in 1848 to supply the whole of the SER. This caused much pollution in Whitstable town, effectively concentrating all the SER locomotive smoke in one place. The SER's transition to coal lasted until 1881 when the Whitstable ovens closed.

The **London & Greenwich** was London's first passenger railway. Opened in 1836, its coke was supplied by the Phoenix Gas Light & Coke Co. from ovens in

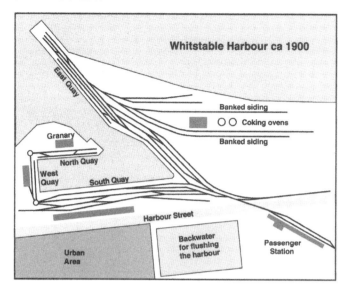

Thames Street near Greenwich pier. The L&G also built ovens of their own at Deptford Creek but with a short life (1836-38), and may never have been used in earnest. They would have lit all the stations and the whole L&G line with gas (Ref. 3).

Running powers over the L&G were granted to the London & Croydon (1839), London & Brighton (1841) and

A covered locomotive coal siding with steam crane at **Brighton MPD**. *Just visiting is GWR Dukedog No. 9017. JJS 1962.*

Gillingham MPD had a covered coal stage with transverse hoist gantry. Classes Q and N attend. Roger Goodrum Collection 1955.

SER (1842). To relieve congestion into **London Bridge**, the SER and L&C opened the **Bricklayers Arms** branch in 1844. These termini may have taken coke from gas works at Bankside or the Old Kent Road. The latter was supplied via the Grand Surrey Canal.

The **LB&SCR** opened wharves at Shoreham Harbour (1840), Deptford Wharf (1849) and Battersea Wharf (1858). Their coke ovens were at Kingston-on-Sea near Shoreham and at New Cross. The latter opened in 1849, managed by Cory and supplied from Deptford Wharf (Ref. 4). We do not know if they supplied Battersea MPD. The LB&SCR subsequently changed to coal delivered via the GWR at Acton.

The **Bodmin & Wadebridge** was Cornwall's first steam railway, opening in 1834 with fuel shipped to Wadebridge. Trials were conducted in 1835 with coke, Tredegar coal and Liverpool coal (Ref. 5). Without a secondary chamber, it is unlikely that Liverpool coal would have complied with smoke regulations.

The **L&SWR** opened Nine Elms in 1838 and Southampton Terminus in 1839. Coke ovens were built at Nine Elms wharf and at Northam MPD. The latter were still there in 1870, supplied via a tramway from Northam Quay. The L&SWR

gradually changed to rail-borne coal, supplied principally via the GWR at Salisbury.

When the **East Kent Railway** opened from Strood to Faversham in 1858, it hired six coke-burning Crampton locomotives from the GNR and bought six new Cramptons in the same year. Coal was already being imported from the North-east at Faversham Creek, the most likely location for coking ovens. It would have been carted to the MPD until the Faversham Creek branch opened in 1860. Rochester was another possible source of coke.

The **LC&DR** reached Victoria in 1862 and the West London line opened a year later. This gave access to rail-borne coal from the Midlands or Wales but we do not know how soon coal arrived this way or the source of LC&DR coke in London. Blackfriars Bridge station opened in 1864 but we do not know what types of goods were handled at its low-level wharf. It is unlikely that coal was hoisted in bulk from this modest wharf.

Records of Southern locomotive coal sources for the next hundred years are sketchy. We get only glimpses. The sheds themselves would not have known every source. It is beyond the scope of this review to attempt a moving picture of all locomotive coal sources. Broadly, the SR sources were mainly South Wales and Kent with the rest coming from the Midlands and the North.

Industrial Coal

The Southern did not have the big manufacturing industries of the Midlands and the North but it did have thousands of smaller works which used rail-borne coal until superseded by electricity, oil and natural gas.

Gas works supplied town gas until natural gas took over in the 1960s. This created major coal traffic for the railways. Inland works were supplied from the Midlands by rail or from the North-east by sea and then rail. Sydenham gas works was supplied by rail from Erith's coal wharves by some circuitous routings (Ref. 6).

During the 20th century, inland **power stations** created railway coal traffic. Croydon power station was supplied originally from Deptford Wharf, then from Betteshanger colliery and finally by road from Durham colliers unloaded at Kingsnorth (Ref. 7). Built by the L&SWR in Wimbledon, Durnsford Road power station took rail-borne coal for nearly fifty years. The LB&SCR, on the

Opposite middle - The high-level covered coal stage at **Redhill MPD** with class H15 No. 30331. Steel barrows transferred the coal from wagon to locomotive. JJS 1960.

Opposite bottom - Ground stacking of coal was sometimes done to create a strategic reserve. At **Folkestone MPD**, class R1 Nos. 31128 & 31340 simmer alongside. JJS 1952.

Above - Deptford Wharf supplied bituminous coal to much of South London for domestic and industrial uses. JJS 1954.

other hand, took power from Deptford power station of the London Power Company using sea-borne coal. If SE&CR electrification had gone ahead, it would have been supplied from a new power station at Angerstein Wharf using sea-borne coal. When the SE&CR suburban system was eventually electrified by the SR, this too was supplied from Deptford power station.

In addition to the wharves already mentioned, there were others at Cattewater, Exmouth and Fremington in Devon and at Medina on the Isle of Wight, all supplying both industrial and domestic coal by rail.

Coalfield Traffic

The **Kent coalfield** was worked from the 1890s until 1986. Principal uses were domestic, gas works, power

*Right: Opened by the L&SWR in 1915, **Durnsford Road** power station was sited between the EMU sheds and the main line. An electric locomotive pushed wagons up the ramp to the boiler bunkers. There was additional storage of coal beneath the concrete section of the ramp. Half a mile to the south, Wimbledon also had a municipal power station whose coal was supplied by rail. The Bournemouth express here is headed by LN class No. 30863* Lord Rodney. *CH 1958.*

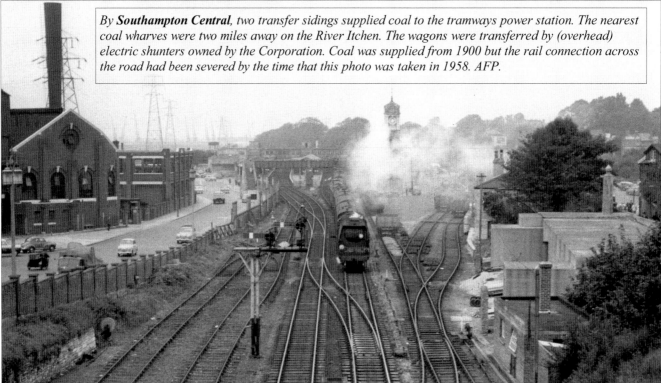

*By **Southampton Central**, two transfer sidings supplied coal to the tramways power station. The nearest coal wharves were two miles away on the River Itchen. The wagons were transferred by (overhead) electric shunters owned by the Corporation. Coal was supplied from 1900 but the rail connection across the road had been severed by the time that this photo was taken in 1958. AFP.*

stations, steel works and local industries. Nearly all the mines had rail connections. Indeed, the EKR (the second of that name) was built specifically to connect mines to the SE&CR. Road and sea transport were sometimes preferred because they were cheaper. Bowater's paper mill at Sittingbourne was supplied by ship from Tilmanstone colliery via an overhead ropeway to Dover. Facilitated by the Dartford tunnel, Kent coal was sent to Newcastle by road for the steel industry (Ref. 8). But Kent coal went by rail to the Sheffield steel industry.

Richborough Port was built by the government during the First World War with a rail connection facing north to Minster. After the war, the EKR built a branch to Richborough from the south but it only carried freight and had a short life (Ref. 9). In the early 1960s, the northern branch was rebuilt to supply Kent coal to Richborough power station using bottom-hopper wagons. Ten years later, the power station was converted to burn heavy fuel oil supplied by rail from the BP refinery at Grain. In a final twist, the port was redeveloped in the late 1980s to import Venezuelan Orimulsion for the

The 4 Principal Mines ⊙ and Rail Connections in East Kent

Dover colliery, also known as Shakespeare colliery, took over the abandoned SER workings of the Channel Tunnel. Located just west of Shakespeare tunnel, it was worked from 1890 until 1915. The mine was never a success, being prone to flooding. The site was reactivated in the 1990s during construction of the Channel Tunnel. Archive Images.

This page - The Dover colliery at Shakespeare Cliff again. In the top view there is what appears to be a Manning Wardle 0-4-0T just visible.

(RCHS Spence Collection.)

power station.

The **Somerset coalfield** had over fifty collieries and produced coal from the 15th century until 1973. The earliest workings were horizontal adits and bell pits (near the surface) with transportation by cart. The Somerset Coal Canal was worked from around 1800 until 1898. It connected to the Kennet & Avon canal and supplied coal as far east as Reading (Ref. 10).

The Bristol & North Somerset Railway opened to Radstock in 1873, becoming part of the GWR which won the lion's share of the Somerset coal traffic. The **S&DJR** line to Bath opened in 1874 and served seven collieries at Radstock, Midsomer Norton and Chilcompton. Most of the SD&JR's Somerset coal traffic ran northwards onto the Midland system. There was also through coal traffic

Right:
*A badly parked wagon at **Tilmanstone**. The axle box castings read GCR, suggesting coal for Sheffield steel making. AFP 1961.*

*Below: **Writhlington** colliery was a mile east of Radstock. The S&DJR 0-4-2 saddle tank was one of three built at Highbridge, working from 1882 until 1929 (Ref. 13). Archive Images.*

southwards of lower grades of coal from the Midland Railway on to the L&SWR system.

It would appear that little **locomotive coal** came from the Somerset coalfield - a survey of October 1943 shows that just 283 tons of locomotive coal were supplied (Ref. 11). But in Kent, railways became the main user of Chislet coal. Both coalfields produced a range of bituminous and anthracitic coals depending upon the particular pit and the seams being worked. The reasons for not taking more local coal may have been technical or price. One paper on the new Bulleid Pacifics describes Kent coal as 'rubbish' but does not say in what respect. Too low in volatiles, perhaps, or too much slack?

During the 20th century, binders were used with slack to make **ovoids** or briquettes but with little success. Ref. 12 reports that ovoids broke into dust during loading and made black smoke. There were also poor results with pulverised coal, mechanical stoking and oil firing.

Domestic Coal

Sometimes supplemented by coke from gas works, domestic coal was predominantly bituminous until the 1956

Top: Bagnall 0-4-0 saddle tank No. 2848 of 1956.
Middle: Pecket 0-4-0 saddle tank No. 2014 of 1951.
Both: Steve Price, 1971, Monorail, Geoff's Pages website.

*Both: Two of the industrial locomotives that shunted coal wagons at **Croydon power station**. Each wagon was emptied on a rotary tippler to feed covered belt conveyors to the boiler bunkers (as seen in the top photo).*

*Bottom - Served by the S&DJR, **Norton Hill** colliery was on the southern outskirts of Midsomer Norton. Archive Images.*

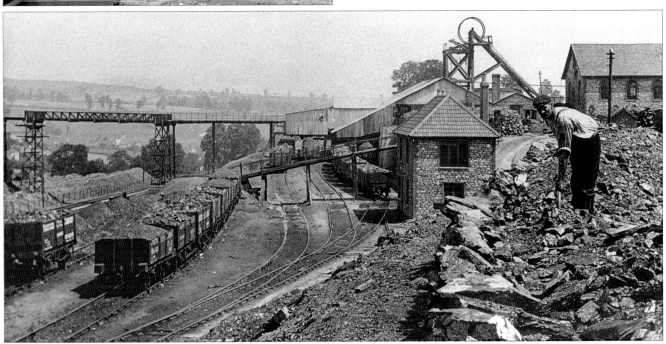

Clean Air Act after which the more costly (but smokeless) anthracite became the norm. Coal was the principal goods traffic at many local yards when they closed in the 1960s and 70s. There were also **foreign coal yards** in South London as follows (Ref. 14):

> Brockley Lane (L&NWR & GNR)
> Elephant & Castle (GNR)
> Falcon Lane (L&NWR)
> Knights Hill (L&NWR)
> New Cross Gate (GNR)
> New Wandsworth (GWR)
> Peckham Rye (MR & L&NWR)
> Walworth Road (MR)

Left: The Midland Railway's **Walworth Road** coal drops opened in 1871. There were three wagon turntables and a traverser to position each wagon on a bottom-emptying side spur (most of which were covered). Photographed from the signal box looking north, the locomotive here is LMS 'Jinty' class 3F No. 47203. JJS 1956.

Below: Journey's end in the old goods yard at **Callington**. The three piles of coal are of different grades including some 'nutty slack'. AFP 1958.

*The coal merchant's facilities at **Brasted** - a 10 ton steel mineral wagon, a heap of domestic coal, a weighing machine and wooden steps to a grounded box van. Full sacks would be stored there for direct loading onto the lorry. AFP 1959.*

*In 1959, coal was the one remaining goods traffic at **Mayfield**. The sylvan setting is idyllic. AFP.*

*In 1940, railway lines surrounded **Tilmanstone** colliery. The bridge in the centre was a public footpath, the miners' only access to their model village at Elvington and to Elvington Halt on the EKR. Subterranea Britannica website.*

*Yorkshire 0-6-0 saddle tank No, 2498 was built in 1951 for United Steel subsidiary Samuel Fox at Stocksbridge near Sheffield. Sold to the NCB in 1959, it worked **Chislet** colliery until 1969. It was bought by the Quainton Railway Society in 1970 and given the name* Chislet. *Frank Jones.*

__Chislet__ colliery was worked from 1918 until 1969 when the market for locomotive coal collapsed. The remaining collieries closed in 1986 following a year-long strike.

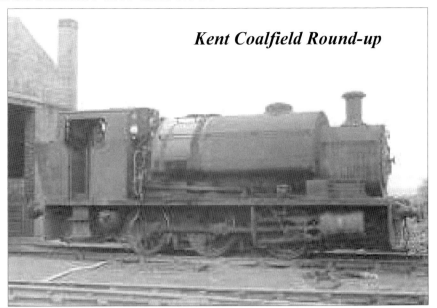

Kent Coalfield Round-up

Above - *With miners dressed for wet conditions, a ceremonial bucket of coal is raised at Snowdon colliery. Archive Images.*

Opposite bottom - Guilford *colliery was a mile to the south-east of Shepherdswell. Its rail connection was to the EKR at Eythorne. Starting in 1906, three shafts were sunk but they never reached productive coal seams and the colliery was dismantled from 1932 (Ref. 15). This photo is from 1910. In contrast to Tilmanstone, the only railway siding here was the run-round loop. Subterranea Britannica website.*

*The loading sidings at **Tilmanstone** colliery in 1940. Subterranea Britannica website.*

*At the time of closure, this new face at **Betteshanger** would have been the next to be worked.*   *Jim 'Overman' collection.*

Bluebell Photographic Credits

Abbreviated photographic credits herein are of Alan Postlethwaite (AFP), Collin Hogg (CH) and John J. Smith (JJS). Their complete collections can be perused on the Bluebell Railway Museum Archive website.

Acknowledgements for Help and Advice

Members of Kent History Forum, KentRail, Southampton Industrial Archaeological Society, Coalfields Heritage Initiative Kent (CHIK), Buckinghamshire Railway Centre and Greater London Industrial Archaeological Society.

References

1. Wikipedia, James Cudworth.
2. Phillips, Terry, *Harbour History and Operations of the Canterbury & Whitstable Railway*, Simply Whitstable website.
3. http://marysgasbook.blogspot.co.uk/2009/08/greenwich-railway-gas-works.html
4. Greater London Industrial Archaeological Society, Journal No. 6, 1996.
5. Whetmath, CDF, *The Bodmin & Wadebridge Railway*, Forge Books, 1994.
6. Postlethwaite, Alan, *St Johns Station, Lewisham*, Southern Way Issue 8, 2009.
7. Catford, Nick, *Disused Stations* website, Mitcham.
8. Davies, Jim, private communication.
9. Cole, Terry, *The East Kent Railway in its Dying Years*, Southern Way Issue 23, 2013.
10. RK Bluhm, *The Somerset Coalfield 1790-1820* website.
11. *Coal Disposals in October 1943*, Bristol and Somerset Coalfield Regional Survey Report, HMSO, 1946.
12. Andrews, Roger, *The Last Steam-age Fireman Part 3*, Southern Way Issue 23, 2013.
13. Atthill, Robin, *The Picture History of the Somerset & Dorset Railway*, David & Charles, 1970.
14. Course, Edwin, *The Foreign Goods Depots of South London*, Railway Magazine, November 1960.
15. Subterranea Britannica website, Guilford colliery.

NEW IMAGES OF 'LEADER'

The story of 'Leader' has been told elsewhere with little in the way of substantive new information emerging since, although occasionally the odd new photograph does appear.

Ironically the views on this page had once resided less than five miles from where I was researching the subject, yet they lay hidden until discovered, quite by chance, at the NRM.

The location is of course Eastleigh, with No 36001 seen (left) running 'bunker first' on the up-through line en-route from the shed to collect its test train from the carriage sidings alongside what was then Platform 4. No dates are given whilst the quality of the images we will admit is not perfect. But on the basis of rarity they are certainly worth including. At bottom the engine has halted at the north end of the station - a signal gantry (out of sight) - would determine when the engine had permission to proceed. Even before the trial has started there is clearly some investigation going on from the man in the 'six-foot' whilst the machine is also the subject of interest from the platform. (Apologies for the 'shading' of the engine, caused by the emulsion lifting on what was a small size glass plate.) All the views show the engine with No 2 (bunker) end leading. This was a condition of the one crew from the 'relief' gang prepared to work the engine. For the fireman it would have made little difference, but the driver at least was saved the heat radiating off the smokebox door which protruded into the cab at the opposite (No 1) end.

No 36001 was eventually 'dismantled' at Eastleigh after the decision was made not to continue with the venture. The word 'dismantled' is used deliberately - and carefully - as it has since been learnt that whilst some parts were certainly scrapped as being of no further use, others were retained. But what might these have been and consequently what might they have been used for? It just goes to prove that the enigma of 'Leader' still persists today. (Nos 36002-4 were 'broken up'(?) at Brighton.)

Further information on No 36001, may be found in 'The Leader Project: Fiasco or Triumph' - 978 0 86093 628 2.

Top - Here No 36001 has coupled to its train, the headcode has been changed and it looks as if it will soon be time for departure. Of particular interest is the existence of the Bulleid coach in the formation immediately behind the dynamometer car - quite appropriate of course. We know that the weight of the test train was slowly increased day-on-day, possibly meaning this was the extra vehicle added for this day. (No dates unfortunately.) What makes the view so interesting is that this is the only time Leader has ever been seen coupled to a Bulleid coach. The number of observers in the cab will be noted.

Middle- ...and getting away. The excess steam escaping from the cylinders at either end could well be an indication this was one of the early tests before the engine was taken into works for new rings to be fitted. Before this the practice had been to run the engine up and down a siding 'light' so everything expanded in the heat, thereby making for a more 'steam-tight' situation. Not surprisingly this was commented upon by the test crew on the basis that to continue attempting to test the engine in this condition was simply not worthwhile - hence the works visit.

Bottom - …and getting away. There appears to have been a lack of consistency over the use of the headcode on the runs north: the use of the electric marker light in the middle image will be noted. In theory after Eastleigh it was 'next stop Basingstoke ('for water and examination'.) And over that 18-mile journey Leader would use more lubricating oil than a diesel did fuel over the same distance… .

The EPB Story Part 4: The Ten-car Scheme

David Monk-Steel

(Previous instalments appeared in SW20, 24 and 25.)

The Ten-car Scheme - The Concept

Following the decision not to proceed with the double-decker, British Railways laid plans to resurrect the idea of using ten-car trains on the Eastern Section. They proposed to start using them progressively from 1954. This decision was reached for a number of reasons, of which the general unpopularity of the double-decker with the general public and the fact that the power distribution system was to be renewed in any case, were prime factors.

Power Supply

The Southern Railway, when providing electricity for traction purposes within each scheme, had adopted the latest available technology. The London and South Western Railway had their own generating station at Durnsford Road, Wimbledon, and distributed power through lineside cables to sub-stations where high voltage (11,000 volts) alternating (25 cycles per second/Hz three phase A.C.) current was transformed to traction voltage (600 to 660 volts) and rectified to direct current using rotary converters. These large electrical machines required constant supervision, and the actual track feed and security of supply was controlled manually at each sub-station. The London, Brighton and South Coast Railway who used A.C. traction did not require the rectification machinery, and purchased their current from an established power generation company, the London Power Supply Co., who had a generating station at Deptford. After grouping the Southern Railway, who had adopted the D.C. system as standard, chose to purchase power from the same source, and therefore all the power for the suburban area was generated either at Durnsford Road or Deptford and distributed along radial feeders.

When the Southern later extended the third rail to outer suburban locations, (and for the main line schemes) in the mid 1930s, power supply technology had moved on, and the Sevenoaks and Windsor schemes were supplied directly from the new National Grid, at the standard industrial frequency of 50Hz. at 33,000 volts. This was transformed at substations to 660 volts D.C. as before but was passed through mercury arc rectifiers to turn it into the D.C. needed for traction. Furthermore the new sub-stations could be un-manned and controlled remotely from Electrical Control Rooms. The supply feeders were also arranged in the form of a 'Ring Main' that gave a more reliable supply.

Both Deptford and Durnsford Road Generating Stations were bombed during World War 2 and although repaired, problems of age and unreliability had been reported with the 11,000 volt A.C., 25 Hz distribution system. A report by the Southern Railway Electrical Engineer C. M. Cock in May 1946 had concluded that the power distribution network in the inner suburban area was becoming inefficient, and following approaches from the London Electrical Supply Co. to decide whether they should renew the Deptford Power Station like for like, or up-grade to supply at the now standard 33,000v 50hz, the Southern Railway concluded that the latter course was more economic in the long term and therefore preferable, but nationalisation intervened, and it was left to the Railway Executive in October 1949 to give it the 'go ahead'. It was finally approved in November 1950 which also helped to sway the decision on 10-car operations, as the power for longer trains would now be more easily provided from an up-graded system.

Frequency change

To implement the plan would require the existing electricity control and distribution system to be replaced, virtually a complete re-electrification of the Southern Region suburban area. The old manned rotary converter substations would be closed and in a few cases demolished, others would be used to house the new remote-controlled mercury arc rectifier sub-station equipment and switch-gear but new sub-stations would also have to be built. Additional track sectioning control switchgear would also be provided either in the original buildings or new brick huts, known as Track Paralleling huts. The old oil-filled lineside cables, which followed each line suspended from concrete posts and which conducted the high voltage A.C. supply from the switch room at Lewisham to the sub-stations, would be replaced. In their place a 'ring main' for the higher voltage would be installed of a similar pattern to that used for the

'Mission critical - Borough Market Junction. The photographer has his back towards London Bridge with, on the right the curve to Cannon Street and, straight ahead, the lines towards Charing Cross. The numerical headcodes are: '16' Charing Cross - Sevenoaks' and '10' Charing Cross - Bromley North'.

This time the service is even more intense with a ten-coach train, including a brand new BR Standard 4EPB at the head, on the elevated approach to London Bridge from Borough Market Junction. Note that on the top of the bridge girder at the extreme left hand side of the picture are the asbestos cement conduits which have been attached. These enclosed the new feeder cables and the 'pilot' cable which carried supervision and control signals.

electrification extensions to the Medway towns and Sussex coast. The new cables would usually be contained in concrete troughs or in asbestos cement ducting, and would be accompanied by a remote control and supervisory cable to enable the Electrical Control Room Operator to exercise absolute control from a new control centre built alongside the old one at Lewisham. This was the arrangement for the South Eastern lines, but similar work would take place for the Central (former Brighton) Section at Selhurst, and at Raynes Park for the Western Section. Each section would however, be interconnected.

The use of industrial frequency at 50Hz rather than at 25Hz would allow the Southern Region to draw power from a number of Central Electricity Authority (CEA) supply points. Power would be transformed by the CEA to 33,000V A.C (or 66,000V at Deptford) from their National Grid, and was already supplied at Northfleet (for the Sevenoaks and Medway schemes), Tunbridge Wells, (for

the Sevenoaks scheme), Croydon, Three Bridges and Fishersgate (for the Brighton scheme), Eastbourne and Hastings (for the Hastings scheme), Byfleet and Wymering (for the Portsmouth scheme), Leatherhead (for the Mid-Sussex scheme), and Reading. For this scheme the supply would come from Northfleet, Deptford [at 66kV to Nunhead, Brockley, Lewisham and South Bermondsey], Wimbledon [replacing Durnsford Road power house], Leatherhead and Croydon.

The new substations were a great deal less obtrusive or interesting than the giant red brick 'cathedrals' that they replaced. The original buildings had a stark industrial grandeur with their clerestory roofs, large metal-framed, arched windows, and cages full of buzzing transformers. The new buildings were squatter, with a flat roof and a very paltry louvred 'turret', where the rectifier lurked. They did not even have the same character as the pre-war rectifier substations, the most visible of which is probably the one on

Chelsfield down platform. The transformer was situated outside the building, attached to it by cables, whilst inside was the rectifier and its associated cooling apparatus, the remote control switchgear and workshop facilities for the technicians who might occasionally wish to carry out maintenance. The buildings were operated un-manned.

Implementation on the Eastern Section

Each scheme was tackled on a route-by-route basis. The Charing Cross to Dartford route via Bexleyheath was ready by June 1954 with good progress on other routes at this time. The scheme was fully completed by 1957. New cables were run out on the line side to supply the mains power. These were placed in the new concrete troughs and conduits, but the old pole-mounted cables remained in place for many years afterwards at a lot of locations. The following table describes the provision of the new sub-stations.

Beyond Gravesend and Orpington the 1935 rectifier sub-stations were retained.

Authorisation of Ten-car scheme

Following the decision to up-grade the power supply, the final decision to abandon the double-decker scheme was taken in December 1950. The ten-car scheme was authorised by the Railway Executive at the same time. The lines between Charing Cross, Cannon Street and Dartford, Gravesend, Sevenoaks, Bromley North, Addiscombe, Sanderstead and Hayes and stations in between would be reconstructed to permit ten-coach suburban trains to operate, and new rolling stock would be provided.

On a line-by-line basis the works required were as follows:-

Charing Cross to Dartford via Bexleyheath (Stage 1)

BERMONDSEY	Built into underline arches	14/06/1954	Beneath line
LEWISHAM	Existing building adapted and new control room built	From 23/11/1953	Down side between St. Johns and Lewisham
ELTHAM WELL HALL	New building provided	05/03/1954	Up side in Goods Yard
SHOOTERS HILL (Eltham Park)	Old building decommissioned and demolished	05/03/1954 (Demolished two years later)	Down side at country end.
BEXLEYHEATH	New building	05/03/1954	Up side in Goods yard
BARNEHURST	Existing building decommissioned, and used as TP Hut	10/02/1956	Up side at country end
SLADE GREEN	New building	14/05/1954	Down side between Station and Carriage Depot
DARTFORD JUNCTION	Existing building adapted	21/03/1955	In fork between North Kent and loop lines
HITHER GREEN	New building	09/07/1954	Up side at London end
GROVE PARK	Existing building adapted	20/01/1956	Up side at Country end
CHISLEHURST	Existing building adapted	26/11/1954	Up side, north of former LCDR line
MOTTINGHAM	Old building decommissioned and demolished	09/07/1954 (demolished later)	Up side alongside station
NEW ELTHAM	New building	09/07/1954	Up side between New Eltham and Mottingham
SIDCUP	Existing building adapted	04/05/1956	Up side between Bexley and Albany Park
GREENWICH	New building	01/10/1954	Up side London side of station
CHARLTON	Existing building adapted	07/12/1956	Down side alongside station
PLUMSTEAD	Existing building adapted	23/08/1957	Down side in Goods Yard east of station.
BELVEDERE	Existing building adapted	03/02/1956	Up side alongside station
STONE CROSSING	New building	16/07/1954	Up side on top of embankment country side of station
NORTHFLEET	Old building decommissioned and sold	14/06/1954 (Sold later)	Down side alongside station.
NORTHFLEET	New building	14/06/1954	Up side between Gravesend and Northfleet
CATFORD	Existing building adapted	08/02/1957	Up side adjacent Catford Loop line flyover
ELMERS END	New building, old building retained	1955?	Down side alongside station
WEST WICKHAM	New building	13/05/1955	

Recorded at Norwood Junction, unit S5247 leads a London bridge to Tattenham Corner service. (If a portion were continuing to Caterham then the service will split at Purley.)
P J Sharpe

In order to accommodate the 10-car electric train services platforms were extended to 674 feet: this work involved considerable track alterations at some places, and also modifications to bridges, retaining walls, etc. Brief particulars are given below-

CHARING CROSS - Nos. l, 2 and 3 platforms were extended at the country end to give an effective length of 675 ft, and provision for 20 ft, sand drags at the concourse end. This entailed re-arrangement of the connections between Nos. 1, 2 and 3 platform lines and the down and up local lines with consequent repositioning of signals.

No. 1 siding was lengthened to accommodate one 10-car train and a 20 ft, sand drag was provided at the signal box end. Due to weight limitations on the river bridge, it was not possible to extend No. 2 siding which was therefore abolished, At that time 357 down trains and 355 up trains were being handled daily, carrying approximate 119,100 passengers (57,800 arriving and 61,300 departing) each weekday.

WATERLOO EAST - The platforms on the up local and down through lines were extended at the country end to give an effective length of 665 ft, and 661 ft. respectively This entailed sluing the down through line, minor alterations to bridges 22 and 24A and the repositioning of automatic signal No. A50 applicable to the down through line. The

platforms were to be further extended to accommodate the new 12-car Hastings line diesels introduced in 1957.

At that time approximately 24,000 passengers were handled (12,100 arriving and 11,900 departing) each weekday.

LONDON BRIDGE - Platforms 1 and 2 (country end), 3 and 4 (both ends) and 6 (country end) were extended to give an effective length of 675 ft, which also extended the effective length of platform 7 to 781ft. Platforms 1 and 2 were raised at the London end,

This work involved:-
(a) sluing of No. 4 platform line, also adjustment to the roofing over platform 4 and the covered ramp approach way at the London end of platforms 3 and 4,
(b) abolition of redundant No. 5 up (through) line [removed March 1953],
(c) abolition of facing connection from down local to No. 3 platform line (operated by Borough Market Jct, signal box),
(d) repositioning and re-alignment of certain connections at both ends of station,
(e) repositioning of signals at both ends of station.

METROPOLITAN JUNCTION - The work entailed the provision of additional facing crossover roads from up through to up local line and from down local to down through line, 261 and 45 yards respectively on the Charing

Cross side of the signal box. This entailed repositioning the existing facing crossover from down through to down local line to a new location 139 yards on the Charing Cross side of the signal box. Signalling alterations were also necessary to suit the altered layout,

The provision of the new down local to down through line crossover entailed some modification and strengthening of the deck of bridge 34B.

NEW CROSS - The platforms were extended at the London end; Nos. 1 & 2 with brick walls containing filling which was finished with a tarmac surface, Nos. 4. & 5 with precast reinforced concrete walls and filling with a temporary gravel surface that was covered with tarmac after final settlement. A new electric light pole on No. 4 platform had to be removed and re-positioned because it was too close to the platform edge. The tracks were slewed and two of the up signals were re-positioned.

St. JOHNS - The local line platforms were extended at the country ends and the main line platforms at both ends. Precast reinforced concrete walls were used to retain the earth filling that was finished with a tarmac surface. A new retaining wall was built on the down side and the Local Line crossover at the country end of the station was moved further out. Two of the down signals were also re-positioned.

LEWISHAM - Both the Mid-Kent and North Kent line platforms were extended at the country ends and the two under-bridges were widened to carry them. Precast reinforced concrete trestles and flooring were used except over the bridges where special construction was necessary. Standard Southern Region concrete panels provided excellent barriers at the backs of the platforms, there being a considerable drop to the street outside. The down signals on both lines were re-positioned.

BLACKHEATH - Both platforms were extended at the London end with precast reinforced concrete trestles and flooring and a concrete precast fence was erected at the back of the down platform. These extensions involved considerable alterations to the down carriage sidings and down line and the repositioning of several of the existing crossovers. The positions of the up starting signals were also modified to suit the new platforms.

KIDBROOKE - The platforms were extended at the country and of the station with precast reinforced concrete walls, flooring and fencing. The crossover at that end and the down starting signals were re-positioned. A new footbridge constructed of reinforced concrete was completed in March 1952 to provide for the increased passenger traffic.

ELTHAM WELL HALL - Both platforms were extended at the country end with precast reinforced concrete trestles, flooring and panel fences. Part of the extension was carried over the road under-bridge, which was widened accordingly and the positions of the down signals and the country end

crossover were also altered. The inspecting officer from the Ministry of Transport was concerned that a section of the ramp at the end of the up platform had to be omitted owing to fouling some signal rodding. He required that the ramp was completed to its full width in order to close the gap in the footway that he considered might be dangerous, especially at night,

ELTHAM PARK - The up platform was extended at the country end with precast reinforced concrete trestles, flooring and panel fencing. On the down platform extension at the London end, a precast reinforced concrete wall contained earth filling. It had to be finished with a temporary gravel surface that was covered with tarmac later. The inspector required that a bump in the platform coping about 1.5 ins high was removed,

FALCONWOOD - Both platforms were extended at the London end with precast reinforced trestles, flooring and panel fencing. An automatic signal was repositioned.

WELLING - The platforms were extended at both ends with precast reinforced concrete trestles, flooring and panel fencing. Some of the signals had to be repositioned.

BEXLEYHEATH - Both platforms were extended at the London end with precast reinforced concrete walls containing filling finished with a tarmac surface. The overbridge at this end was rebuilt and widened to allow for the new platform extensions.

BARNEHURST - Both platforms were extended at the country end with precast reinforced concrete trestles, flooring and panel fencing. The signalbox was repositioned by constructing a new brick base further from the up line and the whole upper section moved accordingly. The crossovers at this end were also moved further out and the signals were re-positioned.

SLADE GREEN - The platforms were extended at the London end with precast reinforced concrete trestles, flooring and panel fencing. The down siding connections were re-positioned and the positions of the signals altered accordingly.

Additional berthing sidings between Slade Green and Crayford Creek Junction,

In order to accommodate the additional electric rolling stock required for the 10-car train scheme, berthing facilities were provided at Slade Green on the up side between Crayford Creek Junction and Slade Green signal boxes. A staff footbridge was also provided to connect the new sidings with the main depot on the opposite side of the running lines, The new sidings consisted of five roads with connections to the up main line at each end, The connection from No. 5 siding (furthest from running lines) at the Slade Green end was, originally, only a temporary measure but after consideration it was retained permanently. The lengths of the sidings became as follows:-Nos.1 & 2 to 827 ft.,

Platforms 1 and 2 at New Cross showing the extended platforms for 10-car trains by day and with night illumination.

Steve Godden

Nos.3 & 4 to 709 ft., No.5 to 675 ft. Nos. 1 and 2 sidings were equipped with staging, lighting and water points for carriage cleaning purposes. Trap points leading to sand drags were provided at each end of the sidings, while access to the sidings at the Slade Green end was by means of a trailing connection in the up main line 88 yards on the Crayford Creek Junction side of Slade Green signal box. The points were operated from the signal box.

At the Crayford Creek Junction end access to the sidings was by means of a facing connection in the up main line 82 yards on the Slade Green side of Crayford Creek Junction signal box: the points operated from the signal box, and considerable new and altered signalling at Slade Green and Crayford Creek Junction was provided.

All the works at Slade Green were completed by June, 1954.

DARTFORD JUNCTION - New track circuiting was installed and re-signalling carried out in connection with alterations and abolition of Dartford No.1 signalbox.

DARTFORD - The platforms were extended at the country end to 675 feet, entailing rearrangement of the permanent way and the widening of bridge No. 822 over the River Darent. The berthing sidings were extended to accommodate

additional rolling stock and on the up side this involved extensive chalk excavation and the construction of a retaining wall. The opportunity was taken to concentrate the signalling at Dartford station in No. 2 signal box and No. 1 signal box was abolished. The points and signals at the London end of the station were converted to power operation.

New facing points were provided from down fast to up line at the London end of the station, 409 yards from the signal box, to enable down trains to run to No. 1 platform. Facing points leading from the down slow to down fast line at the country end of station were repositioned due to the extension of platform. The facing points and the trailing connection in the down line were 108 yards and 34 yards from the signal box respectively. A sand drag was provided at the termination of the down slow line. A new facing connection was provided in the down line, 35 yards on the Littlebrook side of the signal box, leading to the up carriage sidings. The trailing points in the down line leading to the down siding were repositioned 18 yards farther from the signal box. The reception siding was extended 50 yards towards the station, necessitating provision of new facing points in down line 251 yards on the Littlebrook side of the signal box.

At that time an average of 490 passenger and 24 freight trains were dealt with daily by Dartford signal box.

All this stage of the work was ready for use by 14th June 1954.

St. Johns to Orpington and Bromley North (Stage 1)

HITHER GREEN - Main line platforms extended at both ends, and the Dartford Loop line platforms were extended at the country end.

GROVE PARK - All platforms were extended at the country end, and signals moved to accommodate this.

ELMSTEAD WOODS - The down local platform was extended at both ends, but the up local & up/down through platforms were extended only at the London end.

CHISLEHURST - The down local platform was extended at the London end. To permit this the dock siding was abolished.

PETTS WOOD - The four platforms at the London end were extended with reinforced concrete walls and copings retaining earth filling that was finished with a gravel surface. The crossover leading from the down local to the down sidings was moved further out and some of the signals at this end of the station were repositioned.

ORPINGTON - No. 1 (bay) and No. 2 platform were lengthened at the London end with reinforced concrete walls and copings retaining earth filling finished with a gravel surface. This work entailed the remodelling of this end of the station, and in order to give better running facilities, a double line junction between the main and local lines was put in just to the north of the signal box. The new facing connections gave direct access between the local lines and No. 1 up bay platform and also enabled trains reversing at No. 3 down main platform to return via the up local as well as the up through line at the London end. The up sidings were altered and up shunting neck extended. In addition two up sidings were electrified,

The signalling and interlocking was modified to suit the new arrangements and a miniature illuminated diagram was provided.

SUNDRIDGE PARK - The platforms were extended at the London end with reinforced concrete trestles and flooring and the fencing was lengthened with concrete panels.

BROMLEY NORTH - Both terminal platforms were extended with reinforced concrete walls and coping retaining earth filling finished with a tarmac surface. No. 1 siding was electrified.

All this stage of the work was also ready for use by 14th June 1954.

Hither Green to Dartford, via Sidcup (Stage 2)

CRAYFORD - The up platform was extended at the London end in precast reinforced concrete work consisting of trestles supporting a slab floor with a panel wall at the back, and both platforms were extended at the country end with precast walls and earth filling covered with a tarmac surface. The down and up starting signals were repositioned.

BEXLEY - Both platforms were extended at the country end in precast trestle and slab construction with panel back walls, and a trailing crossover was re-laid in 109 lb flat bottom material clear of the extension. The down and up signals at this end of the station were repositioned and a banner repeating signal was provided for the down starter.

ALBANY PARK - Both platforms were extended at the London end in precast trestle and slab construction with panel back walls, and the up home signal was repositioned.

SIDCUP - Both platforms were extended at the country end in precast trestle and slab construction with panel back walls. The down starting signal was repositioned and a banner repeating signal provided.

NEW ELTHAM - Both platforms were extended at the London end in precast trestle and slab construction with panel back walls, and the up starting signal was repositioned. The old platforms were below standard height but were gently sloped to meet the level of the extensions.

The work on the down platform necessitated the removal of the signal box to an alternative site, and the opportunity was therefore taken to dispense with it and install colour-light signalling with continuous track circuits between Mottingham and Sidcup. In accordance with the usual practice on the Southern Region the first colour-light signal in each direction is an "approach" one showing green and yellow aspects only, and is placed under the last semaphore signal. When the semaphore arm is in the danger position the colour light "approach" signal is not illuminated but when the arm is in the clear position the semaphore signal light is obscured and the green or yellow aspect of the colour light is illuminated in accordance with the state of the track ahead.

The trailing crossovers between the down and up lines at both ends of New Eltham Station were removed. and also one of the two siding connections in the up line. There were now no connections in the down line over the colour-light length and only one trailing connection in the up line at New Eltham, for which a new 3-lever ground frame, electrically released from Sidcup box, was provided.

MOTTINGHAM - Both platforms were extended at the London end in precast trestle and slab construction with back panel walls, although not finally completed until the inauguration of the change of frequency scheme, when the spur to the sub-station was removed. To facilitate this, the points were repositioned and improvements made to the layout of sidings so that 'run-rounds' could be carried out clear of the main line.

LEE - Both platforms were extended at the country end in precast trestle and slab construction with back panel walls.

The whole route was provided with B.R. three-position block in place of Walker's one wire, except between Mottingham and Sidcup where track circuit block was provided.

This work was ready for use by 13th June 1955.

North Kent East Junction to Slade Green (Stage 2)

DEPTFORD - Both platforms were extended at the country end.

GREENWICH - Both platforms were extended at the London end

MAZE HILL - The up platform was extended at the London end, and the down platform was extended at both ends. A new subway staircase was constructed, and the loop siding slued, and a trailing connection repositioned.

WESTCOMBE PARK - Both platforms were extended at the London end

CHARLTON - The up and down platforms were extended by 175 ft at the London end. The double junction at the London end was re-laid and realigned. A set of switch diamonds was included in the new layout and a single slip was removed. A new 36-lever frame was installed in the signalbox to replace the original, and additional track circuiting provided.

WOOLWICH DOCKYARD - Both platforms were extended at both ends, Because of the restricted site, the up platform was extended only to 654 ft.

WOOLWICH ARSENAL - Both platforms were extended at the country end. A new facing connection was provided in the up line to the up sidings at the country end. A trailing crossover (motor worked) was moved. The up home signal was re-sited and an additional signal provided for the up loop.

PLUMSTEAD - Both platforms were extended at the London end.

ABBEY WOOD - Both platforms were extended at the London end

BELVEDERE - Both platforms were extended at the London end

ERITH - Both platforms were extended at the London end. The footbridge stairs were rebuilt to allow a full platform width. The trailing connection and crossover were re-sited.

Lewisham - 'diamond' crossing at London end, 20 August 1955. Lewisham Sub-station is visible in the distance to the right of the picture. This original building housed the rotary converters and transformers to supply all the lines in the Lewisham area together with the distribution board receiving current from Deptford power station for the high voltage feeders to the remainder of the Eastern Division suburban area. After the frequency change scheme the mercury arc rectifiers and new transformers replaced the original equipment and a new building on the station side of the original building housed the staff and equipment which operated the remote controls in the new sub-stations and TP huts. Alan A Jackson

Unit S5194 departing from London Bridge with a Cannon Street to Maidstone West via Bexleyheath service. In the background set S5212 leads a Charing Cross to Sevenoaks working. The view shows platforms 1-3 at London Bridge.

Dartford to Gravesend and Gillingham (Stage 3a)

STONE CROSSING - The platforms were extended at the London end (168 ft & 359 ft). To permit this it was necessary to widen the girder bridge (825A) over the APCM mineral branch and move the trailing connection in the down line. A permanent way hut and a siding gate also required removal.

GREENHITHE - Both platforms were extended at the country end.

SWANSCOMBE - Both platforms were extended at the country end.

NORTHFLEET - The up side platform was extended at the London end, and the down side platform at both ends. The trailing crossover at the country end was repositioned.

GRAVESEND CENTRAL
Both platforms were extended at the country end. As a consequence the country end dock siding (at the end of the up platform) was removed. To accommodate longer trains the down siding was extended. The line to the up local platform was re-aligned. A new locomotive coal stage and ash bunker were provided for the locomotives on the Hundred of Hoo service.

DENTON - As electric trains did not call, the platforms were not extended.

MILTON RANGE - As electric trains did not call, the platforms were not extended.

HOO STAFF HALT - Special stopping arrangements applied at Hoo Junction (only the leading coach was at the platform), therefore it was not extended.

HIGHAM - Both platforms were extended at the London end.

STROOD - The platforms at Strood were extended at the London end. A trailing connection from the down line to the sidings was repositioned and a short siding on the down side at the London end was abolished. The barrow crossing was repositioned.

ROCHESTER - The down island platform was extended at the London end. This involved special construction over bridges 153 and 153A over Furrels Wharf Road. The up island platform was extended at the London end. A lamp room and sand bin were replaced.

CHATHAM - Until the signalbox was removed the down local platform was only extended at the country end to 665 ft 3½ ins, and the down main to 637 ft. After removal it was proposed that the platform lengths would be 705ft 3½ ins and 675 ft respectively. The up local platform was extended

No S5179 leads the 12.55 Charing Cross to Hayes via Lewisham service, recorded at Catford Bridge on 13 August 1960. Beyond the bridge carrying the former LC&DR Catford Loop line over the Mid-Kent line the former Catford sub-station which was converted and retained as a sub-station within the Frequency Change Scheme can just be made out .

John Scrace

at the country end to 689 ft 6 ins and the up main to 691 ft 8 ins. The trap siding at the London end of the down local was abolished. Two water columns at the country end of the down platforms were replaced by one standard.

GILLINGHAM - The platforms were extended at the country end, but not by the full amount, pending remodelling for the Kent Coast electrification. A temporary walkway was provided at the London end of the up platform.

GILLINGHAM CARRIAGE SIDINGS (Stage 4 works) - Four additional sidings were provided at the Rainham end together with cleaning stages and lighting. Connections to the arrival and departure lines were adjusted. Pits and additional drainage were provided throughout the Inspection Shed. Cleaning stages were provided on the arrival and departure lines.

Parks Bridge Junction to Addiscombe, Hayes and Sanderstead, (Stage 4)

LADYWELL - The platforms were extended at the country end with precast reinforced concrete trestles and flooring and the fencing was lengthened with concrete panels. The down advanced starting signal was repositioned.

CATFORD BRIDGE - The platforms were extended at the London end. The trailing connection from the down line to the down siding was repositioned.

LOWER SYDENHAM - The down platform was extended at both ends. The up platform was extended at the country end.

NEW BECKENHAM - The down platform was extended at the London end. The up platform was extended at the country end, which required special construction over subway No. 680B.

The up siding was electrified to take ten cars. This required the trap points to be repositioned, a small retaining wall to be constructed and a carriage cleaning stage to be provided.

CLOCK HOUSE - Both platforms were extended at the country end. To permit this the coal pens and a goods roadway were altered as was the access to the signalbox and the Elsan toilet.

ELMERS END - The down and up platforms were extended at the country end, but the up bay was only extended to 328 ft 6 ins. To permit this, the junction was repositioned. (Moving the junction was considered a cheaper option than reconstructing bridge 690 by £25,000). A new culvert and drainage channel was required.

WOODSIDE - Both platforms were extended at the country end. This also entailed repositioning connections to the up sidings, cutting back the slope and alterations to trackwork, fencing and drainage.

ADDISCOMBE - Platforms 1 and 2 were extended to 675 ft and 685 ft respectively, and sand drags provided. The siding alongside No.1 platform was abolished. The connection leading from No.1 platform to the up line was repositioned. Two crossovers near the signal box were abolished and replaced by a new trailing crossover at the London side of bridge 699. Sidings numbered 1, 2 and 3 were slued and the coal pens cut back. No.3 platform was abolished and replaced with an additional siding. The water column was repositioned and a new staff crossing provided.

EDEN PARK - Both platforms were extended at the London end.

WEST WICKHAM - Both platforms were extended at the London end. The trailing connection in the down line to the goods yard and the trailing crossover were repositioned. The up side dock siding was removed.

HAYES - Platforms 1 and 2 were extended at the London end to 673 ft and 686 ft respectively. The down electrified siding was extended to accommodate ten cars. The crossover between No. 2 platform and the down siding was repositioned, and sand drags were provided to both platforms.

BINGHAM ROAD - Both platforms were extended at the London end.

COOMBE ROAD - The down platform was extended at the London end, and the up platform extended at both ends. Special construction was required over bridge 10 on the up side at the London end.

SELSDON - Both the Mid-Kent platforms were extended at the London end.

SANDERSTEAD -The down platform only was extended at both ends. The country end trailing crossover was repositioned clear of the platforms.

Orpington to Sevenoaks (Stage 4)

ORPINGTON - No 5 platform was extended at the country end and the barrow crossing was repositioned.

CHELSFIELD - The down platform was extended at the London end and the up platform was extended at the country end. The trailing crossover at the London end was abolished. The trailing connection from the up line to the siding at the country end was also abolished but was replaced by a trailing crossover from down to up line at the country end with a slip connection into the sidings. The siding was slewed to allow for this.

KNOCKHOLT - Both platforms were extended at the London end. The connection from the down line to the down sidings was repositioned, an additional siding was provided and No.1 up goods yard siding was slewed to match.

DUNTON GREEN - The main line platforms were both extended at the country end, and the barrow crossing repositioned.

SEVENOAKS - All platforms (1 to 6) were extended at the country end. The down bay, engine turntable siding and turntable were abolished. A new facing crossover was provided from the down Orpington line to the up line, at the London end of the junction to Otford. A short electrified

siding near 'A' signalbox was removed. The up dock siding was slued and a retaining wall provided at the site of the new signalbox. Nos. 1 & 2 Quarry sidings were partially electrified, and the country end connections were remodelled.

CANNON STREET - This station, because of its restricted site between the River Thames and the busy thoroughfare of the same name, proved difficult and expensive to reconstruct. The German bombs of the Blitz had gutted 'Southern House' which was the former railway hotel, but which had been in use as offices since 1931, and damaged the overall roof beyond economic repair. The ten car scheme required the five eastern platforms to be lengthened but the track layout on the river bridge prevented southward extension, and the concourse had to be reduced in size and the buffer stops and ticket barrier line moved northward. Platforms 1, 4 & 5 were ready for ten car trains on 4th March 1957. On the morning of the 5th April 1957 the operating floor of the signalbox that was located on the westward side of the station burned down. Temporary equipment was installed in the remainder of the building within a month, but a permanent signalbox was not opened until 16th December 1957. The remainder of the platforms were opened for longer trains in early 1958. In April of that year the station was closed outside the rush hours to enable the remnants of the station roof to be removed. Southern House was eventually demolished in 1963 and replaced by a multi-storey glass and concrete office block.

Platform / Length	
1	668 ft
2	668 ft
3	678 ft
4	677 ft
5	860 ft Platforms 5 to 8 were further extended to cater for 12 car trains planned for the Kent Coast electrification
6	811 ft
7	819 ft
8	810 ft

The final platform capacities at Cannon Street were:

An electrified stabling siding was provided alongside the curve towards Metropolitan Junction, and some trains were berthed in Ewer Street Depot following the removal of Southwark Continental Fruit Depot to a new facility on the up side at Hither Green sidings.

Full ten-car operation on the Eastern Section was operational by June 1957.

'The Old Order Changeth'...at Bournemouth

Jeffery Grayer recalls the end of steam and the dawn of the diesel and electric era at 70B

Above - *Ivatt tank 41320 and Standard Class 5 73115, typical of mid-1960s motive power, seen in Bournemouth yard with the primitive coaling arrangements evident in the form of a mobile crane.*

Opposite top - *A brace of original Bulleids, Nos 34033 "Chard" and 34041 "Wilton", are matched by a couple of elderly M7s seen to the right in this early 1960s view of the shed area.*

Opposite bottom - *No 34100 "Appledore", its glory days hauling the "Golden Arrow" now long behind it, displays a good head of steam alongside Standard 4-6-0 No 75076.*

Right - *Standard tank No 80134 which remained in service on the SR, along with nine examples of its classmates until July 1967.*

Left - *The fireman of No 73115, formerly carrying the name "King Pellinore", relaxes prior to taking his steed to London.*

Opposite top - *Bereft of its ponderous nameplate, No 34090 "Sir Eustace Missenden, Southern Railway" poses on the turntable at Bournemouth MPD.*

Opposite bottom - *A very grimy No 35028 "Clan Line", looking very far from its present day pristine condition in preservation, simmers in the yard at Bournemouth.*

No 35030 "Elder Dempster Lines" prior to departure from Bournemouth Central with a London train. No 35030 powered the final up steam service into Waterloo, the 14:07 from Weymouth, on 9 July, the last day of steam working on the SR.

Ivatt tank No 41224 rests between duties in the shed yard.

3TC trailer unit No 301 alongside the site of a now trackless MPD at Bournemouth Central. The former shed was to be demolished and the area transformed into a car park.

Hymek D7027 prepares to depart Bournemouth station , now no longer dignified with the suffix "Central", with an inter regional service to the Midlands. Note the absence of central roads which were taken out in December 1966 in connection with the electrification programme.

SOMETHING RATHER SPECIAL

Like many I am sure, I have a soft spot for the Island railways. We are delighted then to present a short section of what we hope will be of interesting Island railway images - not all of finest quality (hence their size), but certainly a number of 'rare birds'. We start with this posed view of No W13 'Ryde' complete with Set No 498 consisting of four Billinton vehicles. These are brake-third No 4116, composite No 6371, Third No 2344, and a further Brake Third No 4115. After an active life of nearly 60 years, No W13 was withdrawn in July 1932, the same year the 4-wheel stock seen was also withdrawn from service. It is possible the view was taken on the Bembridge Branch.

NRM / Curl collection

(With grateful thanks to Roger Simmonds for locating the images on the pages that follow.)

Left - Freshwater station, Alan Buckett (standing far left) about to leave the Island ready to emigrate to Australia. He is seen with two unknown friends. (Cty. Dave Buckett)

Above - Bembridge c1911.

Left - Merstone Junction c1914.

Left - The Brading Station master, Mr Wheelaway complete with the all-important train staff. (Cty. Jayne Pidgeon)

Top - Construction at Ventnor 1866-7.

Bottom - Pound Lane Crossing on the Freshwater, Yarmouth & Newport line. (Cty. Anne Buckett)

Sandown to Newport train near to Coppins.

Left - Ryde Pier railway under construction.

Opposite top - Newport station staff, 1911. (Cty. Ken Beazley)

Opposite bottom - Yarmouth c1913.

In October 1909 Ryde Tunnel flooded. Here, on the 27th of the month' pumping operations to clear the line are taking place.

QUESTIONS...?

We all know of the 'Devon Belle' and we also know the route it took: Waterloo to Exeter and beyond. So why is the Devon Belle observation car plus a selection of Pullmans running north on the Bournemouth line in the early 1950s? Test working / special train for which the stock was used / or perhaps even a travel agent publicity tour? It cannot be the 1947 press trip as this was a circular Waterloo to Waterloo tour through Surrey. So, 'Answers on a post-card please...' to..... ('The Devon Belle' featured in SW Issue No 2.)

Left - Although all were taken as 'snapshots' it just goes to prove some such views are worth preserving for their historic interest alone. The train is heading north past St Cross signal box (just south of Winchester), the formation identified as six pullmans in addition to the observation car.

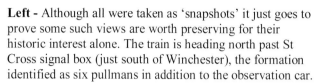

Right - Arguably the working operated on more than one day, as here the view is half a mile north of St Cross on the way to Winchester. This is also the only view where it appears there is at least one passenger in one of the vehicles.

Left - Leaving (or passing) Winchester bound for Basingstoke (I am assuming the train did not 'turn-right' at Winchester Junction towards Alton). Again the same six+one formation will be noted.

Right - We are 99% certain the images come from the camera of enthusiast and one time Medical Officer of Health for Winchester, Dr J L Farmer. This particular view was also amongst a small group of prints purchased some time ago from a stall at a collectors' fair. The circumstances were clearly as stated, with the remains of the recently truncated Meon Valley line in the foreground. If any reader has any knowledge of contacting the family of Dr Farmer we would be grateful

Meldon Quarry

Peter Tatlow

(The author trained and worked as a civil engineer on British Railways, Southern Region from 1957 to 1968 and all photographs are by him.)

An alternative to a photographic permit to gain access to the lineside came about as a result of one's professional duties. Remarkable was a two-day visit by four civil engineer students/graduate engineers to Meldon Quarry in December 1960, as part of their training scheme while in the Permanent Way Drawing Office at Waterloo. A further visit came about when the Civil Engineering Student Association of the Southern Region visited Plymouth for the weekend, during the summer rather than winter conditions, in September 1961.

Meldon Quarry, situated in a cutting beside the line on the edge of Dartmoor beneath Yes Tor, two miles south-west of Okehampton at an elevation of 850 to 960 feet above sea level, was found to produce a hard angular rock, ideal for track ballast. A small quarry is believed to have been opened up to supply local railway requirements in

Opposite and above - The wintery scene of the Devon countryside from an elevated position at Meldon Quarry on the morning of 20 December 1960 following an overnight fall of snow. In the middle distance is the crushing and screening plant feeding the loading hoppers by a continuous belt system to railway hopper wagons on a siding below. In the view opposite, the Meldon Quarry signal box is towards the left above the wisp of steam.

1874, during the construction of the Devon and Cornwall Junction Railway. Re-activated in 1897 by the local district engineer of the L&SWR, by 1905 it was well-established with its own crushing plant to provide much of the company's needs, which at the time amounted to about 100,000 tons per annum. To convey the stone from the quarry to the place of use, 12-ton 4-wheel steel ballast hopper wagons and associated ballast plough brake-vans were brought into use from 1898, while from 1903 the first of a long line of 40-ton bogie hopper wagons was introduced.

With grouping in 1923, the condition of the permanent way of the other two constituent companies – the LBSCR and SECR – left something to be desired. Following the disaster at Sevenoaks on 27 August 1927, as well as questions about the suitability of large tank engines on fast passenger train work, the condition of the track was deemed inadequate. As part of plans put in hand to upgrade the permanent way, Meldon Quarry was now to supply ballast for the entire system, necessitating the installation of more modern plant for winning, crushing and screening the stone, as the track of the Central and South-Eastern divisions was brought up to scratch. This led to the construction of more bogie ballast hopper wagons and the inauguration of a regular pattern of special trains up the West of England Main Line and on as far as Kent, as appropriate, to supply the needs of the relaying programme in each of the engineering districts. Typically eight or nine, rising to fourteen trains, each consisting of up to ten vacuum-brake-fitted 40-ton ballast hopper wagons grossing at over 500 tons, were run out and back per week, together with ordinary wagons loads of chippings forwarded by regular goods train as required.

In 1923 the quarry had been extended to over 200 acres and by 1955 had an annual output of some 320,000 tons. After crushing, the stone would be graded: track ballast passing a 2½ inch sieve; ½ inch chippings were ideal for measured shovel packing in maintaining line and top of the rails, while Meldon dust was employed in blanketing the track formation. The quarry also supplied aggregate for the Exmouth Junction Concrete Works, where the familiar pre-cast concrete units, so much part of the Southern Railway, were produced. From the late twenties it was found expedient to base a small shunting engine at the quarry for which a small shed was erected.

In the 1920s, without road access at the time, a private halt with short platforms on each side of the line immediately east of Meldon Viaduct was provided for some of the 150-200 workmen employed on the site. Later, vehicular access off the Okehampton to Tavistock road (A30) was provided by means of a steep private track that passed under the viaduct. This afforded the opportunity for some of the workers to be transported to and from work by mini-bus. With the cessation of passenger services on the Exeter to Plymouth Line west of Okehampton in 1968, the halt ceased to be used and the rail access to the quarry rearranged to continue to deal with an output of 300,000 tons per year.

As part of the process of privatising British Rail, the quarry operation was sold to ECC Quarries Ltd on 4 March 1994 and subsequently managed by Aggregate Industries, who, it is understood, currently have it on the market.

Left - An Aveling-Barford 12-ton dumper truck deposits its load of rock from the quarry face into the top of a crusher.

Opposite bottom - Maunsell 2-6-0 N class No. 31860 passes Meldon Quarry signal box with a goods train bearing a local engine head code, thought to be for a Class K stopping freight train working up from the Western Region in the North Road area of Plymouth.

Above - More than a year later, in warmer summer weather, members of the Civil Engineering Students Association made a visit to the quarry on 1 September 1961, during which opportunity was taken to photograph 4-6-2 Battle of Britain class No. 34079 '141 Squadron' crossing Meldon Viaduct with an up train from Padstow.

Opposite top - A rebuilt West Country No. 34056 'Croydon' passes the lower quadrant signal with a train for Plymouth.

Opposite bottom - Sister engine No. 34109 'Sir Trafford Leigh-Mallory' with a similar train in the opposite direction. On the left hand side beyond the shunt signal is the short platform for use by the workmen travelling by train and by which the party of students departed.

Above - Another 'Woolworth' Mogul No. 31857 climbs up from Okehampton with a passenger train for Padstow as other photographically-inclined students capture the scene. Beyond them is Adams G6 class 0-6-0T DS682 (formerly No 30328) standing outside the small single road engine shed.

References:

Dendy Marshall CF, *A History of the Southern Railway*, The Southern Railway, 1936, p 584-5.
Griffiths R, *Southern Sheds in Camera*, OPC, 1989, p89.
Hammett RA (Ed), *British Railway Track, Design, Construction & Maintenance*, Permanent Way Institution, 1956, pp 144-154 (Measured shovel packing).
King M et al, *An Illustrated History of Southern Wagons, Volume 1: LSWR and S&DJR*, OPC, 1984, pp 77-81.
King M et al, *An Illustrated History of Southern Wagons, Volume 4*, OPC, 2002, pp 123-132.
Quarrying Stone for Ballasting, Southern Region Supplies from Dartmoor, Sixty-year- old Railway Enterprise, reprint of Modern Railways, Dec 24, 1955.
Tatlow P, *Blanketing Track Formation*, Backtrack Vol 26 (August 2012), pp 506-508.

A prototype for everything, old and new. **Above** *- With a letter headcode looking towards the future, CL71 No 71011 is seen at Hither Green (?) with its pantograph raised.*

Steam shunting of tank-cars but without any barrier wagon. No 30084, believed to be at Dover.

Want to run a railway?

Stephen Grant

(The story of the 1962 booklet distributed to commuters by the Southern Region)

It is December 1962. A long period of economic growth and prosperity is coming to an end as the British Empire shrinks and the more productive industries of France, Germany and even Japan threaten to overtake us.

Though most of us had, as Prime Minister Harold Macmillan assured us, "never had it so good", during the 1950s, this could not be said of the railways. Many of us had spent our increasing disposable income on our first car and now we use the family car as often as possible, using the railway solely for commuting. Industry, too, is losing patience with British Railways' lumbering unbraked freight trains, with consignments lost in the system or damaged by rough shunting in the many marshalling yards. Increasingly

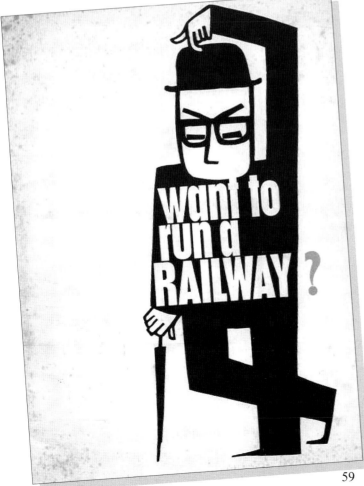

the articulated lorry is moving materials and delivering products.

BR had drifted into deficit in the mid-1950s and its operating loss in 1962 is destined to be £99m (equivalent to £5.3bn at 2013 values). The British Transport Commission, with its abandoned vision of an integrated public transport system, is in its last days of existence and in the New Year the British Railways Board, with Dr. Beeching in the chair, will take control with the authority to take drastic action to return the railways to profit.

Roads seem to be the future but roads cannot carry the 300,000 passengers who commute into central London on the Southern every weekday. Peak-hour crowding has been a problem for many years and successive initiatives - electrification, six-a-side seating, the 10-car scheme on the South Eastern - have each been overtaken by a rising tide of commuters. Now the peak is becoming sharply concentrated in the 8.00-9.00 a.m. band as early morning 'workman' traffic declines and employers resist the idea of staggered office hours. Commuters crammed into narrow compartments designed for half as many passengers are not happy. It is against this background that the Southern Region distributes to its passengers a booklet with the eye-catching title "Want to run a railway?"

"Try taking over the 8-15 tomorrow morning" it challenges, going on to point out that the Southern carries 400,000,000 passengers a year, more than the railways of the United States and Canada combined. "There are *forty* eight-fifteens to Town every weekday on the Southern. There is an 8.15 through the ABC from Ashford, Bookham and Carshalton down to Upper Warlingham, Virginia Water and West Wickham. You've got to take the forty. After all, *we* have to."

Not everybody would approve of the colloquial style. In an editorial the following month 'Modern Railways' magazine will deplore the Southern addressing its customers in the tones of a Peter Sellers night-watchman: "Passengers on 37 trains a minute all bound for London? How does London deal with them?" "You've no time to worry about London, mate. (Mate? Yes- you're one of us now, remember)."

But the booklet sets out in clear, journalistic and non-technical language the scale and complexity of the task with, for example, a small section of a track occupation graph. "You'll have to work 7,000 trains a day. Send more than a thousand trains a day over the points at Borough Market Junction, just north of London Bridge. A hundred in your first hour. You'll have to fit them all in. Allow twenty seconds and no more for each of the stops. Use every section of track, every yard of platform at the London end, to get forty 8.15s (and all the 8.16s and 8.17s too) in their right sequence at junctions, into Town for a quick turn-round and away again."

It urges empathy with the Southern's front-line staff facing customers who believe they could run the railway a good deal better. "Some will try their sarcasm (perhaps the only chance they get to use it) on the ticket collector, doing their best to ruffle a man who has his work cut out all day dealing with enquirers in a hurry and bilkers whose ingenuity is boundless. A man who may be in trouble if he answers back in the same way."

And, it points out, handling the commuter peaks is not the only thing the Southern has to do. "You've got to superintend the running of forty-three cross-channel ships which form the busiest shipping line in Europe. Get scores of thousands of people away to the seaside and the country. Deliver a large part of the food, fuel and supplies which keep the south of England going. Shuttle into sheds, and out again before the rush hour, the daily percentage of stock requiring service and maintenance. Deal with the inevitable breakdowns. (You don't expect to run 7,000 services a day without an occasional failure? Something's got to give - and on the Southern electric there's roughly one breakdown every 23,601 miles run). Keep the permanent way *permanent* by constant inspection and making good. Constantly inspect and make good everything

The train supervision office, known as Control. Here they try to anticipate and prevent confusion when things go wrong. They leave it to the men at the spot to iron out the immediate difficulty while Control looks ahead, sees what timetable snags are likely to occur as reactions to the first difficulty, and alter schedules now in order to get back to the timetable service as soon as possible.

else on the railway where the slightest doubt would endanger people's lives. Run telecommunications. Distribute power. Renew signalling systems. Build bridges. Rebuild stations. Draft timetables. Administer staff. Buy food and materials on a huge scale. You'd better buy yourself a cup of coffee while you send for your next file of responsibilities. Or perhaps you don't want the job any more?"

Time-table drafters. The railway time-table is timed to *split minutes*, not the whole minutes used for public announcements. It takes months of calculations to work out the time-table twice a year.

Motive Power foreman and guards' regulator in conference at Cannon Street. The 9.10 must go out in five minutes, but the crew to take it are still down the line because the 8.15 Hayes has been delayed by a door swinging open against another train. Bill and Charlie must be asked to come off the 9.17 and take out the 9.10. How they will get back to their own schedule, how they will finish at their home depot, who will take out the 9.17 . . . all this must be left until the 9.10 is out on time.

there. Every signalman is continuously making decisions, selecting intelligently from a number of choices. Every stationmaster, train examiner, driver and guard is for ever facing problems and *making up his mind* about them. A railway does not go by clockwork but by the intelligence of its staff.

"A signalman used his initiative and worked trains through. A lineman used his skill, detected an electrical fault and righted it. A motorman 'notched it up' in favourable stretches and made up speed without menacing safety. A guard saved valuable minutes on the turn-round. A stationmaster anticipated trouble, saw a way out, and broadcast an alternative plan to his waiting passengers. Train examiners, fitters, motive power foremen, station inspectors - they are continually co-operating to get work done and trains out. They work on good will and good sense, not under High Command orders. Nothing is less like an army than a railway."

The booklet rather contradicts this assertion by introducing 'Control' - the train supervision offices at Orpington, Redhill, Woking, Southampton and Exeter - with a detailed account of the operational issues faced by Orpington Control on a typical weekday morning. In fact the pace of operations on the Southern would prevent fully effective, real-time centralised control until the advent of panel signalboxes each controlling large areas later in the 1960s.

Occasionally the booklet risks a derisive snort from the reader. "Nobody 'runs' the Southern, minute by minute" it admits. "The job of getting you to work is done in the only way possible - by a team of thousands of responsible men and women. They are taking decisions. NOW, as your train speeds along they are taking individual decisions, making individual adjustments that will ensure you get

It goes on to describe "strictly among friends" some of the things that can go wrong. It points out that fail-safe signalling can mean that a trivial and harmless defect can hold up trains over a wide area. Fog is a major problem - whilst the busiest sections of the network have colour light signals, much of the network still relies on Victorian-era semaphore signalling and block telegraphs. And not everything can be explained in detail over the loudspeakers. "'An incident at...' rarely means a serious accident. It could well be a tragedy on a personal scale - someone who has fallen in front of a train." Snow and ice, defective brakes (fail-safe again), broken rails "...Sounds really dramatic but it is usually a simple fracture in a steel rail length".

Rather bravely, the booklet gives contact details for the three Line Managers responsible for each of the Southern's newly-formed Divisions and their top teams (from a 21st century perspective one is struck by the modesty of

WHO IS THIS MAN, ANYWAY?

Who is the genius who has made thousands of spot decisions in the day, referring to work in thousands of places?

WHO IS SUPERMAN?
WHERE IS HE?

NOWHERE.
AND IN 600 PLACES.

'HE' DOESN'T EXIST.

NOBODY 'RUNS' THE SOUTHERN, MINUTE BY MINUTE

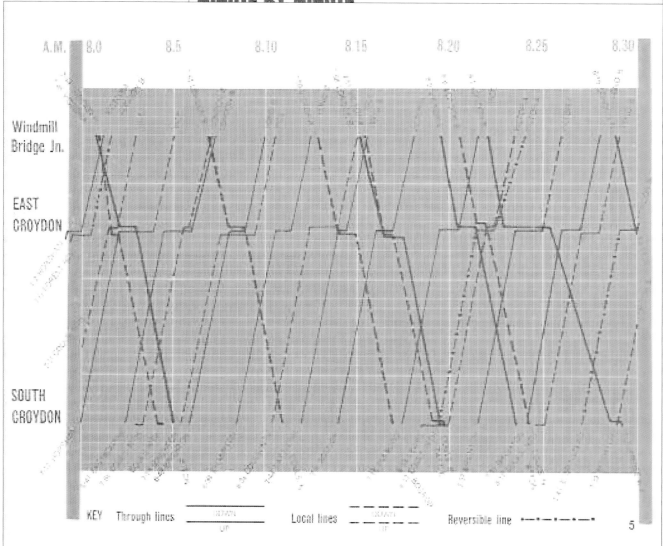

KEY   Through lines   Local lines   Reversible line

5

inform commuters about the complexities of the system they rely on to balance working in central London with living in the suburbs or beyond.

It is difficult to assess the success of a public relations initiative such as this - most of the Southern's customers will probably glance at it and then consign it to the waste paper bin. But some will no doubt find it interesting enough to read through and will be a little better informed and a little more understanding next time the 8-15 to 'Town' is running late.

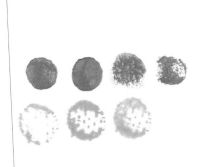

Stephen Grant is also author of:

THE BRIGHTON ELEVATED ELECTRIFICATION: a pictorial view of the construction.
£10.00

64 pages b/w
**ISBN
978-1-906419-65-3**

Paperback 270mm x 210mm

titles such as "Traffic Superintendent" and "Passenger Officer").

The booklet concludes with a gallery of images of the Southern at work - a ganger checking gauge at Borough Market Junction, a train and its crew starting the day's work in early-morning darkness, a pile of litter swept from compartments, a shunter with his pole, a train examiner, a fitter, a mound of discarded cast-iron brake blocks, linemen tracing a track-circuit failure, a platform inspector helping to ensure the Southern's 20-second station dwell times are achieved, Control with its track diagrams and vintage telephone equipment, signalmen, time-table drafters, a motive power foreman and a guards' regulator, ticket inspectors, a ticket collector ("universal uncle") and finally "The Man in the Bowler Hat - S.T. Stanbridge, station-master at London Bridge, stands inconspicuously among the hurrying crowd (51,847 in one rush-hour) missing nothing, ready to move in with crisp instructions the moment action is needed."

Although the booklet strikes a few wrong notes - "We put our trains, equipment, stations and track to more use in one hour than they were built to stand in a day" does not say much for the skills of BR's design engineers - it is on the whole a creditable attempt to

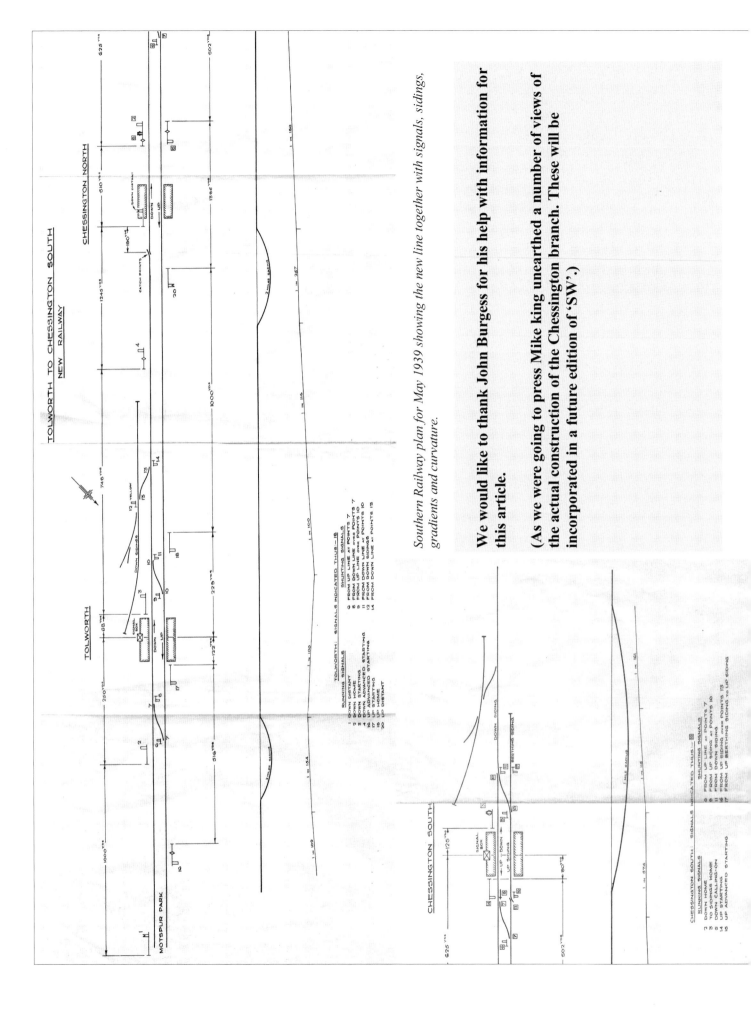

Southern Railway plan for May 1939 showing the new line together with signals, sidings, gradients and curvature.

We would like to thank John Burgess for his help with information for this article.

(As we were going to press Mike king unearthed a number of views of the actual construction of the Chessington branch. These will be incorporated in a future edition of 'SW'.)

The Chessington Branch
An Ambition Unfulfilled

Jeremy Clarke

The many small villages that closely ringed London were changed irrevocably by the coming of the railway, so much so that, without a second thought, we classify them nowadays as inner city suburbs. Within only a few years those south of the Thames, such as Deptford, Peckham, Brixton, Clapham and Battersea and their like, had seen extensive and rapid housing development on what had been up to that time agricultural land. There came also the concomitant supporting infrastructure, shops, schools, churches and public buildings, until the individuality of these villages had been completely subsumed into a single agglomeration which now saw its inhabitants travelling cheaply by rail to their places of work in London rather than walking to the field or forge or byre as their forefathers had done for generations. The row upon row of Victorian terraces that cover much of inner London and seem nowadays to be largely 'on the up' are the direct result of improved travel opportunities the railways provided.

In a short time other villages further out saw a similar, though perhaps rather different, style of development. Wimbledon, sitting on its plateau above the Thames Valley, retains much of its character and charm and its unspoilt Common because the railway lies more than half a mile away and well below it. Development has, therefore, spread out, more conveniently for its users, from around the station instead. The same applies to Georgian Richmond which, similarly, sits high on its hill above a bend in the Thames while the station with its subsequent surrounding development is in the valley, the railway having followed the river quite closely all the way from Waterloo.

Kingston, Surrey's County Town at the time and for centuries an important and convenient stop on the Portsmouth Road, also retained its isolation from the railway despite being handily at the level of the Thames. But that was because its good burghers successfully objected to the London & Southampton's plans to pass through on the basis it would harm the profitable coaching trade. The line therefore went by to the south, the company opening a station about 1½ miles away and cunningly naming it 'Kingston-upon-Railway'. The station and the area around it are now far better known as Surbiton, a settlement that owes its present position and status almost

Tolworth in the up direction towards Malden Manor, Motspur Park, Raynes Park and Waterloo. A small goods yard was provided on the down side of the line behind the photographer. A squat concrete signal was provided just to the right of the photographer. 16 March 1968.   *R F Roberts*

entirely to the railway.

The County of Surrey in general provided a rich vein to be mined by the Brighton and South Western Railway companies. It prospered on good agricultural land on a variety of soils with a spread of well-established market towns both supporting and nourishing trade, from Farnham in the west to Reigate in the east. The railways were naturally keen to exploit both the freight and passenger traffics these could provide. Beyond the main routes, the South Eastern line from Redhill to Guildford put Reigate and its neighbouring market town Dorking on the railway map in July 1849. The South Western's branch from one market town, Woking, reached another, Godalming, in October that year, dallying there until the independently-sponsored Portsmouth Direct line via Haslemere and Petersfield continued southward: that route opened almost ten years later.

The Brighton was even earlier in the field, extending in May 1847 from West Croydon to reach Epsom, whose wide main street still regularly features an open market. It was to be another twelve years before the South Western got there too and a jointly-worked line went onward to connect yet another market town, Leatherhead, to the railway network.

Not unnaturally, improving rail services brought about a not-so-subtle and quite distinct change to places like these. Even quite small towns started to develop their own 'suburbs' as the wealthier segment of society began increasingly to find how congenial country-town living could be, particularly when allied to good transport connections into 'The City'. The railways, in return, set out to encourage the growth of the 'dormitory town' by offering attractive season-ticket rates and reduced journey times in what became 'the rush hour'.

Electrification south of the Thames, beginning with the Brighton's South London Line in 1909, came about largely as a result of the need to move rising numbers of people in a shorter space of time at each end of the working day and to do so at a reduced cost to the company as well as fostering continuing growth in travel to justify the investment. It has been written elsewhere that the incentive to the Brighton was provided by electrification of local tramways. The fact is, the plans were being drawn up when horses still hauled the trams though, with a much lighter electrification infrastructure to deal with, the trams got there first. Unlike the Metropolitan Railway however, the southern companies did not become directly involved in property development, leaving that to others with the necessary skills and capital.

But this burgeoning increase in population around the capital had a knock-on effect on local road transport too. Even before the turn of the 19th century the volume of and delays to traffic in and around Kingston, for example, were so severe that ways of relieving the crush in the town's streets were already being explored. Not only was local traffic abundant but the longstanding and busy Portsmouth Road added its contribution.

Portsmouth had been established by Henry VII as a base for the Royal Navy in 1495. By the middle of the 18th century it had grown into the world's largest industrial organisation. Communication with the Admiralty in London, built in Whitehall in 1726, was vital and the need for easy and swift travel by naval officers between the two being quite as important as it was for the couriers carrying orders. The Portsmouth Road could be traced as a single entity by the late-16th century and had been turnpiked throughout between Kingston and Portsmouth and thus much improved by 1746.

Fifty years later, messages between capital and coast started to be passed largely by a shutter telegraph, although this along with several other shutter systems (London to Deal, Great Yarmouth, etc.) were closed in 1816 after the end of the war, the Admiralty reckoning they didn't need to pass urgent messages in peace-time. The line was rebuilt, and re-opened as a two-arm semaphore system in 1822, and then stayed open until 1847 when superseded by the electric telegraph. The various hills were called Telegraph Hill after the original Murray six-shutter telegraph, rather than the later semaphore (though a purist would say - correctly - that both systems are telegraphs).

Portsmouth was first reached by rail in November 1841, when the South Western opened its line from Eastleigh to Gosport, though the Brighton managed to breach the outer landside fortifications to get into the heart of the town in June 1847. Though two routes between capital and naval base were now provided by the railways they were not always the first choice for people in a hurry. A post chaise on the 67 miles of the Portsmouth Road with regular changes of horses and a given right-of-way was often still considered to be superior in timing to the railways' 95 mile-long wanderings, in the one instance via Eastleigh and Basingstoke and in the other via Brighton. So long as the South Western and Brighton companies continued to pool receipts and share them 50/50 there was no reason for either to disturb the *status quo* by open competition. It was only when the South Western began to work the Portsmouth Direct line in January 1859, and particularly once doubling had been completed in 1878, that

Opposite top - *Chessington South. In the platform No 4680 forms the 16.05 service Waterloo train. The second platform was used for shunting run round purposes. 17 February 1968.*

Opposite top - *Chessington South looking in the direction of what would have been Leatherhead. This time unit No 4680 forms the earlier 15.35 to Waterloo on 17 February 1968. The squat signal box will be noted, to the same design as that at Tolworth. The grass covered platform 'up' platform has never seen regular use by passengers.* *Both R F Roberts*

The 15.05 Waterloo train at Tolworth on 16 March 1968, formed of unit No 4660. All the stations on the line had the same design of platform canopy known as 'Chisarc Cantilever', which afforded a completely clear platform surface. These were also amongst the first stations to have fluorescent lighting, which was provided in different colours.

R F Roberts

a real advantage was gained by the railway, especially as town roads *en route* became increasingly congested. Despite this, Portsmouth's rail services continued to be poorer than might have been expected, for although the Brighton's Mid-Sussex line opened throughout in August 1863, the South Western still had the advantage of a shorter and easier route if a more heavily graded one. And because receipts were still pooled, though now divided ⅔/⅓, competition was more in name than in fact despite the Brighton's best efforts.

So far as Kingston is concerned definite plans for the Portsmouth Road to by-pass the town were finally proposed in 1912. However, the First World War intervened before these had been legally formulated. But they came to the fore again in the early 1920s when traffic through the town had more than doubled in a mere ten years. In part this had been caused by the rise in private motoring particularly with the increasing use of motor vehicles for the distribution and delivery of goods over longer distances than had ever been possible with horse and dray. And it was not just in Kingston itself, for serious traffic problems were also being encountered along the route of the approaches to it through Coombe, Surbiton and the Dittons as 'through' traffic vied with local vehicles for limited space.

By 1923 the by-pass route had been established and

authorised, work on it starting the next year. The new road was to be some 8½ miles long, running through countryside, first in a great southward and then westward loop from a junction at the foot of Roehampton Vale to another on the old road a mile above Esher at the Scilly Isles. (The name comes from the layout of the roundabouts at the junction, still a novelty at the time and then called 'traffic islands'. Their peculiar complexity, still the case, caused them to be nicknamed 'the silly islands', hence over time, Scilly Isles!)

Even before the road opened, land around its route was being snapped up by enterprising builders for speculative residential development, so much so that the Southern was able to take advantage of the new traffic offering from these estates by opening Motspur Park station on the Raynes Park-Epsom line as early as July 1925, concurrently with electrification through to Dorking North. By the time the Prime Minister, Stanley Baldwin, came to perform the opening ceremony of 'The Kingston By-Pass' on 28th October 1927, a great rash of typical three-up two-down semis had already appeared right alongside it and up to a mile away. By the early 1930s these semis and bungalows had been erected by the tens of thousands together with the shops and schools and other infrastructure to support them, great swathes of open land being lost with virtually continual residential development from Raynes Park to Ewell and Tolworth to the south of the by-pass, and New Malden to Long Ditton to the north. Increasing traffic demand saw the Southern open Stoneleigh station on the Epsom line 1¼ miles south of Worcester Park in July 1932. Berrylands, on the main line between New Malden and Surbiton, followed in October 1933 to serve an area that had been largely countryside only a decade before. But by this date motorists and traders were already complaining about delays caused by heavy local traffic on the by- pass. If further indication of the busy state of the Portsmouth Road as a whole is needed, the idea of the recently opened tunnel at Hindhead was first raised as long ago as 1936.

So far as the Southern was concerned, the continual growth in demand for services brought about by this vast new residential area was to be welcomed until it became clear that usage on the local suburban trains was close to saturation point in rush hours. This was particularly so on the Raynes Park-Epsom line with especially heavy traffic at Worcester Park and Ewell West stations, a situation the opening of Motspur Park and Stoneleigh was designed to relieve by the use of staggered stopping patterns in rush hours.

The question has to be asked; how unusual - if not unique, certainly in relatively recent times - is the construction and opening of a new road responsible for spurring on the building of a new railway line? Also, how much was the introduction and sanction of the Ribbon Development Act 1935 due to this vast swathe of new building brought about directly as a result of the planning and construction of the by-pass? By then, of course, the damage had been done by the formation and virtually uncontrolled growth of these new south western outer suburbs. It was left to various post-war Green Belt Acts to ensure there was no repeat of it on this scale in the outlying rural areas.

Herbert Walker's solution to the overcrowding on the trains was to propose a virtual four-tracking of the line between Raynes Park and Leatherhead by construction of a new route from a point south of Motspur Park via Hook, Malden Rushett and Ashtead Common. The Board accepted this recommendation at its meeting in October 1929, at the same time as it approved his proposal to electrify to Brighton. The Bill for the new line received Parliamentary sanction the following year, though Walker did not recommend work start until the Board meeting in June 1934 and it was to be early-1936 before it actually commenced. The long delay between conception and construction is indicative of the financial problems facing the country in general after the Wall Street crash of 1929 and the slow recovery that followed and, from the Southern Railway's point of view in particular, prudently finding the necessary capital for the project and ensuring an adequate return on it, despite the abolition of Railway Passenger Duty in that year's Spring budget. This had brought a saving for the Southern of around £112,000 on 1928's figure.

Not only that: in the interim speculators who had got hold of the land now required for the northern end of the line were proving very reluctant to sell to the railway except at a fat profit until the law came to the Southern's aid. Whether the line would have been completed throughout but for the sin of greed is impossible to know. But the eighteen months or more it took before those necessary purchases were finalised may well have denied the residents of Leatherhead an alternative route to Waterloo.

Following consultations with the London Passenger Transport Board, which had come into being in 1933, it was decided to construct an initial 4¼ miles of the line to Chessington, the limit of the LPTB area, from a junction thirty-four chains south of Motspur Park. Walker had, however, been authorised at the November 1933 Board meeting to purchase the rest of the land needed for the final 2¾ miles of route, between Rushett's Lane, Chessington and the site of the junction at Leatherhead. The estimated cost was £17,800 though £7,000 of this had already been authorised to buy a lineal area of a little less than fifteen acres.

The line as built has stations at Malden Manor (Malden Road), Tolworth (Kingston Road, within yards of its crossing the by-pass), and two in Chessington, at Moor Lane and Church Lane. Together with goods yards at Tolworth and Church Lane the estimated cost was put at £439,147 plus another £120,700 for five eight-car trains to permit a 20-minute headway service to be maintained.

Double-track throughout and electrified from the start, the line opened as far as Tolworth on 29th May 1938 and onward to Chessington one day short of a year later, the near half-mile southward extension to and through the goods yard being completed on 1st July 1939. The two Chessington stations were initially to be suffixed 'Court' and 'Grange' but the more informative if unimaginative and prosaic descriptions 'North' and 'South' were added instead. The delay caused by the War and securing an allowance from the London Transport Pooling Scheme as well as the incipient onset of nationalisation saw the remainder of the line to Leatherhead abandoned together with the expected relief it would have yielded to the Worcester Park route. Despite recent hints that this portion could be resurrected it seems highly unlikely since post-war Green Belt laws have kept the area south of the present terminus more or less clear of development, which means the near-three miles of line would pass through virtually open country alongside the A243 Kingston-Leatherhead road with little if any traffic offering. The only obstruction of consequence is the B280 road at Malden Rushett, a mile beyond Chessington South, which, at the time the line was planned, would have been little more than a country lane that could have been crossed on the level. If the project should, by the remotest chance, go ahead that might still be possible given that a half-hourly train service prevails now and is unlikely to change significantly while there is no longer any freight traffic to be considered. But it should also be noted that that road is now

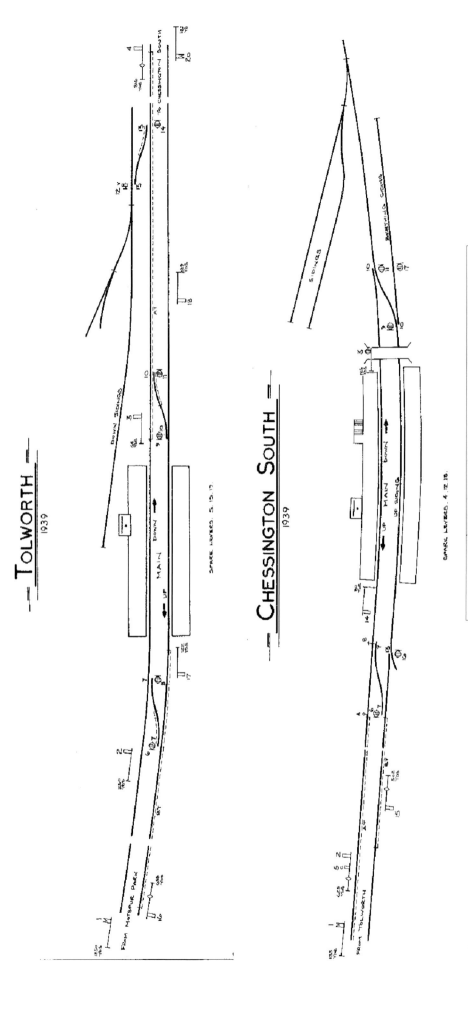

— TOLWORTH —

1939

SPARE LEVERS. 5, 15, 17.

— CHESSINGTON SOUTH —

1939

SPARE LEVERS. 4, 12, 15.

Uncompleted bridge on the abandoned section of line near Chessington.

There were two signal boxes on the line, at Tolworth and Chessington South. Malden Manor and Chessington North were not provided with sidings or crossovers and consequently did not warrant a signal box / ground frame. Had the route been completed then the situation may well have changed. Beyond Chessington South earthworks were completed as far as Chessington Woods whilst stopping places were proposed at Rushett and Leatherhead North, and an intended junction made just north of the original 1859 - 1867 Leatherhead station. Both signal boxes on the line closed on 30 January 1972.

Courtesy Signalling Record Society

very busy and any level crossing would not be far from its traffic-light controlled junction with the even busier A243. Moreover a section of the planned approach to Leatherhead itself is now covered by part of the A243's slip roads to Junction 9 of the M25 though finding an alternative way in at a junction slightly further north might just be possible.

Motspur Park station lies three chains short of 9¾ miles from Waterloo. It consists of a single island platform standing on a low embankment with access from both sides of the line by footbridges, though the one over the up line was not added until June 1938 when the platform canopy was also extended, indications of still increasing usage of this relatively new station. No goods yard was provided here. The surrounding area is known as West Barnes – Motspur Park itself lies a little way to the south west - the line crossing West Barnes Lane on the level immediately to the south of the platforms which retain their SR-style buildings of the period. The signal box, a typical LSWR-pattern brick-built one placed on the up side and to the west of the road, was opened originally as Blue House Crossing and renamed Motspur Park some four years after the station opened. As well as local signals it controlled the junction with the Chessington branch from the first and the branch as a whole from 30th January 1972 until its duties were taken over by the Wimbledon Signalling Centre in July 1990. The crossing gates had been superseded by lifting barriers in November 1974.

Thirty-four chains south of the station and on a downgrade of 1 in 264, the Chessington branch turns west at Motspur Park Junction. There was a serious accident here on the evening of 6th November 1947 when a fog-signalman wrongly exhibited a green light to the 16.45 from Holmwood to Waterloo which then collided with the second carriage of the crowded 17.46 Waterloo-Chessington South service crossing its path. There were four fatalities and twelve people injured.

Leaving the junction in a cutting and climbing at 1 in 99, the line straightens and then runs out on to embankment where the gradient eases. In the course of this section the track crosses the Malden Road (A4203) on a bridge considerably wider than the carriageway itself. The bridge appears to be constructed in reinforced concrete but is, in fact, of steel girders encased in concrete to protect them, a common feature of all such bridges on the branch. From here on the line forms a long, rather uneven almost 90° arc so that at Chessington it faces just west of south.

The first station, Malden Manor, is reached at 11 miles and 5 chains from Waterloo, the building being toward the down end on the up side with the forecourt facing Manor Drive North, which the line bridges. The station lies on the northern edge of what is now Old Malden, a village appearing in the Domesday Book of 1086. In 1846 the London & Southampton Railway opened a station, 'Malden and Combe', about midway between the two villages it purported to serve but the best part of 1½ miles away from both of them, one to the north of the line, the

other to the south. As elsewhere, and for that reason, the station began to attract new development around it, particularly toward the end of the nineteenth century, though the naming distinction between the established and upstart Maldens does not appear to have been in common usage until about 1870. Malden & Combe station itself went through a bewildering series of name changes, New Malden not being finally settled on until September 1957. Old Malden's manor, from which the Chessington branch station takes its name, is now Grade II-listed while the adjoining church of St John the Baptist is of Saxon origin. Both, naturally, appear in Domesday. (Worcester Park station, opened with the line to Epsom on 4th April 1859, was originally titled 'Old Malden & Worcester Park', indicative of the relevant importance of the two places at the time.)

All four branch stations are built in the concrete 'Odeon'-style – or 'Marine' as the Southern called it - considered very modern and up-to-date at the time, with sweeping curves to the roofline and the pillars of the triangular-shaped building at ground level. It has not worn well. Luggage lift shafts were provided at Malden Manor as they were also at the other three stations, arguably as simply a design feature since the machinery was never installed in any of them. Unlike the stations on the 1929-built Wimbledon-Sutton line with their island platform lay-out or the two similarly constructed by the Southern on the Epsom route, those on the branch were provided with wide 520'-long side platforms in anticipation of projected heavier usage. The concrete canopies here and at the other three branch stations were revolutionary, being cantilevered out from the back wall on the Chisarc principle to leave the platforms completely clear of obstructing pillars. As well as modest rectangular windows in the back wall and two rows of small, glazed portholes in the roofs of each section, they were fitted with fluorescent lighting, one of the first such installations on the Southern and much improved by the use of tubes of different colours. Neither the windows nor the portholes survived, the former being blocked off, the latter capped with concrete.

Shortly after leaving Malden Manor the track drops down at 1 in 100 to cross the Hogsmill River, a tributary that meets the Thames a little way upstream of Kingston Bridge. The three-span viaduct is 140' in length. There follows a climb out of the valley at the same inclination on embankment built mainly from material recovered from London slum clearance. That gives way to a cutting as the gradient eases slightly before the line comes to Tolworth station at a little over 12 miles from Waterloo. This also stands on embankment immediately west of the bridge crossing the dual carriageway A240 Burgh Heath-Kingston road only yards from its roundabout and slip roads at the notorious Tolworth underpass. This station, with its building on the up side near the London end and facing Kingston Road, is a replica of Malden Manor except that a goods yard was provided closer to ground level on the down side at the west end of the station. At first this consisted of

71

Coal concentration yard at Tolworth. 16 March 1968.   *R F Roberts*

four sidings with a shunting neck but wartime saw it increased to one of seven roads, the increase believed to be for the purpose of storing Pullman cars withdrawn for the duration.

Tolworth yard ceased handling general goods traffic in May 1965 but had already seen work carried out to make it an NCB coal concentration depot. The crossovers at each end of the station were retained and another crossover laid between two sidings in 1970. Mechanisation in the form of a conveyor speeded up transition from rail vehicle to storage from 1971, two of the sidings being lifted to make room for it. The five remaining sidings varied in length between 206 yards and 286 yards with a rather longer shunting neck. At its height the yard received seventeen coal trains per week but this number gradually declined as the demand for solid fuel diminished until the NCB's interest ceased in 1989. Subsequently marine aggregates were unloaded when it became a base for London Concrete, three sidings being retained for the receipt of these necessary raw materials. But a bus garage was opened on the site in 2002 by the Transdev Group as a replacement for the town centre – and therefore valuably sited! - Kingston Garage.

Tolworth signalbox, a flat-roofed, slab-sided concrete structure quite out of keeping with the graceful curve of the canopy cantilevers, stood at the western end of the down platform. It closed at the end of January 1972 with the takeover of branch signalling by Motspur Park box.

A 12-lever ground frame commissioned two weeks earlier assumed responsibility for the yard connections.

From Tolworth the line falls for about ¼ mile at 1 in 100 before the start of a gentle climb that continues to the terminus, almost entirely on embankment until a short distance beyond Chessington North, which stands 13 miles and 25 chains from Waterloo. Though in the same basic style as the stations that precede them, the two in Chessington show quite distinct differences. Though of concrete construction the buildings are faced in red brick, now much weathered to a pale grey/brown, and the platform canopy cantilevers are much more angular, lacking the smooth curves of the true Chisarc design and, therefore, far less satisfactory from an aesthetic point of view.

The buildings are on the down side at the country end with the forecourt facing Bridge Road, presumably a renaming of the western extremity of Moor Lane as the line 'bridges' it. There is a Station Road to the west of the route though it appears to have no connection to it whatever, the properties on its east side turning their backs to the railway. Bridge Road, which leads to the main A243 Leatherhead-Kingston road and another notorious underpass, at Hook, runs beneath the railway at the down end as the line climbs away on the final stage of its journey. It is soon into a lengthy cutting made through unstable London Clay which required a thick 'mat' of ash and hardcore to be laid on the floor to prevent the clay seeping up through the track ballast.

A southward view from the road bridge at Chessington South station showing the electrified double track heading hopefully towards Leatherhead. Coal wagons and a classic lorry stand in the goods yard. The whole area either side of the track is now heavily overgrown but note the pristine 14th milepost on the left. 1 August 1959.

A E Bennett.

Chessington South station is 13 miles and 75 chains from Waterloo and was the only one on the branch to have the platforms at a lower level than the booking office, though a ticket office was provided on the platform in 1971. The down platform alone is in use, the up one, though completed and with its now very dilapidated canopy, never having been commissioned. The line beside it is, however, electrified for berthing purposes. The entrance to the station is at the country end on the down side actually facing Garrison Lane – Church Lane is some way to the east - which bridges the line immediately to the south. At the opposite end of the station, on the up side, is the electricity substation that feeds the branch and sited centrally enough on it to have also supplied the planned remainder to Leatherhead. The 18-lever signalbox, another uncharacteristic concrete structure halfway along the down platform, closed at the end of January 1972. Double track extends southward from the station for another 39 chains of which a length of 20 chains was electrified. It is still *in situ* though stop blocks are now placed about halfway along the

section. But the route of the unused line and a small part of the proposed extension beyond are still made evident by the rank of trees either side of it until they become part of Chessington Wood.

The goods yard of three sidings was on the down side beyond the Garrison Lane bridge. Charringtons opened a coal concentration depot here in May 1963 making use of two of the sidings. Coal drops were installed together with capstans to move wagons about by rope haulage and so without the need for motive power. At the start the yard received seven trains per week but as at Tolworth demand for solid fuel steadily declined. Following some further use by EWS, the yard closed at the end of the 1980s though the sidings remain in place but out of use. Coal is still retailed here but it now comes in by road.

Though local traffic provided the principal reason for the station's construction: it also acted as the alighting point for visitors to Chessington Zoo, about ½ mile away and on the west side of the A423. This had been established at Burnt Stub, a mansion originally built in 1348 but razed to the ground by Cromwell, which gave it that name. It was rebuilt as Chessington Hall in Gothic style from the eighteenth century: the zoo opened in 1931. This was as much a funfair as a zoo and included a 12" gauge miniature railway opened in 1932 that took visitors round the perimeter of the grounds. Power was provided by two internal combustion locos whose outline was based on outside-framed GWR 4-4-0s. (Alighting from and boarding the trains took place where the line ran wholly unfenced right through the middle of the main pedestrian circulating area between the entrance and the animal cages, a situation to give today's Health & Safety officers nightmares!) It closed in 1984 for re-gauging as a 2' steam-powered line though that was lifted at the end of the 1996 season. The whole site now forms part of the Chessington World of Adventures theme park opened in 1987 by the Madame Tussaud's organisation and still an extremely popular attraction today. The great bulk of its visitors, however, scorn use of the station.

At opening the branch was provided with a 20-minute headway service seven days a week which gave six trains an hour on the Raynes Park-Motspur Park Junction section of the Epsom line. The service was reduced to two trains an hour from September 1958 and remains so to this day, including during rush hours. At the time of writing the first up train to Waterloo departs at a relatively late 06.39, the last at 23.39 though this requires a nineteen-minute wait at Wimbledon and the intervals in the late evening are hourly. The first down departure from Waterloo is at 05.50, also requiring a change at Wimbledon, the last at 23.00, one and a quarter hour after the previous down train. Some compensation may be provided by the No 65 bus route that runs half-hourly all night between Kingston, which has four trains leaving Waterloo after 2300, the last at 23.57, and Chessington.

And what of the road that caused the Southern to seek a new path to Leatherhead? In time its several crossroads were equipped with traffic lights which, in turn, were superseded by roundabouts which, later still, had cuttings dug out beneath them to form underpasses with the inevitable widening being undertaken piecemeal over much of its length. It was also extended, a new six-lane dual carriageway opening in the 1970s from just west of the Hook underpass, looping around Esher through open country and not regaining the original route until south of Cobham and within shouting distance of the later M25 junction 10. But at certain times of day heavy traffic still moves along it in a more or less solid and speed restricted phalanx that shows no signs of ever diminishing, while the trains to Epsom and Chessington have never got beyond the Southern's standard 8-car length. There's surely a lesson there somewhere!

Bibliography

History of the Southern Railway, C F Dendy Marshall, Ian Allan Ltd., 1963 (1982 reprint.)
Sir Herbert Walker's Southern Railway, C F Klapper, Ian Allan Ltd., 1973.
The London & South Western Railway, O S Nock, Ian Allan Ltd., 1965.
Railways of the Southern Region, (PSL Field Guide) Geoffrey Body, Patrick Stephens Ltd., 2nd edition 1989.
Wimbledon to Epsom including the Chessington Branch, Vic Mitchell and Keith Smith, Middleton Press, 1995.
Railway Track Diagrams no 5, England South and London Underground, TRACKmaps, 3rd edition 2008.
Ordnance Survey 1:50,000 maps nos. 176 and 187.
Ordnance Survey 1" to 1 mile map 'Greater London', 1966.
Master Atlas of Greater London, Geographers' A-Z Map Company Ltd., 7th edition 1995.

A number of websites have been consulted to obtain or confirm information, particularly concerning the history of places the branch line passes through and the background to the planning and construction of the Kingston by-pass. The timetables on sites provided by National Rail and London Buses have also been consulted.

On 2 and 16 December 1962, the RCTS and SLS jointly organised a special train covering a number of branches in the London suburban area. Former LSWR 'H16' 4-6-2T No 30517 took the train down to Chessington South and is seen running round before the return trip to Wimbledon.

George Smith

From the SOUTHERN RAILWAY MAGAZINE, June 1938

SOUTHERN RAILWAY MAGAZINE

with which is incorporated the SOUTH WESTERN GAZETTE (first issued 1881)

Vol. XVI. No. 186.   June, 1938.

SOMETHING NEW IN STATIONS!
Malden Manor, one of the two new stations of the Chessington extension, opened on May 29th. Note the roof lighting and the freedom of platforms from pillars and other obstructions.

Surrey's New Railway.

MOTSPUR PARK TO TOLWORTH SECTION OF CHESSINGTON LINE.

It is very rarely in these days that a new bit of railway is constructed in Great Britain. It is still more rare to find such a construction within a few miles of London, although the new Wimbledon and Sutton line opened in 1930, was certainly an indication that other developments would be necessary in this growing residential part of Surrey. The continued extending of the population has now resulted in another new line, leaving the Epsom line at Motspur Park, eventually to join it again at Leatherhead, but for the present reaching as far as Tolworth.

Not only will the new line which the Southern Railway are constructing between Motspur Park and Chessington help to develop the district round Tolworth and Chessington, but it will also cater for the growing population in the Surbiton and Malden areas. The census figures for the year 1931, as compared with 1921, show that the population of these two urban districts increased from 19,547 to 29,396, in the case of Surbiton, and from 14,495 to 23,412, for Malden. Since 1931, the growth has been even more rapid.

This increase is also reflected in the number of season tickets issued from stations in the locality. A comparison between the year 1927 and last year is as follows :—

				1927	1937
From Surbiton	...	...	...	16,061	45,607
,, Malden	...	...	...	12,043	31,643
,, Worcester Park	...	...	8,201	31,984
,, Motspur Park	...	...	2,061	12,808

OPENED ON SUNDAY, MAY 29TH.

On Sunday, May 29th, the first section of the new railway was opened for traffic, and provides services between London (Waterloo) and Tolworth, the two new stations being Malden Manor and Tolworth, respectively.

The new railway has been built under powers obtained by the Company in 1930, and will serve, in the main, the rapidly growing residential area south of the Kingston By-Pass Road.

The railway begins a short distance south of Motspur Park Station and bends to the right in a south-westerly direction, and after passing through Old Malden, Tolworth and Chessington, will terminate for the time being at a point near a road known as Garrison Lane, which leads from the Kingston-Leatherhead Road to Chessington Church, quite close to the well-known Chessington Zoo.

The four stations on this section of the railway, at intervals of approximately a mile, are Malden Manor, adjoining a new road named Manor Drive North on a new building estate ; Tolworth, on the Surbiton-Ewell-Reigate Road, a few yards from the Kingston By-Pass ; Chessington Court, adjoining Bridge Road, which is a new road leading from the Kingston-Leatherhead Road to Epsom ; and Chessington Grange, adjoining Garrison Lane, referred to above.

Chessington Court and Chessington Grange Stations will be opened, it is anticipated, in about a year's time.

At Tolworth and Chessington Grange Stations, commodious Goods Yards are being constructed.

The railway, a small, but important addition to the Southern Railway's great electrified suburban system, is being constructed to full modern standards, so far as permanent way, bridges and stations are concerned.

THREE TRAINS AN HOUR.

A service of three electric trains per hour connects Tolworth with Waterloo. These leave Tolworth at 2, 22 and 42 minutes past the hour on week-days, and at 4, 24 and 44 minutes on Sundays. In the Down direction, the trains leave Waterloo at 16, 36 and 56 minutes past the hour on week-days and at 6, 26 and 46 minutes on Sundays. The journey occupies 29 minutes.

ENGINEERING FEATURES.

The new line runs for the most part on embankments and through cuttings, as none of the

Malden Manor Station—platforms and roofing.

Southern Railway Magazine,

76

track could be laid at the original surface level.

The local soil is clay, of a type liable to slip in wet weather. For this reason it was unsuitable for the embankments, although it was possible to make use of a certain amount to form the "core". The embankments were therefore completed with large quantities of dry filling material, obtained from slum clearance and other demolition works in London. This contained large quantities of brick rubble, sand, ordinary soil and debris, and

Malden Manor Station.

Tolworth Station.

was excellent material for the purpose, as it allowed the slopes to be trimmed to a much steeper angle than is possible with clay, while it is also free from the liability to slip. The surplus clay was used to fill in a large lake on the Company's property near Teddington Station.

NEW STYLE STATION ARCHITECTURE AND LIGHTING.

The four stations are in keeping with the modern character of the neighbourhood. At each place the station buildings adjoin the main roads, the platforms being reached by staircases. As will be seen at the two stations already constructed, the buildings are of attractive appearance, and there is an extensive forecourt as well as a car park at each station. Waiting rooms are provided on the platforms.

The platform roofs at Malden Manor and Tolworth are of a novel type in reinforced concrete work, giving an *unobstructed platform free of columns,* and having also the advantage of involving no cost in periodical painting. The illumination of the platforms under these roofs is by means of florescent tubes.

EIGHT BRIDGES IN 4¼ MILES.

There are a number of bridges under the railway and one over the railway, viz., that carrying Garrison Lane. All these bridges have been constructed of steel girders completely encased in concrete, and are of a very modern design.

Tests have proved that there is a good deal of latent strength given to the bridges by protecting them with concrete. The primary object of encasing the steel in concrete is, however, to avoid periodical painting, a considerable item in railway maintenance expenditure.

The most notable of these bridges is that over the Ewell Road, which is now being reconstructed by the Surrey County Council as a double carriage way with cycle tracks and footpaths on each side. The bridges over Moor Lane and Cox's Lane are of considerable span compared with the width of the existing roadways. Bridge Road is an entirely new road, and the main girders which span it are over 90ft. in length and weigh about 60 tons each.

In addition, a viaduct, 140ft. long, has had to be constructed over the Hogsmill River.

MINERALS IN THE CLAY.

About the time that the railway was first projected, it was discovered that the clay in the neighbourhood was very strongly impregnated with sulphates, viz., Magnesium Sulphate (Epsom Salts), Sodium Sulphate (Glauber Salts) and Calcium Sulphate (Gypsum). All these have a very deleterious effect on Portland Cement concrete where water is present, and for that reason all the drainage works in the clay have been constructed with a special cement concrete which is unaffected by sulphates.

At Chessington Grange, where deep excavations had to be made, rock was found full of small fossil shells said to be 20,000,000 years old.

PROTECTIVE FENCING.

Throughout the new railway, wherever building development has taken place or is in con-

An inaugural run along the new line was made on May 25th, in which representatives of the local authorities and trade associations participated, including the Mayor of Malden and Coombe (Ald. F. S. Wagner), the Town Clerk (Mr. J. W. Johnson), Alderman Dumper of Surbiton and the Town Clerk (Mr. R. Baskerville).

Mr. E. J. Missenden, the Traffic Manager, and Mr. G. Ellson, the Chief Engineer, were accompanied by Mr. H. E. O. Wheeler, the Superintendent of Operation, Mr. C. Grasemann, Public Relations and Advertising Officer, and Messrs. W. S.

Top: Double span bridge over Ewell Road.

Left: The bridge over Manor Drive North.

Right: The bridge over Malden-Worcester Park Road.

Bottom: The 140ft. viaduct over the Hogsmill River.

templation, the railway is being fenced with the Company's new standard diamond mesh fencing, with a view to preventing trespass either by children or animals.

MATERIAL STATISTICS.

The principal quantities of materials dealt with on the works are as follows:—

Earthworks.

Excavations	...	200,000 cubic yards
Embankments		550,000 cubic yards

Bridges.

Steel	...	600 tons
Concrete	...	17,000 cubic yards
Pipe Drains.	...	6,000 lin. yards
Fencing	...	15,000 lin. yards

Mr. Missenden, Mr. Ellson, Alderman Dumper, and the Mayor of Malden on the inaugural run.

The new protective diamond mesh fencing—a preventative measure against trespassing.

England, S. W. Smart, W. M. Perts, C. S. Cobley, C. Gribble, J. R. Scott, H. I. Bond, S. G. Morgan, R. W. O. Hartridge, and D. G. Williams.

Mr. E. J. Missenden, the Traffic Manager, gave some interesting figures to the gathering to show that the new line should prove a good venture. The Southern Railway Company, he said, has the most intensive electrified suburban service in the world. In America, with a population of 125,000,000, the number of passenger journeys in 1936 over a route mileage of 241,822 was 490,000,000. On the Southern Railway last year, with a route mileage of 2,200, the number of passenger journeys was 378,000,000.

Hitherto, when electrification schemes have been carried out, it has been necessary to assume that the traffic would increase to justify the cost of the work, and in all cases electrification has led to a large extension of the built-up area and a large increase in the number of passengers. A census taken last month showed that the number of passengers conveyed in one day to and from the London stations of the Southern Railway was 733,506, 41.7 per cent. more than 10 years ago. The number of people arriving at and departing from Waterloo Station was 151,571, an increase of 15.1 per cent. as compared with 1928. Of this number 47,051 arrived between 7 a.m. and 10 a.m. and 24,296 arrived in the busiest hour. On the same day 1,421 trains arrived at and left Waterloo Station.

In the case of the new line to Tolworth and on to Chessington the circumstances are different from previous cases of electrification. The traffic is already there waiting for the railway. Since the Kingston by-pass was constructed and the new railway was started building development has proceeded rapidly; a resident in the district for 40 years said that if he went away for a few weeks he found so many new streets that he had to ask the way. The new line will not only provide for this growing traffic, but will relieve the congestion on neighbouring lines.

Just to show that the recent terrible winter flooding has not been confined to the present century. This was the scene at Mitcham on 16 February 1902.

REMEMBER

HORSHAM?

The view from within the deserted locomotive stalls shows across the turntable an 80xxx tank, with valve and cylinder head removed, awaits attention – perhaps a failure dumped there. A solitary railwayman strolls round the table – one of the very few people seen that day. (Photograph and captions by Bill Allen)

REMEMBER HORSHAM?

Opposite top - *No 84026 on the turntable. It was built at Darlington in April 1957 and first allocated to Ramsgate. By 1961 the Southern Region had replaced aged H & M7 0-4-4Ts on the Brighton – Horsham and Guildford – Horsham lines with the modern tank engines, both the original ex – LMS Ivatt, and later BR 2-6-2T 84XXX locomotives. Very well liked by the enginemen, they had a brief time on these services before the lines closed. The headcode on the bunker indicates Horsham – Guildford and No 84026 looks somewhat work soiled, with white scale all over the cylinders. The engine was on the allocation of Brighton (75A) from June to September 1961 which helps date the visit. That autumn re-allocation took the loco back to the north at Newton Heath, Manchester. After service in this area, No 84026 was due to be transferred back to the S.R. in November 1965 as one of the 84xxx proposed for use on the Isle of Wight. This did not transpire however, and the RCTS book on BR Standard Tanks confirms that the loco stayed in the north with withdrawal following in that year.*

Opposite bottom - *Ivatt on the turntable. No 41291, an Ivatt 2-6-2T, poses on the turntable. A long time Stewarts Lane (73A) engine, the Kent electrification brought transfer to Brighton (75A) in the spring of 1961. The arrival ended, as The Railway Observer commented, an Indian summer for E4s and M7s on the Horsham services.*

Bottom - *Coaling Stage - No 84026 taking water at the coaling stage on the lines leading from the turntable to the station approaches. The shed was on a very restricted site – to the right the driver adjusts the water crane and on the tank the fireman waits to receive the bag. Another 84xxx lurks on the left behind the coaling stage, and to the right the large water storage tank sits on its brick tower. In the immediate foreground is a travelling crane that had been located here to make the back-breaking job of coaling a bit easier.*

Top - *EmptyTurntable. The old shed looks fairly trim in this view across the turntable – the tender in shot may be a K class, by this time in her last six months of life before the "Accountant's cull" in December 1962. To the left is the 80xxx tank seen previously.*

Bottom - *Q in the shed. No 30545 Q class 0-6-0 lurks in the shed - in steam and with a well filled tender, this Q had been allocated to Horsham at nationalisation and only transferred to Three Bridges in July 1959 as part of the downgrading of 75D. I remember this loco as a regular visitor to Bognor on the "goods". Initially the engine was fitted with a Maunsell chimney followed in 1949 by a Lemaitre blastpipe and large diameter chimney to improve steaming. Ironically this was replaced in 1958 by more conventional arrangements and a BR Standard Class 4 chimney when it was discovered that steaming was improved over the Lemaitre!*

TUNES OF GLORY?

*Musical compositions that attempt to portray railways often seem to miss the mark somehow. On the other hand, music which has different aims can sometimes be much more evocative. This is of course an emotional response and, as with poetry, can vary from one person to the next. **Nick Pallant** nevertheless risks the wrath of all concerned by suggesting a variety of music which, for him, evokes the Southern.*

I was once in conversation with an ex-Hither Green fireman who recalled a night in the very early 1960's when he worked a freight train from South East London to Tonbridge. It was an uneventful run but when he and his driver went to start their rest break the Shadows' **Apache** was playing on the lobby radio. It had ever since reminded him of that occasion and now when I listen to that immortal hit I don't imagine Native Americans but an N class tackling the climb to Knockholt with a long string of wagons as the sound of the exhaust echoes across the suburbs and the countryside. From much the same era came the Tornados' **Telstar**. There is a weird sound effect at the beginning and end of this tune which is supposed to represent a satellite in orbit (noise in space?) Not a bit of it. To me it has always sounded like the engines of a Hastings diesel and the rhythm of the piece can certainly evoke the sight of a 6L unit heading at speed across the Weald.

Not long afterwards, ITV used **Sibelius' Intermezzo to the Karelia Suite** as its theme tune for the *World in Action* programme. There is something in the faster renderings of this piece which to this day reminds me of 'spotting' at Ferring level crossing on Coastway West as a Spamcan appeared from the Goring-by-Sea direction with a Brighton - Plymouth train and thundered westwards followed by the sight of the last vehicle disappearing into the distance. Similar scenes can also be evoked by (inevitably!) Ron Goodwin's **633 Squadron**. That composer's work of course includes the **Battle of Britain Theme** which, to say the least, can be heard as suggestive of something other than certain noble fighter aircraft.

Moving forward with Bulleid Pacifics, one cannot omit Ray Davies' wonderful **Waterloo Sunset**. Yes, I know he originally wrote it about Liverpool but was persuaded to move the setting to London. Did the 'persuaders' realise that both making the change and releasing this Kink's song in the summer of 1967 was going to gain them a few more sales? I know I'm not the only person who regards that sixties classic as something of a Southern anthem. A few years later came the Return to Steam programme on the national network. The Southern contribution began in April 1974 when Merchant Navy Class *Clan Line* left the erstwhile Ashford Steam Centre at just after midnight. It was recorded at the time that, as she headed through Ashford, Jerry Goldsmith's **Theme from Patton** was playing on the support crew's car radios (no dedicated support coaches in those days). The slow build up of this music and the gathering pace to a purposeful march perfectly matches the progress of that magnificent locomotive as she headed towards Tonbridge and on to the West of England, carrying with her all the hopes and aspirations of the Southern heritage groups.

To come back to the classical tradition, Ralph Vaughan Williams' **Wasps Overture** would make excellent background music for a video about today's Isle of Wight railways – the buzzing about bits for the ex-tube trains, the statelier passages for the Steam Railway and the gentle tune in the middle for the ferries across the Solent. Similarly the same composer's **Fantasia on a Theme by Thomas Tallis** always brings to mind standing on an upper deck of Sealink's *St. Helens* and watching the spire of St. John's rise out of the morning mist as the ferry made its way past wooded shores rolling down to the sea whilst anticipation of the 'Island of Dreams' once more worked its magic. Vaughan Williams' friend Gustav Holst of course wrote **Jupiter from the Planets Suite.** Now there are all sorts of things in there which have railway-like rhythms and the 'big tune' (*I Vow to Thee My Country*) is surely a tone poem for the rolling landscape of Southern England.

No doubt some readers will regard all the above as mawkish nonsense (and musically illiterate). On the other hand, maybe you have your own selection of pieces which remind you of the Southern?

'Bridge over Troubled Water' perhaps? (Sorry - Ed)

VARIATIONS ON UTILITY VANS

Part 2: Covcars and Luggage Vans post 1939, Gangwayed and Scenery Vans

Mike King

In part one we traced the development of the four-wheeled Covcars and luggage vans from inception until the end of 1939 – now we will continue the story through to the final productions of 1955, moving then to the gangwayed bogie luggage vans of 1930/31 and ending with the three small batches of vans built specifically for theatrical scenery traffic.

As previously recounted, the 2+2 planking made its first appearance on Covcars at the end of 1938 and on the luggage vans around six months later. No official documentation has ever been found to explain this form of construction but it was probably O. V. Bulleid's first contribution to the utility van design apart, maybe, from some livery changes. Whatever the politicians may have been telling the country at large ("peace in our time" - and all that), the railways had been advised to prepare for war and it was anticipated that some sources of timber, in particular from eastern Europe might be disrupted or cut off altogether. Bulleid was asked to investigate alternative forms of construction that might overcome these restrictions and this may have been the first step in making greater use of home-grown timber by allowing smaller sections to be used and also to reduce wastage. This begs the question – why not use smaller sections throughout instead of the mixed alternate width planks? But perhaps sufficient strength could not be guaranteed if this was adopted. As the war progressed, Bulleid and Lynes would investigate these aspects further and come up with several more alternatives, as we shall see.

Luggage Vans 1940-1947

Production of Covcars had halted at the end of 1938 and would not resume until BR days but construction of luggage vans continued right through the war and after. Many of these were identical to the last pre-war productions, having 2+2 planking. Details are as follows: -

1821-1920	Built Lancing/Eastleigh, Feb-Aug 1940
1053, 1692-1730, 2083-90	Built Lancing, May-Sept 1943
1501-1560	Built Ashford June-Aug 1947

As before, Diagram 3103 was allocated – the different planking being of no consequence whatsoever to anyone except a railway enthusiast! Notice how all three works were now involved and that the numbering was becoming fragmented as existing gaps in the luggage van series were being used up. During this period most of the last pre-Grouping passenger luggage vans were withdrawn as well and by 1945 the Southern's non-passenger coaching stock fleet became, with the exception of horseboxes and a few specialised vehicles, almost wholly made up by utility vans of all descriptions.

However, between August and December 1942, 120 luggage vans were completed at Lancing using pressed steel "U" channels in place of the usual "L" and "T" angle body framework, combined with even planking. There must have been some concerns about the strength of the channels as these were reinforced by having stout timbers bolted to one arm of the "U" framing – resulting in a most peculiar appearance. The bodyside timbers must also have been fractionally narrower than the pre-war even planks, as there was a narrow make-up plank (about 4 inches wide) about halfway up the bodyside. Clearly this was another Bulleid/ Lynes idea to overcome wartime shortages. Numbers of these vans were 1781-1820 and 2091-2170. Van 2140 suffered fire damage soon after construction and was re-planked in 2+2 style, so exhibited what was probably a unique combination of planking and framing.

The Bulleid livery changes had so far been largely missed by the non- passenger coaching stock – although it is possible that some vans received the short-lived Dover green colour around 1939 – that which weathered to a khaki hue rather too quickly. However with the general levels of grime and extended repainting periods during the war, none of this might have been noticed much anyway. Some vans numbered from 1821 onwards received the company title (now without the word "Railway") in Bulleid style when new, yellow with the black "in-line" instead of the previous gilt-shaded black but the van numbers continued in the older format. Just how many received the new Bulleid malachite green is open to debate – likewise those overhauled and repainted during this period seemed to be largely out-shopped in Maunsell green. Vans definitely noted in malachite are confined to just 1075 and 2062 (both on 2nd July 1940) and 2124 (on 1st January 1944). However Frank Foote noted Covcar 1766 in "sage green" during February 1947 – whatever that might signify? Others noted in grey between 1942 and 1946 include 1157/66, 1265 (the first one recorded, on 26th July 1942), 1808/93, 1927/50/57, 2111, 2224 and 2385, most being seen during 1944-46. These were lettered normally on the light grey finish. Quite possibly full repaints during this period were few – patch

Uneven-planked van 1915 when new in August 1940. It may be malachite green and has the new Bulleid company title in yellow with a black "in-line" but the numerals are still shaded black. The word "Railway" has been omitted. This van would not enter ordinary traffic until August 1945, instead becoming the drawing office stores van 1572s to Diagram 3104. Once in normal service, it ran until October 1981.

SR Official

painting and re-varnishing being the order of the day.

Van 1915, new in August 1940 was officially photographed on completion, only to be immediately modified as a mobile drawing office stores van, numbered 1572s in the departmental stock and allocated Diagram 3104. This diagram shows that it was equipped internally with 33 cylindrical metal drawing canisters at each end and had a reference bench with filing cabinet and cupboard underneath between the doors along one side. The interior was lined with asbestos sheeting, as was the roof. The windows were also covered with asbestos but those two panels above the reference bench could slide sideways to admit light into the vehicle. Clearly this was used for dispersal of Chief Mechanical Engineer's drawing office records and the van was also fitted with secure locks . It was released from these duties and then retook its traffic department number in August 1945. A handful of other luggage vans were transferred to departmental service during the war years but all were returned to normal traffic afterwards.

The "Plastic" luggage vans

In 1943 Bulleid and Lynes contributed the greatest change to utility van construction – although it was destined to remain something of an experiment. The last ten vans on order L1659 (placed in April 1941) were subsequently amended as sub-order E1659A, dated August 1943, for the construction of "Ten lightweight 4w luggage vans", so it looks likely that this was something of an afterthought as the

war progressed and things began to look brighter. These vehicles; numbered 1401-10 to Diagram 3105 emerged from Eastleigh in December 1943/January 1944 for Nos. 1401/2 and between May-September 1944 for the remainder. Much coverage was given in the railway press of the time and "The Railway Gazette" went as far as producing a separate 4-page pamphlet entitled "New Southern Railway Passenger Luggage Van", available for the purchase price of one shilling (five pence), giving full technical details. This actually reprinted the contents of their 7th April 1944 article but clearly the Southern felt the publicity would be worthwhile.

The criteria behind the design were as follows: -
To reduce weight while maintaining strength
To avoid sudden shocks to passengers or goods in the event of impact
To use new materials such as plastics, where suitable
To use new methods of fabrication, where applicable
To keep maintenance costs down

A combination of light steel channels (like those used on the Lancing-built 1942 vans), welded assembly and timber roof sticks were used for the body framing with the body panels themselves constructed from reinforced plastic sheets – the reinforcement being provided in the form of woven high-tensile steel wire and cotton fabric laminated into the pre-coloured plastic material. Wartime restrictions constrained the size of the panels and black was the only colour readily available but it was hoped that once peacetime had returned

Top - *PMV No. S1899S in BR green livery at Yeovil Junction on 18ᵗʰ February 1965, showing the standard lettering layout adopted from at least 1955 onwards, probably earlier, with full dimensions and wheelbase quoted at the lower right-hand end. This one also has overhead live wire flashes. Built in May 1940, it too ran until 1981.*

these two matters might be addressed. The doors were constructed from light sheet steel material. The lightweight body demanded that some form of spring cushioning or shock absorbing mechanism was needed, so the 33ft underframe was 12 inches longer than the body to allow for movement. This did not have conventional solebars but instead had two middle longitudinal girders spaced about 2ft 3in apart, from which the body supports, headstocks and axle-box assemblies were cantilevered. Two sets of cushioning springs were provided, arranged so that one set came into play immediately, the second having a delayed effect, allowing the complete body to move up to a maximum of 11 inches, be arrested and then return to the centre-point smoothly. Shock absorbing wagons had been introduced by the LMS in 1937 and the other companies had built similar small-bodied wagons but this was in a different league altogether. The resulting van had a most un-British appearance but Bulleid never owed much to convention!

However, the design was not multiplied beyond the original ten vans, so any saving in weight (2¾ tons per van combined with an increase in capacity of 40 cubic ft compared to a standard luggage van) was hardly noticeable while at least half were later repainted in BR Southern Region green livery so any maintenance saving was lost there too. None has been noted in BR crimson (that would look interesting!) so one assumes those repainted were done from 1956 onwards once the original finish deteriorated. Eastleigh Works would go on to manufacture GRP (glass reinforced plastic) doors, EMU cab ends and, of course, the "plastic-bodied" suburban coach S1000S so maybe this early development work was not altogether wasted.

All ten vans remained in existence – if not all in traffic – until the 1960s while the last, No. 1402, was withdrawn in 1972, by which time it was green but had replacement steel doors of a rather heavier pattern fitted. When seen by the author at Micheldever sidings in October 1972 one of the destinations chalked on was Colwyn Bay, so no special allocations or restrictions were applied to the vehicles and they could turn up in a van train anywhere. That said, one was regularly rostered for the *Golden Arrow* duty in 1946/47. Otherwise, they were simply noted in carriage working appendices as luggage vans of 10 tons tare, instead of the usual 12, 13 or 14 tons for conventional vans.

Luggage Vans – Post 1948

Production of conventional luggage vans was not interrupted by the development of the plastic-bodied vans and the last Southern Railway-ordered vehicles took to the rails in August 1947. One might have thought this would be the end, but it was not the case and two further orders were

placed after Nationalisation. The first was for 111 vans - the odd number probably allowing for 21 replacements for those converted for the War Department – not that this is noted against the order description (it would have been in Maunsell's day!) and these appeared from all three SR workshops between April 1950 and January 1951 – painted BR crimson with 'S' prefixes to the numbers but with plywood bodysides and ends in the manner that ordinary covered goods wagons had been constructed since 1945. However, the side doors remained in the 2+2 uneven planking, perhaps for strength. This did give a small saving in weight and the tare of these vans was reduced from 13 to 12 tons. Running numbers were 1561-1671, again to Diagram 3103.

The last batch of 50 vans was constructed, rather surprisingly, at the former LNWR carriage works at Wolverton during January-August 1951, numbered 1451-1500. These reverted to the uneven-planked bodywork, perhaps because Wolverton was not geared up for plywood construction methods but like the recent SR-built vans were also recorded as 12 tons tare. This brought the number of luggage vans completed up to 990 vehicles (including 45 of SECR origin and the ten plastic-bodied ones) but by this time a few were already in departmental stock, so at no point were all in traffic together. A little bit of rough computation suggests that the maximum in service might have been around 920 in 1952 – but do not take this as gospel!

By now the existing vans were steadily being repainted in BR crimson with black ends – but many were just plain dirty anyway and could now be seen almost anywhere in the country. The older vehicles, plus a few new ones, were now being transferred to departmental service in increasing numbers and this would continue through until the 1980s. Seven vans were shipped to the Isle of Wight in October 1950, repainted crimson and became the most modern carriage stock on the Island during the steam era. These were from different batches and some were even-planked, others had the 2+2 arrangement. They were renumbered 1046-52 but were classified PLV (passenger luggage van) whereas the mainland coding was PMV (parcels and miscellaneous van). They just had 'S' prefixes to the numbers and never received a suffix letter, unlike their counterparts on the mainland. These were Westinghouse-fitted and also had side lamp-irons provided in case they were included in Island goods trains. All survived to the end of steam operation in December 1966 and all subsequently entered departmental use. Several were later sold to the Isle of Wight Steam Railway.

The five ex-SECR air-control PP vans were

Opposite - One of the Lancing 1942 vans with pressed steel channel body framing. Notice the timber bolted to one arm of the channel and how this has to break at window/door hinges. Van S1813 is in crimson lake livery with black ends at Stewarts Lane on 21st July 1951. The number is low down at the left-hand end and minimal dimension details are given at this end, together with the minute P.M.V. code (complete with full stops) on the lowest plank. The extra four-inch make up plank may be seen at door handle height.

A. E. West

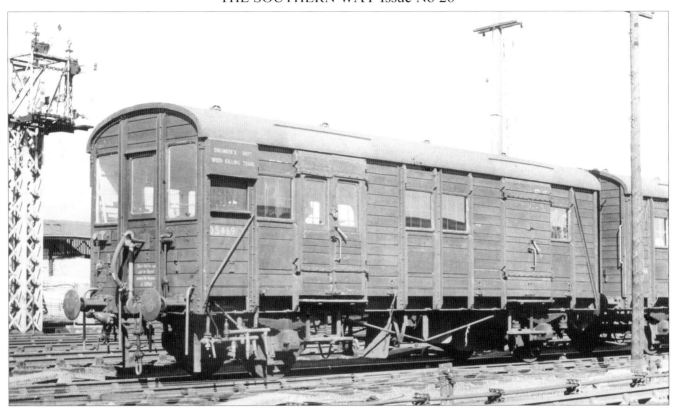

Four of the Lancing 1942 vans entered departmental use for weed killing train vans as soon as May 1947. These were Nos. 1787/91, 2127/64 that became, respectively 466s, 469s, 470s and 471s. All were considerably modified for this work and were originally based at Blackheath. Their first departmental livery was malachite green, including the leading end of the spraying van but they were later noted in black and finally brown. This is spraying van DS469 with mess van DS466 coupled behind it at Eastleigh on 17th September 1959. The rest of the train comprised six tank wagons and a 15-ton "pillbox" brake van, with the locomotive pushing from the rear. Vans 470/71s formed a separate train. Their later base was at Horsham.

J. H. Aston

withdrawn in 1962 but there was still some need for the vans, particularly on the Brockenhurst-Ringwood-Wimborne- Bournemouth West service, so the pull-push equipment was taken from the SECR vehicles and fitted to plywood-bodied vans 1621-25 between October 1962 and March 1963. This effort was somewhat wasted as the M7 locomotives providing the pull-push motive power were withdrawn just over a year later so the vans were returned to ordinary traffic soon after. Five more plywood-bodied vans (Nos. 1562/76, 1613/18/28) were hurriedly altered as security vans in September 1963 for Southampton Docks bullion traffic, for which purpose they had the side glazing replaced by steel sheet (invisible because of the usually dirty state of the windows!) and a second single-leaf door was fitted inside the double doors – which could only be released with a special key once the outer doors were opened. The sides and outer doors were also lined with steel sheet, causing the door hinges to fail under the extra weight and all required new stronger hinges to be fitted during 1973! Diagram 3104 was allocated (the second use of this number) and the vans remained on these duties until 1978. They were then stored at Micheldever sidings where they

remained pending departmental transfer, which took place during the early 1980s. The diagram records the fact that the tare weight was increased to 15 tons 16 cwt (an increase of almost four tons) by these security measures and carrying capacity had to be reduced to five tons to compensate for this. It is not believed any special labelling was applied – the Great Train Robbery of August 1963 prompted the conversions and they were done extremely rapidly after authorisation – so their duties were hardly likely to be advertised in any shape or form, even amongst railwaymen. Presumably before September 1963 any ordinary van was used but having been caught out once….

Vans 1537/58 were fitted for dual heating in October 1961 for use on the electrically-hauled *Golden Arrow* service, eventually having air brakes added. About ten others (including Nos. 1455/77/82/95/96/99, 1626/47) were similarly equipped between 1965 and 1968 for Central Division loco-hauled services – mostly on the Reading-Redhill-Tonbridge and Oxted lines and other overnight duties but how much use was made of these fittings is debatable as most seemed to sit in a line at New Cross Gate yard until they were transferred to the Western Region in

One of the Isle of Wight transfers of October 1950, seen here at Newport on 21ˢᵗ May 1957. Nearest the camera is 2+2-planked S1048 – ex-mainland no. 1720 – while just visible behind is an even-planked van so must be one of 1046/47/49/50. Note the lamp irons high up at each end and the absence of an 'S' suffix letter. Van 1048 went on to become departmental DS70257 in December 1966 and internal user 082056 at Sandown six months later. It was finally sold to the Isle of Wight Steam Railway in 1985 for its underframe to be shortened and reused under ex-LCDR brake third no 4112.

H. C. Casserley

1973 All these were eventually repainted rail blue, including the ends, as were many survivors from 1967 onwards. Some remained in Southern Region green, which began to replace crimson from April 1956 onwards (in fact before the press release announcing a return to regional colours had been made). Early green repaints had black ends but later, in association with the introduction of airless spraying techniques, green ends became more common. Of course, some vans remained crimson and a few could still be noted in the early 1970s – hidden beneath the dirt. One other interesting allocation was van 1567 modified for Kellogg's cornflake traffic in March 1965 – but the nature of these or if any markings were carried are unknown.

General withdrawal of the newer luggage vans began in the 1970s but many were still in traffic until 1981 when mass scrapping commenced. The last PMV in traffic was 1940-vintage no. 1865, which was actually withdrawn in 1981, reinstated and finally taken out of service in July 1986, then being sold to the Midland Railway Trust at Butterley for its underframe to be reused under an ex-Midland Railway coach body. This was typical and just one of many that have been purchased by heritage railways for further use in some form or another. Others remain in departmental stock to this day while other bodies have been grounded for use as stores huts and the like.

Covcars – post 1948

As noted at the start of this instalment, production of Covcars ceased, as far as the Southern Railway was concerned, in 1938. Again, this was not the end of the story and a further 150 CCT's (as they would now be coded) were built between 1951 and 1955. Like the luggage vans these utilised plywood bodyside construction together with 2+2 planked side doors – the end doors remaining vertically planked as before. Again, all were to Diagram 3101 and the tare weight was reduced from 14 to 13 tons with the use of plywood. Numbering details are 1411-50, 1977-91, 2006-20/73-82, 2171-80, 2231-40, all built at Ashford between October and December 1951, entering traffic in crimson livery with just an 'S' prefix to the running numbers; and 2501-50 completed at Lancing between June and December 1955; these being the final batch of "utility van" construction and were presumably amongst the last in crimson, with 'S' prefix and suffix letters. This brought the

An official view of "plastic" van 1401, taken in December 1943. "Sunshine" lettering on black with grey slate destination panels below the four windows. Despite the unusual appearance the general design follows the conventional van layout. The underframe is probably more unconventional than the bodywork. Note the lethal-looking hand brake wheel – soon to be replaced by one of normal pattern but probably not before some knuckles had been skinned! This van was taken out of normal traffic in August 1958, the first to be withdrawn but was used as a store at Eastleigh Carriage Works, eventually renumbered IU082186 until the works closed. Van 1405 was later to join it.   *SR Official*

No. S1407S at Clapham Junction around 1957 carrying standard insignia on a green paint finish. This ran from August 1944 until December 1966. Nos. 1402/4/7/9/10 at least were repainted green after 1956 while No. 1405 had some of its panels painted grey during its days as a stores van at Eastleigh Carriage Works.   *Author's collection*

Plywood PMV no. S1651S some time in the 1960s. Built at Lancing in September 1950 on an underframe from Ashford Works, this van lasted until BR ceased its parcels delivery service in 1981, which hastened the demise of all non-passenger coaching stock. No dimension or tare weight plates seem to have been provided on plywood-bodied vans; these are now painted on instead. Just the route restriction 0 plate remains. Author's collection

Plywood CCT no. S1431S in green livery at Bournemouth Central on 31st August 1962. Built in December 1951 this ran until March 1981. The side elevation is identical to contemporary PMV's except for the provision of steel strengtheners top and bottom of the diagonal strapping to give added support to the corner stanchions where the door hinges are located. The tare weight of 12 tons is one ton lighter than most plywood CCT's. A. E. West

One of the 1955 batch, no. S2543 (now without the 'S' suffix letter – this was dropped from the early 1970s) in rail blue with the lettering in white in the BR style. Dating from November 1955, just a month before final production ceased, this ran until February 1983. By this time many vans had lost their roof ventilators.   *D. Larkin*

number of covcars to 390 and quite probably in 1955 this was also the total in service. Notice how fragmented the numbering has become and also that vans numbered between 1977 and 2016 reused those of the former SECR luggage vans – a trap to catch the unwary enthusiast! The final batch also used numbers formerly allocated to LSWR horseboxes, most of which had been scrapped by 1955.

With the exception of a few accident victims, most of these CCT's ran until post-1980 but probably the shortest life of all may be claimed by van 2523, new in September 1955, which met its end in an accident at Horsham in May 1958 after less than three years' service. The last three in traffic were Nos. 2010, 2239 and 2516, all withdrawn in February 1986. These are likely to have been rail blue at withdrawal and about 20 of the final survivors had their end doors plated over at the bottom, meaning that they were in effect, PMV's and had their TOPS code altered from NOV to NQV as a result. Again, some have passed into departmental service or were sold for preservation.

Gangwayed Bogie Luggage Vans

The South Western had invested heavily in new steam-hauled suburban rolling stock between 1903 and 1912, only to decide to electrify their inner suburban network in the following year. From 1914 onwards many of these new "bogie block" 4-coach sets were rebuilt as electric stock and this process was re-commenced by the Southern Railway from 1927 onwards. However, whereas the LSWR had reused the whole coach, the Southern took only the bodies and mounted these on new 62ft long underframes, splicing and adding new sections to suit the longer length. This left them with 120 relatively new underframes capable of reuse. The Southern was not given to wasting anything, so it was suggested that the underframes could be utilised towards the construction of bogie luggage vans. There was a small complication since the LSWR coaches did not have conventional buffing gear (hence the "block" description which referred to the within-set coupling arrangements) – and there were two different lengths, viz. 49ft and 51ft. However, by splicing on new sections at each end of the frames they could be made suitable for reuse at a fraction of the cost of new underframes. As a result there were three different diagrams allocated to the new vans – not that this would be immediately apparent to an observer.

Initial proposals were for 50 bogie passenger luggage vans without gangways – this order being placed in July 1928 for vans 2281-2330. Second thoughts prevailed and in April 1929 this was revised to 50 vans with gangways and it was not long before two more orders brought the number up to 120 vans. Details are as follows: -

Diagram	Length of U/frame	Bogie centres	Date Built	Running Numbers
3098	51ft 3in	34ft 3in	11/30-4/31	2331-2354
3098	51ft 3in	34ft 3in	-9/31	2482-2491
3099	53ft 3in	36ft 3in	1-4/31	2355-2370
3099	53ft 3in	36ft 3in	7-8/31	2461-2481
3100	51ft 3in	36ft 3in	3-10/30	281-2330

Corridor luggage van 2467, to Diagram 3099 and photographed not long after entering service in July 1931. This shows the original lettering with the word "Luggage" repeated on each double door. One of the longer vans - 53ft 3in over headstocks with bogie centres at 36ft 3in – the underframe dates from 1905 and came from a 51ft bogie block brake third. The van became ambulance car 6804 in 1944/45, receiving droplights in the centre doors so returned to the Southern to become Diagram 3097. Withdrawn in July 1959, the underframe gave almost 55 years of service. SR Official

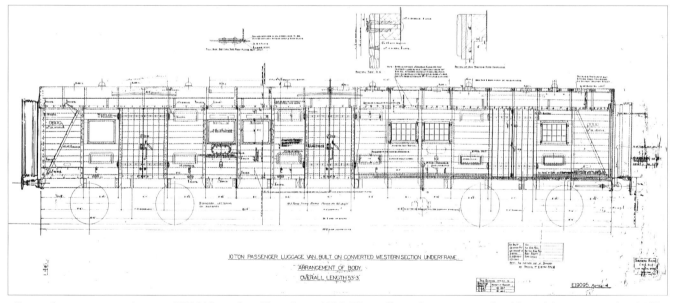

General arrangement drawing E19095, undated but about 1930. This tells us that it was applicable to 16 vans on order A467 (nos. 2355-70) and 21 vans on order A573 (nos. 2461-81) to Diagram 3099. The extra two feet were incorporated into the panels either side of the outer pairs of double doors – six inches wider in each case compared to the 51ft 3in vehicles.

51ft 3in long van 2319 to Diagram 3100, recorded for posterity in July 1933. Completed at Ashford in September 1930, it received its first repaint in November 1932, when the lettering layout was changed. The word "Luggage" now appears in primrose yellow script at the lower right hand corner instead of on the doors. The small lettering above this is a cast plate reading-"Distributed Load 10 Tons" and was a standard fitting on all SR-built utility vans (with, of course the appropriate tonnage shown) but whereas the GBL's kept these throughout, BR removed the plate from other types of van. The gangway adaptor clips are visible. SR Official

All were constructed at Ashford Works and were described as GBL's (gangwayed bogie luggage vans). Tare weights varied from 25 to 27 tons and carrying capacity was 10 tons. British standard gangways were fitted – which might seem unusual since the Southern had standardised on the Pullman pattern – but it was easier to fit the smaller BS type onto flat-ended vans without the complication of the Pullman buffing gear which would in any case only be used when coupling up to standard SR coaches – and not to most pre-Grouping stock or when included in van trains. However, it would be necessary to fit adaptors to enable them to couple with vehicles having Pullman gangways.

One area where these vans proved useful was for services to the West of England branch lines, especially the overnight newspaper train from Waterloo, since this split into portions during the journey and each portion might include both a coach and a van intermixed down the train. The gangway, in theory, would allow passengers to move along the train as necessary, although just whether it was possible to negotiate piles of luggage and newspapers in the van was another story. For this reason they were more often coupled at the front or rear of passenger services and all had roof board mounting brackets and were often kept cleaner than other types of utility van, receiving regular re-varnishings to keep them looking spick and span. Some were also permanently allocated to milk traffic in the late

1930s – Nos. 2341/42 were reserved for Messrs Aplin & Barrett's dairy traffic between Yeovil Town and London while Nos. 2300/15/22/26 and 2470 were marked "To be returned to Chard Junction" for Wilts United Dairies milk churn traffic. This regularly took these vans off the Southern to locations including Bristol, Crewe, York and Glasgow via the Chard branch to Taunton and onward via the GWR. Van 2351 was regularly allocated to the SR Royal train during the 1930s.

As World War 2 approached, the Southern was asked to make up three casualty evacuation trains, nos. 32-34. These were each formed of a SECR "birdcage" corridor brake composite at each end with ten GBL's as stretcher cars between them. Others were converted as ambulance cars during the war and had droplight windows provided in the middle pair of doors for this work. On return to the Southern in 1945/46 these were re-diagrammed as 3096(ex-3098) and 3097(ex-3099). No Diagram 3100 vans were selected for conversion. After the war the underframes were found to be showing signs of age and most needed reconditioning at Lancing between 1945 and 1948 – this usually resulted in the wooden-centred Mansell wheels being replaced by those of steel disc pattern. The first to be withdrawn was No. 2297 in March 1946, which became a stores van renumbered 300s - but in this form it still lasted until 1961, as long as most of the others.

Van 2463 was one of the first utility vans to receive

Just one GBL was war-damaged sufficiently to require replanking, which was done in the 2+2 style. Van S2353S is seen in red livery at Exeter Central on 29ᵗʰ October 1959. This is to Diagram 3098 and was built in April 1931. After withdrawal in May 1960 it became stores van 081254 at Lancing Works until November 1965.

A. E. West

Sir Winston Churchill's funeral train hearse van, S2464 stored inside Longhedge/Stewarts Lane carriage sheds during its period in waiting but as it is marshalled between Pullman cars, maybe just before 30ᵗʰ January 1965. Built in July 1931 to Diagram 3099, it became ambulance car 4705 in 1944/45, then receiving the droplights in the centre doors. On return to the Southern it was reallocated to Diagram 3097 and was reserved for pigeon traffic between 1959 and November 1961. It was repainted as seen in July 1962, the date being visible on the solebar. It was sold to the USA for £350 and left Britain in October 1965 to become an exhibit at the "City of Industry" in Los Angeles but was later stored and returned to the Swanage Railway in 2007 for full restoration.   *The Lens of Sutton Association*

Departmental van DS70041 at Stewarts Lane in the 1960s, marked up as a carriage & wagon department stores van allocated to Clapham Junction. The livery may still be green, grey or possibly brown. Formerly Diagram 3098 van 2348, this also became an ambulance car in the 1940s, number 3702, returning to the SR with droplights fitted as Diagram 3096. It was taken out of service in June 1959; being converted for departmental use five months later – losing its gangways in the process. Final withdrawal is recorded twice – in July 1965 and October 1970. Official records cannot always be relied upon!

The Lens of Sutton Association

the new British Railways crimson lake livery in April 1949, as part of the Newhaven Continental set. Although a corridor vehicle, so in theory it should have been painted crimson lake and cream, wiser counsel prevailed. The BR code was now Corr PMV. Otherwise, front-line traffic remained and one van could regularly be seen at the head of the *Golden Arrow* in the late 1950s – firstly in crimson and later repainted green. Nos. 2296 and 2480 were permanently roof-boarded "Newspaper Traffic" from July 1953, being used between Waterloo and Bournemouth. Final withdrawal came between 1958 and 1960 as the Southern received a similar number of BR standard bogie CCTs as replacements. The bodywork of van 2291 was reconstructed on the underframe of former Maunsell Hastings line coach 6897 in September 1960, allocated running number 4501 and Diagram 3183 but quite what this set out to prove is unclear, however it had official sanction and a legitimate order number. It was initially classed as a motor car van (code MCV) but was later reclassified as a CCT. It remained unique and was finally withdrawn in March 1966. This was the final design in the "utility van" family to appear.

Twelve corridor PMV's, numbers 2290, 2331/33/44/47/49/56/58, 2464/76/87/88 were retained for

pigeon traffic until November 1961 and one of these, No. 2464 was selected to be used as the hearse van for Sir Winston Churchill's funeral train, for which purpose it was repainted umber and cream (to match the Pullman cars) in July 1962. It was then stored ready for this duty, which it performed on 30th January 1965. The author recalls seeing the train pass through Barnes on that bitterly cold Saturday watched by many other mourners, so this may be regarded historically as important as the original Nurse Cavell van. The van was then sold for preservation in the USA but, after a period in the doldrums, was returned to Britain in 2007 and has now been restored to its 1965 condition at the Swanage Railway. Six other vans passed into departmental use and two have subsequently been preserved while a dozen others were employed as internal user stores vans at such locations as Eastleigh and Lancing Works, Newhaven Harbour, Orpington, Weymouth and West Moors stations. Nos. 2315/44 were sold to the War Department and may be those later noted at the Marchwood Military Railway, on the west bank of Southampton Water.

Theatrical Scenery Vans

These were true covered carriage trucks, characterised by a high roof profile and end doors, through which road vehicles and large items of equipment, including scenery could be loaded. In the 1920s and 1930s there were many travelling repertory companies touring the country visiting provincial theatres and these often made use of the railway to transport themselves and their props. Depending on size, this could range from a complete charter train to just a single coach and a van added to a normal service. The Southern inherited a mixed bag of (mostly) four- and six-wheeled scenery vans/ CCT's from the pre-Grouping companies and built three batches, each of ten bogie vans, for the traffic.

The original 10 were actually the first non-passenger van stock ordered by the Southern Railway after Grouping; order E103 in May 1925 but were then deferred until 1928 – probably because other needs were more pressing. When built they shared some commonality with the gangwayed bogie luggage vans that followed, as these too made use of second-hand underframes. In this case they were 50ft ex-LBSCR – chosen because the vans were to be dual-braked and the Brighton underframes would already be Westinghouse-equipped. They were numbered 4577-86 – most definitely in the covered carriage truck portion of the

van list – and to Diagram 3181. The original LBSCR bogies were replaced by LSWR pattern in 1932-34 and the Westinghouse gear was stripped out between 1934 and 1939. Van 4586 was equipped to carry elephants in December 1933 – you may laugh but travelling circuses were another traffic that presented itself in those days – and the revenue was not to be ignored. For this, stronger springs, steel plate flooring and stout tethering rings were provided. These 10 vans remained in traffic until 1959-62 and none saw any further departmental service.

The next batch was ordered in May 1930 but again there seems not to have been any urgency and they were deferred until 1937, appearing in the following year. The bodywork was almost identical to the 1928 vans but these were on new underframes, causing the diagram number to be amended to 3182. Running numbers were 4587-96 but it is not certain whether these appeared in Maunsell or Bulleid green livery, although the official photograph shows the normal Maunsell style lettering. The underframes were standard Southern products on the usual 8ft wheelbase bogies and identical to those under the Van B (to be

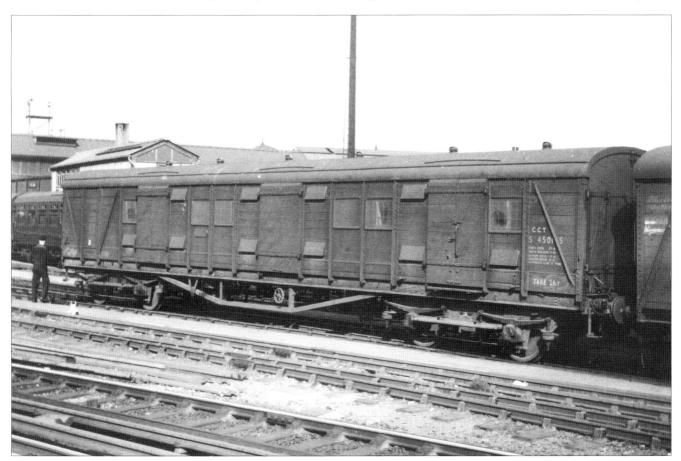

Apologies for using this picture for a third time, but there are few photographs of Diagram 3183 motorcar van conversion S4501S. Seen at Clapham Junction on 17th May 1961 it is already classed as a CCT (was it ever coded MCV – as the diagram describes it?). Unique in all respects, it has BR CCT-type end doors, retractable buffers and buckeye couplings. The additional make-up bodywork is at the far end. A lot of effort just to reuse 25+year-old components!

D. Cullum/The Lens of Sutton Association

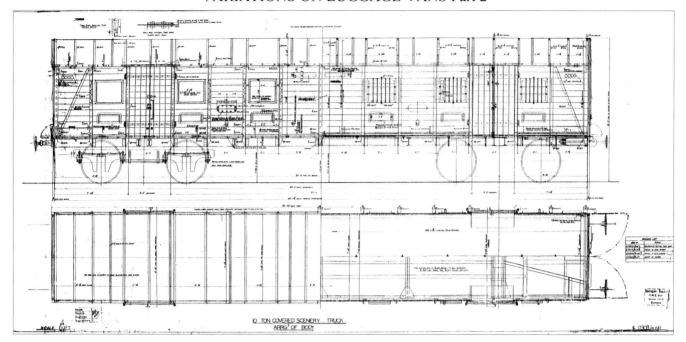

Above - *General arrangement drawing E17303 dated May 1928 showing the first batch of theatrical scenery vans to Diagram 3181. What this fails to show clearly is the domed roof profile but at 12ft 8in above rail level this was eight inches taller than a standard profile van. The originals were at first lettered "Scenery Truck" on the centre panels; fifth plank down, below the company title.*

Opposite top - *Diagram 3181 scenery van S4580 at Rotherhithe Road carriage sidings on 17th June 1950, in Southern Railway green (of what shade?) with the number newly prefixed 'S' in Southern style. The code "Scenery" may just be read low down on the right hand side.*

D. Cullum/The Lens of Sutton Association

Opposite bottom - *1949-built scenery van S4600S at the back of Woking yard soon after repainting in Southern Region green livery, about 1956. The usual dimensional data is now painted on the side – there is just the route restriction 0 plate on the end – the SR code "Scenery" remains but now repositioned at the left-hand end. The code is CCT but some were noted GUV (General Utility Van) once the scenery traffic ceased. The van was withdrawn in April 1980, and then became CC99014 in the Chipman weed-killing fleet until sold to the Isle of Wight Steam Railway in August 2012 – almost certainly for reuse of the underframe under one of their pre-Grouping carriage bodies.*

T. A. Barry

described in part 3 of the article), minus the internal handbrake. No Westinghouse brakes were provided as by then almost all air-braked stock had been eliminated. No. 4589 was eventually equipped to carry elephants. The final batch was completed at Lancing in December 1949 and was almost identical to the 1938 vans, numbered 4597-4606. These were finished in crimson livery, but Frank Foote noted No. S4604 at Weymouth in June 1950 lettered, not in yellow but in white. In due course Nos. 4598 and 4601 became "elephant" vans.

Those in SR green livery would have steadily been repainted crimson until 1956, after which BR green would have been applied, replaced by rail blue from 1967. The

scenery traffic declined during the 1960s and the vans began to be used for general parcels services. Withdrawal of the later batches spanned 1976-81, with van 4601 being the last in service. Several entered departmental or internal use while at least three became part of Chipman's weed killing train, based at Horsham for a number of years. Several are now in preservation, some just for their underframes to be reused under pre-Grouping coach bodies.

Part 3 of this article will deal with the remaining 388 utility vans that included guard's accommodation – the ferry van, Van B and Van C plus a quick look at the special cattle vans and some "might have been" designs proposed but not built.

'GOODBYE 700'

Images by Mark Abbott

At the end of 1962 the era of the Drummond 700 class on regular workings finally came to an end. The seven members of the class still active were withdrawn and so became another statistic in the wholesale cull of steam at the time. On the opposite page Mark Abbott has recorded the end for possibly the very last one in steam, No 30689, withdrawn from Exmouth Junction at the end of the year but then subsequently worked up to Eastleigh where the fire was ignominiously thrown out and the engine subsequently positioned for scrap. It was cut at Eastleigh in March 1963. Although an occasion without ceremony, possibly the two men were indeed aware of the occasion. Meanwhile below, we see No 30700 itself dumped on the scrap road and with various fatalistic chalk markings describing what was to come. The running plate of the engine also bears witness to a previous altercation. Meanwhile alongside an unidentified 'W' has been made ready to meet its own fate, the rods having been removed from an engine a sure sign the situation was likely to be terminal.

Terry Cole's Rolling Stock File No. 26
SR Rebuilds of LSWR Non-corridor stock

The Southern Railway did not design any new non-corridor steam stock but it did rebuild a large amount of pre-grouping stock for both electric and steam use. Bodies were lengthened by splicing in extra compartments or other pieces as appropriate and then remounted on newly built underframes. The vast majority of the steam stock conversions used ex LSWR vehicles and it is some of these that we will be looking at in this 'file'.

Above - *Here is S 2 S originally a 48ft LSWR Composite built in 1899 which was rebuilt in 1935 on a 58ft underframe as a 9-compartment Third to SR Diagram 33. It was paired with Corridor compo brake 6429 to become two-coach push-pull set 653. Initially allocated to the Eastern section, the set stayed together (although occasionally gaining an additional Third) and S 2 S is seen here at Guildford on 13 July 1957. It was withdrawn in February 1961. The photo clearly shows some of the key features often present on an ex LSWR 'Rebuild': the standard Southern underframe and bogies and the carefully panelled over void in the centre of the coach (between the 4th and 5th compartments counting from the right). This is where the extra compartment was added and the space 'made up' to fill the length of the underframe. Also characteristic is the triangular piece of wood running the length of the coach where the body 'joins' the underframe. Often, as in this case, rebuilt vehicles retained their prominent original roof ventilators.*

Opposite top - *This is Non- corridor lavatory composite S4750S seen here at Sidmouth Junction on 24 August 1957. It started life as a 48ft Composite built around 1900 and was also rebuilt on a new 58ft underframe in 1935. Its first SR number was 4809 becoming No.12 on rebuilding to a Third. However, in 1939 two of its wider compartments were up-rated to first class and it was renumbered as Composite 4750 to SR Diagram 287. As such it ran with Lav. 3rd Brake 3072 in two-coach local set 58 until withdrawn in 1958.*

This page, bottom - Compartment lavatory brake 3rd S2611S is seen here at Bude on 31 August 1957. Originally LSWR 48ft Lav. compo 2803 it became SR 4836 and was rebuilt as Third brake 2611 to SR Diagram 97 in 1936. It ran with Lav. compo brake 6486 in set 21 until the set was withdrawn in 1948. After a period in set 257 it became a loose vehicle based in the West Country and was withdrawn in early 1959. *[All photos David Wigley]*

Stephen Collingwood Townroe

A brief look at the new book
'Southern Way Special Issue No 10'
released at the same time as this issue of 'SW'.

Stephen Collingwood Townroe was a remarkable man. A gifted engineer he was equally talented and knowledgeable in other areas, including ornithology and as a musician. In the opinion of many, his own railway story together with his remarkable collection of both colour and black and white photography has lain unseen for too long, hints alone being published from time to time. 'Southern Way' is delighted to redress that balance, achieved through the assistance of the Townroe family, together with Colour Rail and Rod Blencowe, the respective custodians of 'SCT's colour and black and white images.

As a taster for the main work, we present four sides of sample images, most of which will never have been seen before:

Opposite top - *'T9' No 715 entering Templecombe in 1938, coupled behind is coaching set No 146.*

Opposite bottom - *Oil storage facilities at Eastleigh in 1952.*

Above - *Testing 'Kelbus' re-railing gear at Eastleigh, 18 March 1952. The locomotive being used is 'Q1' No 33019.*   *(All R Blencowe collection)*

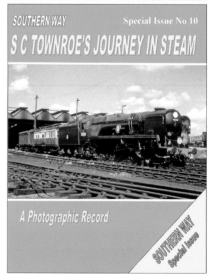

This page - Attaching the extension jib to the Eastleigh steam crane in 1959. The use of this jib was necessary when it was required to add or remove one of the four tall chimneys from the forge. The only disadvantage that it took a whole day to add or remove this jib extension, meaning the crane was out of commission so far as major breakdown work was concerned. (CR 109856ST)

Opposite top - The iron foundry at Eastleigh works, June 1954.(CR 105398ST)

Opposite bottom - Non steam but still a fascinating image. Unrecorded so far as detail information is concerned, but clearly component repair / replacement on diesel shunter No 15233 outside the front of Eastleigh shed. Working conditions were not exactly ideal for this type of repair. (CR 221779ST)

We start this time with two letters from John Raggett:

"Going back to issue 22 if I may and the excellent article on the Battersea Tangle, I noted with interest the picture of the gas train at Latchmere Junction on page 17 which shows a passenger brake van on the rear. Not unusual in itself, but this is one of three vans built by the Southern Railway at Ashford in 1933 for use on the Night Ferry. They were numbered 1 - 3, (later S1S, S2S and S3S.) They had low roofs and birdcage lookouts and were fitted with dual brakes, electric light and had rings on the frames for attaching the chains which secured them to the deck of the train ferry. They were painted dark blue to match the Wagons-Lits sleeping cars. The Night Ferry (along with the Golden Arrow) was suspended when war broke out in September 1939 but the vans continued in use for mail traffic until the Germans invaded France in May 1940. George Behrend and Gary Buchanan's book 'Night Ferry' (first published 1985) shows a photo of No. 1 at Paris Gare du Nord in early 1940. One presumes it returned to the UK before the train ferries stopped. Not being fitted with train heating jumpers, all three vans were demoted in 1959 and repainted SR green when electric locos started working the Night Ferry. I remember coming across S3S several times in the early 1970s in use as an ordinary parcels van. It was withdrawn in 1974, the other two having gone in 1969."

John continues, "The Southern Way issue 24 and once again thanks for a fascinating insight into the past! I read with interest Jeremy Clarke's article, 'Some Gems from a Working Timetable' and I remember this working time table when it was published by Ian Allan - indeed, a colleague of mine bought a copy. I was particularly pleased to find a photograph of Fort Brockhurst station on the Gosport line. This solved a mystery for me. The 1954 film, 'Cockleshell Heroes' features the level crossing at this station and I had long wondered where it was. Cockleshell Heroes, made at Shepperton Studios, stars Trevor Howard, Jose Ferrer and a supporting cast which includes Victor Maddern, David Lodge etc. It is inspired by a true story of a Royal Marine commando raid on shipping at Bordeaux in France, 1942. As part of an initiative test, Major Springer (Jose Ferrer) takes his volunteers on a plane and they are dropped by parachute 'somewhere over England', dressed in German uniforms, their task being to find their way back to barracks over 300 miles away! The Major himself steals a bicycle, while one of his trainees hitches a lift in a fish lorry, (driven by Sam Kydd.) A freight train headed by an S15

class loco is seen approaching an over bridge on an electrified line, which looks like it could be where the (A318) Chertsey Road crosses the line on a skew arch, near Addlestone. Another trainee is standing on the parapet and supposedly jumps into an empty coal wagon as it passes underneath. Chertsey station features, with a 2-NOL electric train on an up service drawing into the platform as one of the trainees runs across the bridge at the London end of the station. The level crossing at Fort Brockhurst is featured,

its gates swinging across the road just as the fish lorry approaches. The Major riding his stolen bike also happens to pull up alongside the fish lorry. The Up train which passes is a T9 4-4-0 number 30729, running tender first with a solitary SR 'BY' type 4-wheel passenger brake van. The gates swing open again, the lorry continues, the Major having jumped in the back while it was waiting at the gates. Having identified some of the locations, the level crossing eluded me. There is no third rail and the gates are typically LSWR style. I scoured several books but could find no photos of a station with crossing that matched that in the film until I looked through this latest issue of Southern Way and there it was! The location made sense, as much of the film was shot at Southsea including Eastney Barracks and the Gosport branch had lost its passenger service in 1953, which made it an ideal place to film this sequence. Chertsey station again features. The fish lorry pulls up outside a pub and while the driver (who fails to immobilise it) and the hitch hiking trainee go inside for a drink, the Major jumps out of the back and drives off. The fish lorry is then seen driving into the forecourt of Chertsey station, where the Major abandons it and continues his journey by train. And the film is shot in glorious colour. The T9 loco, 30729 is itself interesting as it was allocated to Brighton in 1928 and given a 6-wheel tender. It was only there for 2 years before retuning to its home territory but it retained the 6-wheel tender until withdrawal in 1961. (Now I wonder what pub that was where the fish lorry pulled up?!)

Jeremy's article also mentions Addlestone Junction and delivery of coal and supplies to signal boxes, (also touched on in issue 20.) I was a signalman there briefly

until the box closed in March 1970. There was no electricity, water or gas. Lighting was by paraffin Tilley lamps, heating was a coal stove, and a paraffin stove was provided to boil a kettle or for cooking. Supplies came from Addlestone and the 08.28 (SX) Waterloo(W) to Weybridge was booked to stop at Addlestone Junction to drop them off. Most of the trains were worked by 2-EPBs but this was diagrammed as a 4-EPB unit, so was guaranteed to have a brake van at the front. Supplies on Saturday were booked to be dropped off by the 08.43 ex Waterloo, worked by a 2-EPB which might not have the van at the leading end. (The presence or absence of an inverted yellow triangle on the front would indicate which way round the train was!) Water was delivered daily and all the other stuff as needed. If paraffin was required, the empty can was put on the down train and returned the next morning. Empty water cans and coal scuttles would also be loaded on to the train and returned to Addlestone via Weybridge. Traffic notices came round from Weybridge in the evening. The Station Foreman would phone up to say, 'Notices on the next Up Branch,' and to ensure they arrived intact, would be obligingly placed inside a tightly wrapped copy of the 'Evening News', which the Guard would lob out of his van as the train went by. There were no deliveries on Sundays, the water delivered Saturday had to make do until Monday."

Going back to Issue 18 and Jeffery Grayer's article on 'Final BIL', Andy Sturt has kindly sent in two images of the farewell working of 25 September 1971. Andy comments that he believes one of the sets ran hot at Twickenham and was detached.

(With apologies - space and all that - more next time, Ed)

A moment of good fortune. Seen from the approach to the flyover at Worting Junction in the up direction (from Bournemouth), one of the SR main line diesels passes underneath on a West of England train. The flyover here is of course one of several on the Southern system - and with another planned for the up Portsmouth line at Eastleigh but never built (although the earthworks were provided). This would make for an interesting topic in 'SW' if anyone were interested..... (S C Townroe)

THE
SOUTHERN WAY

C000235919

CONTENTS

We regret the caption that should have appeared under the image on p12 of Issue No 28 was omitted: S15' 4-6-0 No 30824 at Wokingham with a Reading South to Feltham freight on 6 June 1964. The chalked crosses on the buffers are not explained. No 3 headcode is a beautifully portmanteau sort - 'All stations to Feltham', BUT - that is followed by a rider. 'except via Mortlake'. The implication is then that anything from the London end will have to go via Weybridge and Staines. (The direct route would demand No 12, 'Nine Elms and Feltham via Mortlake'.) Edwin Wilmshurst

© Kevin Robertson (Noodle Books) and the various contributors 2015
ISBN 978-1-909328-27-3
First published in 2015 by Kevin Robertson
under the **NOODLE BOOKS** imprint
PO Box 279
Corhampton
SOUTHAMPTON
SO32 3ZX
www.noodlebooks.co.uk
editorial@thesouthernway.co.uk

Printed in England by
Berforts Information Press Ltd.

Above - Omitted due to space constraints from 'SW28' was this third view of Rudgwick from the Wallis collection. Signalman P H E Nye is seen. The date is not reported. (For more stunning views from the collection see below.)

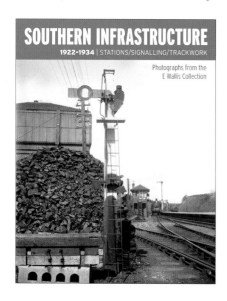
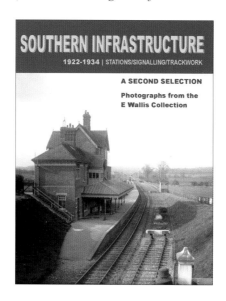

Editorial

I was brought down to earth with a bump a few weeks ago. In reading, writing and producing railway history it is all too easy to become complacent without realising it and certainly without intending to. What started this off was an email from a SW reader, John Cooter. John asked with all innocence what a particular set of initials we had used in a previous issue meant. I was glad to help him but shortly afterwards came another question, again on a topic that might appear to some as basic, but of course anything is if we as individuals know the answer. There cannot be anyone reading this who has not shouted at the television or radio quiz programme, "That's easy, everyone know's that…". Well yes, easy to those of us who do know, but the poor contestant under a glare of lights and with accompanying nerves may find his or her mind has literally gone blank. I am sure if we will admit it, we too have had similar experiences similar, perhaps not on millionaire quiz shows but certainly in some business, social or, (think back), an examination situation.

So this got me thinking - a dangerous occupation I know. We need to encourage people to return to the hobby and also to encourage new interest. The questions thus raised by Jon (and others) are genuine and we fail to answer them at our peril. I/we as hobbyists need the support of new blood into the hobby; as I have said before, how many more times can we disseminate the same information to those of us who already know it but that same information takes on a whole new meaning if presented to a new generation. I use the word 'generation' carefully here, for it could equally apply to an individual of similar age but who is taking up railways again after a lapse. I believe what we should then be doing is to encourage new interest and as a result we will probably find some coming on board with a new perspective for research and learning, and their studies can also only benefit us all.

As I indicated above, age should also not be seen as a barrier here. I referred to 'new blood' but that can be anyone with a new perspective. The temptation is to say hobbies, clubs, societies need young members as indeed they do, but (and I hope he will forgive me for saying this) my good friend Jeremy Clements who produced an article on Maunsell a few issues ago is not a teenager but instead a man whose passion for railways was perhaps constrained by a professional life for many years and now that has passed, he can use his skills to great effect. Maunsell was good (so was his book on William Dean which we have published) but if you want to read something absolutely remarkable then you should take time out to look at his new 'Collett and Hawksworth' tome just released by Ian Allan. (I have had the privilege of a preview and it will literally make your hair stand on end.) This is certainly not intended as a slight to our Great Western friends: come on, all us probably like all railways but we are also allowed some favourites. What Jeremy has achieved is to look at Swindon's locomotive development in a totally new light, one I would never have considered and which, if you have an open mind, will certainly give a new insight into the locomotive policy of the GWR (Jeremy even wonders if there was one, AND this is not based on bias or pure supposition but instead on hard economic fact using research no one seems to have considered before). I cannot say I dread to think what he might come up with if he ever tackled a Southern subject, but he has already threatened me with all sorts of retribution if I dare suggest he write anything further. But if anyone else fancies, for example, a new look at Mr Bulleid I would be very interested. However be warned, we enthusiasts can be conservative as well and we do not always like our icons held to account. I have personally found this to my cost, we criticise at our peril even if such criticism is explained and justified. Personally I stand by every word I have written on the man. I would have loved to have met him and just asked one question, 'Why?'.

So to return to my initial theme, expect to see within future issues, sections explaining railway terms and if there are areas you may not be familiar with please let us know. You note I have mentioned Jon's name, but not his exact query, I will do the same with others or provide anonymity if required.

It could even develop into a regular 'Q and A' similar to the wonderful 'The Why and the Wherefore' of the 'Railway Magazine' for many years. The only criteria I would set is, it must be Southern (and constituent) based.

Kevin Robertson

Front cover - In the days when Templecombe was indeed a junction, Standard Class 4 No 75027 arrives with a local off the S & D. Sad to relate, it is fast approaching half a century since closure of this wonderful railway occurred.

Pages 2/3 - Approaching 11.00 at Waterloo and the departure time of the westbound 'Atlantic Coast Express'. Due to the length of the train, Merchant Navy No 35020 'Bibby Line' is of necessity waiting beyond the platform starting signal,. Meanwhile the fireman has not quite timed his build-up of steam to perfection as both safety valves have lifted. No date, but probably very late on into the life of the train as the engine is embellished with white dots on various bolt/rivet heads. In the background the sidings have long disappeared under what became the (temporary) Eurostar terminal and which also contain an interesting variety of rolling stock.

Rear cover - Gone but not forgotten. Stoneham Sidings signal box, south of Eastleigh.

1.**Harmonious Settings. (above)** This push-pull train could have been photographed in the station purely as a technical record. By moving a hundred yards up the line, however, we capture the starting plume and we can frame the train with trees, grasses, bushes, a telegraph pole and a platelayers' hut with its coil of wire. The story is completed by a glimpse of the station, footbridge, starting signal and a bridge over the River Medway. In May 1963, class H tank No. 31005 restarts from Ashurst towards Oxted near the triple junction of Kent, Sussex and Surrey.

3. **Artistic Framing. (opposite, bottom)** This locomotive is similar to that in the upper image on the same page but it has been brought to life by heading a train. There is even a wisp of safety valve steam. It is the setting, however, that adds artistic merit, using a great telegraph pole on one side and the closed goods yard on the other, complete with L&SWR shed, loading gauge and double slip point. In May 1961, class MN Pacific *Elder Dempster Line* heads an Up Bournemouth express through Shawford.

SOUTHERN STEAM PHOTOGRAPHY
Alan Postlethwaite

2. Technical Records. Many technical books are satisfied with front three-quarters shots of locomotives with little or no attempt to encompass peripheral detail or atmosphere. Here the pits and scattered ash tell us that this is at an MPD but the picture remains 90% locomotive. The crewman is the only sign of life and not a single wisp of steam can be seen. Artistic merit approaches zero but as a technical record, it is first class. In September 1959, class MN Pacific *Channel Packet* stands at Exmouth Junction, fresh from Eastleigh's paint shop after rebuilding.

4. Signals and Spring Flowers (above). The Down 'Bournemouth Belle' looks immaculate and would look fine as a technical record. The setting, however, creates a composition of merit which might the stir the soul - not just for railway enthusiasts but for anyone with an eye for beauty and harmony. The framing comprises SR signal arms on a lattice post, a telegraph pole and the shallow cutting with banks of wild flowers. The safety valve steam plume and the wave of a crewman were fortuitous bonuses. In May 1963, MN class No 35015 *Rotterdam Lloyd* approaches Shawford.

5. Grime in a Grand Setting (opposite, top). Although the locomotive is grimy, the Somerset setting is grand - a gentle cutting, a distant signal arm on an S&D rail-built post, a few trees, the telegraph poles and a double-arch road bridge. In July 1963 near Shepton Mallet, standard class 9F No. 92233 heads a holiday train to Bournemouth.

6. Silver Birch and a Bracket (opposite, bottom): For improved visibility on curves and over sidings, signal posts could be bracketed to one side. This SR example provides a perfect frame, balanced by the bank of silver birch. In May 1963 at Horam, standard class 4MT tank No. 80146 heads a 'Cuckoo' line train to Tunbridge Wells West.

7. Trees as Frames. This picture is beautified by a winter sycamore. The tree converts a narrow horizontal into an interesting L-shape. Try covering it up to see how plain the picture becomes. In April 1960 near Ashey, class O2 tank No. 27 *Merstone* heads a train of pre-Grouping stock to Ryde with Ashey Down in the background.

8. Trees in Silhouette. The SER line between Redhill and Guildford has some long straight stretches between stations with limited peripheral interest. Here, a dramatic composition is created by using a strong silhouette of foreground trees. They are balanced by more distant trees and undergrowth on the sunny north bank of the cutting. In 1963 near Gomshall, class N Mogul No. 31851 heads a Down train of flat-sided Maunsell stock.

9. Full Framing with Trees. This composition was the result of battling up the bank through jungle and taking great care with the camera position. It proved worthwhile because a fine panorama of the distant station emerged. The train provided a nice plume of starting steam and a Southdown bus crossed the bridge at just the right moment. In August 1959 at Horam, LMS Fairburn tank No. 42087 heads a Maunsell train to Eastbourne.

10. Laurel and Hardy. In July 1963, use is made of Salisbury's canopies to frame class M7 tank No. 30033 and class S15 No. 30842. The valance, canopy curves and knobbly chimney stacks make interesting geometry.

11. Through Traffic. In July 1961, Eastleigh provides an open setting for standard class 3 tank No. 82015 with a long train of oil tankers bound for the ESSO refinery at Fawley. We focus on the train but peripheral interest is provided by the great footbridge, William Tite's station building and passengers sitting patiently on both platforms.

12. Full Power on the S&D. In July 1963, a pair of standard class 4MTs charge through Shepton Mallet with a train to Bath. Our attention focuses upon the lead engine, No. 75009. The wisp of injector steam and the twin plumes of light exhaust provide a strong impression of power and speed. The event is enhanced by the station setting, especially the S&D bargeboard and two gents on the platform who are captivated by the approaching beasts.

13. Rural Tranquility. This Maunsell push-pull train is framed by a whole station - the SER clapboard building, lamp hut, coal siding, loading gauge and two sidings which disappear behind bushes. A scattering of trees enhances the beauty of this quiet corner of Kent. In May 1961, a class H tank departs Brasted towards Dunton Green.

14. Railwaymen at Work. The Isle of Wight was a working museum of pre-Grouping trains. Passing at Shanklin with SE&CR and LB&SCR stock are L&SWR class O2 tanks No. 31 *Chale* and No. 25 *Godshill*. The scene is brought to life by railwaymen looking on and exchanging single-line tablets in pouches with hoops. April 1960.

15. Trimming the Bunker. In August 1959 at Hawkhurst, a fireman performs acrobatics along the roof of class H tank No. 31266. A young passenger wants to help with bunker trimming but his mother is unimpressed and urges him to leave. The platform canopy and trees provide framing but it is the human story that captures the imagination.

16. Engine Spotters. In May 1961 at Eastleigh, something has caught the attention of this band of spotters. They are ignoring grimy class H15 No. 30475 in the sidings. This would make a nice technical record of a steam engine at work but it is the young enthusiasts who bring the scene to life. The SR barrow provides additional interest.

17. Conifers and Valancing. Exchanging the token - this time a staff. A feast of peripheral interest is provided by the second train, signal box, an onlooker, his bike, a silhouetted valance and tall conifers semi-shrouded in morning mist. In August 1960 at Cranleigh, the contrasting 0-4-4 tanks are class H No. 31543 and class M7 No. 30049.

18. Tavy Viaduct. This major civil work is on the L&SWR main line to Plymouth. The graceful curve and fine detail in stone and steel make the train almost superfluous. Taken in September 1959 with class M7 tank No. 30036.

19. Wealden Meadow Bank. The train is almost side-on in this peaceful scene, testing the author's shutter speed which at that time was limited to 1/200 sec. The train is framed by the River Teise, reeds, a grassy bank and a great tree. In August 1959 at Goudhurst, class H tank No. 31322 works a push-pull set of L&SWR Immigrant stock.

20. Thomas Hardy Domain. In July 1963, the placid River Stour offers a perfect reflection of trees and masonry. Once again, the train is almost superfluous - Great Western stock plying northwards through rich Dorset countryside. Thomas Hardy is best known for the romantic novels set in his beloved Wessex. He also wrote poems and short stories, some of which have railway settings. *At the Railway Station, Upways* is a reminder that the GWR also ran through Dorset. It ends with "And so they went on till the train came in, the convict and boy with the violin".

21. Brighton Infrastructure (above). Like the Midland Railway, the LB&SCR built its civil works to last a thousand years. This massive buttress was built to retain unstable earth just north-west of East Grinstead. In July 1959, class C2X No. 32521 is part-way through a complex reversing sequence via St Margaret's Junction. It will now run forward to the Tunbridge Wells line and reverse down the incline to pick up its goods train from the low-level yard. This was a perfect time of day for sunshine and shadow across the buttress and to silhouette the engine under the bridge.

23. Poole Level Crossing (opposite, bottom). In July 1963, framing is taken to the extreme for the arrival of standard class 4MT No. 75007, threading its way gently with a train to Bath. Peripheral items include a wooden paling fence, a lorry, commercial buildings, a gas holder, level crossing box, waiting pedestrians and the lattice steel footbridge. One can study such compositions for ages. It is a piece of social history from an era when we did not mind walking and queuing and when stations, signal boxes and local yards were a-buzz with railwaymen.

22. Spanning at Eastleigh. This strong horizontal composition features two long bridge spans carrying signals and road traffic respectively. Note the echo effect between the ground signals, headcode discs, track-circuit diamonds and route indicators. In May 1961, LN class No. 30861 *Lord Anson* heads an express to Bournemouth.

24. Vectis Watering Hole (above). Like Bembridge, Ventnor once had a turntable beyond the platform until the SR replaced it with points. The enlarged bunkers of the class O2 tanks were somewhat ungainly so one sought to enhance a back end view with interesting peripherals. In September 1958, two coaches frame No. 31 *Chale* while it takes water. Evening sunshine reflects off the clean sides of all three vehicles. Beyond the trees is the glorious seaside.

26. Medway at Eventide (opposite, bottom). In March 1961, a study of the Medway Valley near Yalding with evening sunshine bringing out the texture of the grass. The central feature is the back end of a BR Mark 1 coach, part of a three-coach set en route to Maidstone West. The composition is 'made' by peripheral posts which carry a gate, telegraph wires, a signal and cast iron warning signs. The meandering river is visible beyond in a setting of winter shrubs and trees. This as an example of meticulous care with tripod location and focusing for a long depth of field.

25. Stoking near Ryde. Some spectacular photographs of steam are the result of good fortune rather than planning. Such was the case in April 1960 when class O2 tank No. 16 *Ventnor* made dark smoke after departing St Johns Road. It is a reminder that the days of steam were not clean. When stoking, any dust could pass through the boiler to be scattered over town, countryside and into the coaches. Such displays were nevertheless impressive and the little steam trains of the Isle of Wight gave pleasure to generations of holidaymakers regardless of occasional smuts.

Just One Hour at
WORTING JUNCTION
September 1962

Images by Henry Meyer

Variety in workings at Worting Junction in September 1962. Henry Meyer (whose work will certainly be familiar to regular readers of 'SW') spent an hour with his camera recording freight and passenger trains. By this time, steam workings were invariably in the hands of Bulleid and Standard locos, with (opposite) No 75076 working hard as it heads south with an Eastleigh freight.

This page top - Now it is the turn of a 'Standard 5' on a stopping train of Bulleid stock also on its way south.

Right - One of the ubiquitous rebuilt 'Light Pacifics', identified at least as a member of the 'West Country' breed (likely to be No. 34037 'Clovelly'), taking a Bournemouth/Weymouth working of 13 vehicles, including Maunsell, Bulleid and BR Mk1 stock. 50+ years later and housing from Basingstoke has started to infill the land on the right.

Services to and from the west were never as frequent as Bournemouth line workings, although captured here is the prestigious West of England train, the 'down Atlantic Coast Express'. This working ceased in 1964 although in the train seen above passengers could reach Exeter from London in a few minutes under three hours. In charge is No. 35014 'Nederland Line', the No 6 on the duty board indicating that this was a Nine Elms top-link working.

Opposite top - *Coming the other way and climbing the 1 in 106 to pass over the top of the West of England line, No 34025 'Whimple' is eased slightly as it approaches the Worting Junction up distant at 'on'. As far as the Bournemouth line was concerned, this was the last flyover on the route although there had been plans and even some earthworks constructed for a flyover to take up Portsmouth line trains over the main line at Eastleigh. West from here there was of course the flyover for the Lyme Regis branch at Axminster.*

Opposite bottom *- No 35019 'French Line CGT' coming down the other side with what is almost certainly a Waterloo service. Whilst these views were taken more than half a century ago, then and certainly now, knowledgeable passengers are cautious over any drinks they may hold near this point. At the end of the down gradient there is the option to join the up fast line by means of a high-speed facing turnout. The facing arm will cause the carriage to give a slight lurch but that is nothing to what follows a few seconds later at the trailing end. More than one beverage has ended up spoiling an expensive garment. As might be said, 'Twas ever thus'.*

Non-Stop:
Southampton Central to
Wimbledon and then Waterloo

Richard Simmons

Staff at both the London West and Southampton divisional offices attempted to keep the memory and spirit of these two divisional offices alive by holding annual reunions. Southampton held theirs in early October on the basis that such a date was as near as practicable to the September closure. The Southampton people met at a hotel in the city for a buffet lunch and when that closed, moved to a hotel at Sway then owned by an ex-Wimbledon office member of staff who gave favourable prices, but the most recent have been at a Brockenhurst public house. Initially attendances were good, numbering approximately 40 but over the years inevitably numbers declined because of deaths, increasing immobility and people moving away from the area. With declining numbers it was intended to "call it a day" in October 2013 so coinciding with 50 years since the office closed. Sadly that goal wasn't reached because attendance declined rapidly at the end and the last such happy gathering was in 2011. Woking managed to continue theirs, at least in 2012. I have included this account of former office life to illustrate the camaraderie that existed in those days amongst a large number of railway staff, plus the desire to keep in touch with former colleagues following numerous reorganisations which over the years often widely dispersed people. In so many railway positions there was a job for life if one wished. With perhaps the exception of drivers, signalmen and guards I think that opportunity has much diminished with privatisation especially in clerical grades, with so many TOCs doing their utmost to reduce opening hours and even close many ticket offices.

But back to Wimbledon. Naturally from October 1963 the first months of Line Managers' full operation were months of consolidation. Each former district had its own practices which had to be ironed out. One such practice with which I was involved was attendance at banana meetings with Elders & Fyffes (E&F). In addition to Southampton their boats unloaded at Avonmouth, Barry and

Garston whilst Southampton-destined vessels often discharged at weekends. When this came about, a meeting was convened at the E&F office in Stratton Street close to Green Park underground station. Attending were two E&F representatives and no less than three people from BR comprising myself from the Southampton district, one from the London West district and one from Waterloo HQ. The majority of work from the railway angle was done by district representatives and I never really fathomed out why an HQ person was there. I was told it was to adjudicate at times of disagreement between E&F and BR but I don't recall such a situation arising, we resolved any major or minor problems. But on the other hand perhaps the HQ person reported back to the rolling stock section how many banana vans were required, for it was Regional HQ who liaised with BRB HQ on such matters. Once at Wimbledon, however, BR representation was reduced to one person - usually me.

"Q" (if required) pathways were principally used for banana trains, but over the years my predecessor had worked out pathways for other specials of which E&F were aware and which they sometimes used. From time to time however it was necessary for me to find pathways and on one occasion whilst still at Southampton, such a train did cause delays but not because it was a "clash" pathway with passenger trains.

Up Mondays-Fridays morning "business" trains were sacrosanct. These comprised principal main line trains arriving Waterloo before 10.00 and whose timekeeping was reviewed - nowadays it would be termed monitored - on the 11.00 passenger telephone conference chaired by a Regional Operating Manager's officer with all divisions partaking. Trains from the Southampton district were the 06.04 ex-Southampton Terminus, 06.22 ex-Bournemouth Central, 07.07 and 07.20 ex-Bournemouth West, 07.22 ex-Eastleigh and 07.34 ex-Weymouth ("The Royal Wessex"). On one particular morning E&F requested a special leaving the Old Docks (as the Eastern Docks were known then) at around

We are delighted to continue the story of Richard Simmons and his recollections of working in the Control Office - this time at Wimbledon.

The previous instalment appeared in 'SW28'.

'S15' No. 30839 passing the long disused Bramshot Halt between Farnborough and Fleet with the 10.00 Nine Elms to Southampton (Old Docks) on 19 April 1965. At the time the photograph was taken freight workings had recently been re-timed. The halt here had opened in 1913 but closed in 1946. Despite the platforms being seen intact, the remains have since been removed. Notice at this stage the 3rd rail is only present on the up and down slow lines. This was a time when electrification continued on the slow lines only past Pirbright Junction (for Farnham and Alton services) to Sturt Lane Junction and around the now defunct spur to Frimley Junction for the handful of peak-period trains from Woking to Ash Vale and Ascot which were discontinued at the conclusion of the 1964 summer timetable. Afterwards the junction at Sturt Lane was relaid with plain track for the main line only. The fast lines were later electrified with the coming of the Bournemouth electrification. (A curiosity was that the little used spur from Frimley Junction to the main line facing towards Farnborough also had the third-rail but which then terminated abruptly in the vicinity of the overbridge carrying the main line over the Reading to Redhill route and so really led to nowhere. Tucked down at the bottom of the embankment on the up side of the main line at the aforementioned overbridge is an SR designed sub-station still there today. I can only conclude that the conductor rail terminating adjacent to it was something to do with feeding supply to the Ascot route - interesting!)

06.00 via Basingstoke and Reading West to the LMR. I timed it to follow the aforementioned 06.04 ex-Southampton Terminus passenger and go "over the top", as Worting Junction was nicknamed, before the 07.22 Eastleigh-Waterloo. But alas, the engine - a Q1 I believe - was shy of steam and the train had to go into Wallers Ash loop to raise steam. The 07.22 Eastleigh was delayed which did not go down well on the conference that morning. The Chief Trains Clerk told me not to use that pathway again whilst fortunately I do not recall E&F repeating the request.

My first position at Wimbledon was in the freight section dealing with banana trains and other special traffic

arrangements, by which time the 1963 Channel Islands tomato traffic season had just about finished. At that time there was a curious exercise underway known as "pin and string", which had actually started before the Line Manager's organisation had come into being, having been set up with a representative each from Regional HQ and the Southampton and Woking district offices. The exercise was centred upon efficient utilization of Class 33 diesel locomotives which were then being delivered and introduced as they became available in a rather piecemeal way into steam diagrams. Basically a large chart was affixed to a wall with a single strand of string or cotton used

'Bulleids' in quick succession on the down fast line at Raynes Park, 4 July 1964. Left is No. 34071 '601 Squadron' with the 11.05 SO Waterloo to Bournemouth West. Right is No. 34077 '603 Squadron' this time with the 11.15 Waterloo to Padstow service.

for each locomotive from which the most economical use of locomotives was plotted. It should be remembered this was for freight trains only as little or no use of these diesels could be made on passenger trains during winter months because of their lack of provision for steam heating. The result was some quite radical revision to freight train timings but some freight services would also have been revised or cancelled altogether, even if steam had remained supreme due to freight facilities being withdrawn at smaller stations.

The 1965 public timetable saw the change from 12 to 24 hour clock format and I became involved in its implementation. The method used in those days was to use proof copies of the previous year's timetable and amend it with ballpoint pen by hand where necessary so that the printer (the Southern Region timetable was still printed in time-honoured tradition by Henry Blacklock of Manchester), could easily spot where amendments were required. Should a timetable recast be introduced, eg, the Hampshire diesel scheme, then that was a different matter. 1965 also saw other timetable production changes. The usual separate summer and winter editions were replaced by one issue per year and the 1965 one was operative from 14 June 1965 until 4 September 1966. In my opinion this was a retrograde step for two principal reasons. First, production was changed from one regional timetable to three divisional timetables with some tables included in all three books. Second, with the Beeching plan getting into top gear, line and station closures were proceeding at an alarmingly quick pace, necessitating all three divisions producing two supplements during the timetable currency Fortunately sense eventually seemed to prevail and production of a complete SR timetable was resumed with the May 1968 edition. But, dear readers, that is not the end of the saga of a non-regional timetable which is continued as part of life at Waterloo!

So how was I involved in this rigmarole? Proof copies of a 24-hour-style timetable format were required for printing purposes, so two new temporary clerical positions were created for the compilation and I was fortunate enough to be appointed as the senior of the two. Together with my colleague we re-wrote the complete South Western Division services by hand in 24-hour format! As far as I can recall one of us did down pages and the other up pages. Today I expect such a job would be done by some electronic process. At about the same time the decision had been made to do away with those wonderful sheet timetables which were pasted on to large size bill boards and adorned station platforms or at station entrances. They gave a complete line of route only to be replaced by the rather - again in my opinion - less than informative departure posters which only show departure times from the station in question to adjacent stations. For example, departure times are shown from station A to station B with an approximate journey time but to station C, journey times are xx minutes more than to station B. The successors to these departure posters are still in use. My colleague and I were not involved with departure poster preparation.

As this work was only of a temporary nature, when completed I wondered whether I would revert to my freight train section position. The answer to this was no, because I was promoted to a vacant position in the Electrification & Planning section. Quite why electrification was included in the section title I don't know because in 1964 Bournemouth electrification had still to be announced. Its work was largely based on timetable planning for future schemes and had been involved in the "Tadpole" Reading-Redhill-Tonbridge scheme when these units ousted steam in January 1965. Before the creation of Line Managers and while such work was still done at Waterloo, at least one member of its staff had worked on the Hampshire diesel scheme which I'm sure many readers will recall revolutionised south Hampshire local services. It provided good connections at St Denys between the Netley line and diesel services on the main line, as well as at Eastleigh between main line diesel services and Alton together with those between Portsmouth & Southsea and Andover Junction via Chandlers Ford. Unfortunately the original withdrawal of Chandlers Ford line services together with the Mid-Hants line closure started to unravel that pattern and it has to be said the pattern of main line stopping services that came with Bournemouth electrification virtually completed that process.

When Bournemouth electrification was announced in September 1964 the section was re-designated the Electrification section and was enlarged to deal with facilities at stations within the scheme's remit. It was also involved with the introduction of the first Guildford panel box together with the original Eastleigh and Basingstoke installations. Following electrification it was involved with the Surbiton and Feltham schemes. Whilst the Signal and Telecommunications did the technical and design work, the Electrification section drew up local signal box instructions such as level-crossing working etc and any intermediate sidings which the new panel boxes would control. Some of these instructions were quite lengthy and I recall involved spending many hours with the signalling and rules and regulations expert reading out loud with him these instructions to check for typing errors. Nevertheless I gained a lot of knowledge from this type of work. Quite a lot of work was done on the electrification timetable but as already explained, this was taken over by the newly created Central Timings Office at Waterloo.

Before electrification commenced one scheme developed by the section was the use of Western Region (WR) DMMUs on stopping services between Salisbury, Basingstoke and Woking. I was called in one day to one of the operating hierarchy and was informed that the WR could provide sufficient units to the Southern to work these

services. I was amazed that the WR had such resources spare, the South Western certainly had no DEMUs to work on these services (at least on weekdays), some already having been "poached" by the Central Division to replace steam on the Steyning line. The scheme as outlined to me was that in off-peak periods, steam Waterloo-Basingstoke-Salisbury stopping trains would be replaced by DMMUs operating between Woking, Basingstoke and Salisbury, connecting at Woking out of Waterloo-Portsmouth Harbour fast trains and into corresponding up trains, and I was given the task of developing the scheme. Whilst this would give a regular interval service to and from intermediate stations between Woking and Basingstoke, although Brookwood was already served by half-hourly Waterloo-Alton electrics, passengers to and from Waterloo would be required to change at Woking. I suspect this move was not very popular. The reason given for the scheme was that fast lines between Woking and Basingstoke were to be re-laid for electrification which was to be done in sections eg Basingstoke-Hook, on weekdays and not just at weekends or nights, with all trains using slow lines over the affected sections. Replacement of steam traction would release locomotives to work ballast trains and with steam traction due for elimination within a few years, at the time a shortage of serviceable locomotives was emerging and it was reckoned such a shortage would be relieved by using DMMUs. But at the time I remember wondering if the real objective was to release enginemen for ballast trains rather than engines themselves for there was a shortage of footplate crews.

There was also a problem on summer Saturdays because Waterloo-Portsmouth Harbour fasts still conveyed a considerable number of Isle of Wight holidaymakers. The scale of these numbers can be gauged by the fact that when the scheme was introduced in June 1965 between

Western Region DMU set S708 with the 11.54 Waterloo to Basingstoke at Clapham Junction, 24 July 1965.

Note:

DMU = Diesel Multiple Unit
DMMU = Diesel Mechanical Multiple Unit
DEMU = Diesel Electric Multiple Unit.

Each refers to the type of transmission used in the sets although DMU and DMMU were often used to describe the same type of set.

At Clapham Junction on the same day was No. 82019 on ecs from Waterloo. (The 11.28 from the terminus to West London sidings.)

approximately 07.00 and 16.00 there remained up to four fast Waterloo-Portsmouth Harbour services each hour. Also remaining was the rump of the Saturday peak period when London commuters finished work at midday. Whilst during off- peak periods, on changing at Woking passengers had to use what services they could to reach Waterloo, the 09.39 Salisbury-Woking was extended to Waterloo, returning to Basingstoke at 11.54, so affording the unusual sight of a DMMU at Waterloo. Steam Waterloo-Basingstoke and Salisbury trains invariably included in their formation a van for mails and parcels necessitating van trains to be included in the scheme to convey this traffic. For example on weekdays two such trains departed Waterloo at 11.54 and 15.38 to Basingstoke and Eastleigh respectively.

It goes without saying that several liaison meetings were held with the WR at Paddington to tie-up loose ends and agree pathways for empty stock workings between Reading diesel depot and Basingstoke and vice-versa to position units into and out of their workings. Sunday services were unaffected as from the winter 1962/63 timetable most steam Waterloo-Basingstoke stopping trains had been replaced by a two-hourly Woking-Basingstoke service formed of a Hampshire DEMU which was spare on Sundays. This departed Eastleigh empty at 07.55 for Basingstoke, but in the evening, the last train from Woking conveyed passengers throughout to Eastleigh. Two up steam-hauled Sunday morning services remained, serving intermediate stations between Basingstoke and Woking. In mid-winter one from Southampton Old Docks was the inward Le Havre boat train and it would be interesting to have found out the opinion of cross-channel passengers of the trains's sedate and tedious progress between Basingstoke and Woking. The other train was the 07.10 Yeovil Town-

Waterloo. Otherwise, apart from the 01.35 (advertised 01.30) Waterloo-Yeovil Town passenger and news which called at Overton (not advertised), Whitchurch North (as Whitchurch was then known) and Grateley, smaller intermediate stations between Basingstoke and Salisbury had been closed on Sundays since the summer 1963 timetable. It should be remembered that Oakley and Hurstbourne had closed with the winter 1963 and summer 1964 timetables respectively, being joined by Idmiston Halt and Porton on 9 September 1968.

While referring to the fate of smaller intermediate stations, at this point I hope our editor will permit me to digress with what I consider to be a fascinating curiosity concerning Oakley. Way back at the time of nationalisation, the 20.54 Waterloo-Salisbury stopper, which departed Basingstoke at 22.16, did not call at Oakley. But all was not lost for the inhabitants of Oakley wishing to return home in the late evening, as from the summer 1949 timetable an additional facility was introduced to enable passengers to reach that north Hampshire village. This was by using a Venture bus on weekdays which departed from Basingstoke (The Barge) at 21.30 so connecting out of the 19.54 Waterloo-Basingstoke. This bus also operated on Sundays so the same bus journey was shown in the Sunday timetable page, which perhaps demonstrated that on the Sabbath Oakley had "something over" other intermediate stations between Basingstoke and Salisbury where the second of the two sparse Sunday trains – while they still had them - departed Basingstoke at 20.37. Two features of this arrangement seem unusual in that Venture Ltd was not listed as an "Associated" bus company (of which more later) with the Southern Railway or BR, neither did the timetable show that railway tickets would be accepted on that

No. 73089 'Maid of Astolat' entering Wimbledon on the 18.09 Waterloo to Basingstoke. 10 August 1962.

particular bus journey, but the company did participate in the road and rail ticket availability arrangements. By the 1951 summer rail timetable the bus journey was shown as being operated by Wilts and Dorset who had absorbed Venture; that is, the Thomas Tilling Wilts and Dorset and not the present operator of that name. The bus journey was last advertised by BR in the winter 1953 timetable with no alternative train or bus replacement thereafter. It was a good job such an arrangement had ceased to exist for it would have had to be taken into account when developing the Woking-Basingstoke-Salisbury diesel scheme.

There remained one further position at Wimbledon which I occupied before promotion beckoned, and that was in the Special Traffic section which arranged all special trains including Southampton boat trains, which still existed in those days, bank holiday service alterations, timed ballast trains and revised services for engineering work. Freight train special workings were dealt with by the Freight section, but freight service revisions arising from engineering work were made by the special traffic section in conjunction with the freight section.

Within the special traffic section there was a sub-section dealing with engineering work service revisions both at weekends and week nights. Staffing was a clerk in charge, four or five (depending on availability) on weekend work and two for week nights. I slotted in as one of the weekend team and found the work very interesting and absorbing. A quarterly engineering works programme was produced following a meeting attended by technical departments involved (Chief Civil Engineer, Chief Signal & Telecommunications Engineer, Chief Mechanical & Electrical Engineer etc), plus divisional representatives from Special Traffic and Rules & Regulations etc. At these

meetings times and limits of possessions were agreed, points of single line working, diversionary routes and bus substitutes. Staff were given a copy of the programme and allocated a specific weekend to revise train services, produce a special traffic "P" notice - hand written - solely for that one weekend. This was passed to the senior clerk for scrutiny and when agreed after amendments if necessary) was forwarded to the printer. This was to a certain printer in Southampton who over the years, I imagine, made much money from BR work. I don't know if this printer remains in business but very probably has been absorbed into a larger printing group. There was a few weeks' respite from the hectic nature of this work for no major engineering work took place over the three or four weekends before Christmas, because of the heavy programme of additional Christmas mails and parcels trains - vastly different from today.

Bus operators used were confined to those "In association with British Railways (Southern Region)", as public timetables in early nationalisation days described them. So in so far as the South Western was concerned, buses were ordered from London Transport Executive (LTE), Aldershot & District Traction Co Ltd, Hants & Dorset Motor Services Ltd, Southdown Motor Services Ltd, Southern National Omnibus Co, Thames Valley Traction Co Ltd and Wilts & Dorset Motor Services Ltd (the original Tilling company). The municipalities of Portsmouth, Southampton and Bournemouth were not approached but if "associated" companies were unable to cover railway requirements from their own resources and went to municipalities or outside operators, they did so under their own arrangements. Hard to believe that virtually all these bus companies have been subsumed by large combines. At the time I was on engineering work (1970) many bus operators were, like railways, suffering from staff shortages: in particular, it seemed, LTE who frequently went to private coach operators. We had station to station bus schedules so had to produce bus timetables which were submitted to bus companies concerned who scrutinised and agreed them. Also to be arranged with the commercial cartage section were lorries to be available at both ends of engineering possessions to convey perambulators and such luggage as could not be conveyed on buses. From today's engineering works posters no such luxury is provided, posters proclaiming that bicycles, prams and bulky luggage cannot be conveyed on buses although that fact is regretted. It was also necessary to draft posters detailing engineering works which were exhibited at stations involved and which were - if I recall correctly - passed to the Public Relations & Publicity Officer at Waterloo who arranged printing.

It may be imagined that with a basic Herbert Walker inspired "clock face" regular interval timetable, when revising services it would be easy to plan a regular interval "clock face" revised timetable. On most lines this was the existing situation but there were, nevertheless, some timetable quirks which could so easily catch out timetable clerks. Naturally as time progressed one would become familiar with them and plan the timetable accordingly but for an example let us look at the Sunday Portsmouth Direct line service.

Normally Waterloo-Portsmouth Harbour trains did not call at Milford and this situation prevailed in the late 1960s when I was on engineering work, but on Sundays the 12.50 ex-Waterloo did - at 1335: why? In those days there was a hospital in the Milford vicinity which drew visitors from beyond the immediate local area, and a sufficient number of them travelled by rail to justify a stop there on the 12.50 ex-Waterloo. In the opposite direction a similar arrangement applied with the 15.20 Portsmouth Harbour-Waterloo calling at Milford at 16.13. On the West of England line, by then truncated at Exeter St. Davids, several stations were closed on Sundays among them being Whitchurch North and Grateley which both had a call in the "wee small hours" by the same train, the 01.30 Waterloo-Yeovil Junction. The principal purpose of these two stops was to unload newspapers but passengers could make use of them as well, neither being restricted to 'set down only'. I wonder how many people availed themselves of this facility. We tended to memorise much of the service but had to look out for these quirks by referring to the WTT. In passing it is interesting to observe that Overton and Whitchurch North stations seemed to just about escape total closure in the Beeching cull as even on weekdays, the number of calls were restricted to four Mondays-Fridays and two on Saturdays in the down direction , and in the up direction to three every weekday whereas Grateley had considerably more. Consider that level of service with today's when these stations are served hourly on weekdays and two-hourly on Sundays!

Move to Waterloo
My work at Wimbledon came to an end in 1970. By then

amongst the many re-designations to affect or should I say be inflicted upon, railway departments, was one to rename the Commercial Superintendent at Waterloo as Passenger Manager. Other regions had Chief Passenger Manager but not on the SR where the prefix 'Chief' was not added for several years. I don't know the reason why this should have been the case when on the SR passenger traffic had always dominated freight.

At Waterloo the Passenger Manager advertised a position on his Services Section. A colleague in the Wimbledon Special Traffic section and myself both applied for this job as it would have meant promotion, although I have to admit that with seemingly innumerable reorganisations taking place, neither of us really knew what the job entailed. My colleague did establish that it was a "commercial" job rather than "operating", the latter being more familiar to both of us. This demonstrated again the long standing operating and commercial cultural division established on the railway. Therefore as we had both been operating for many years we immediately dismissed much hope of being appointed but even so we both got interviews. Following the interview I was therefore totally surprised to receive a letter informing me of selection to fill the position at the grand annual salary of £1,265 plus £70 annual London allowance. I was instructed to report at 09.00 to Room 313, Waterloo, starting there on 4 May 1970. I must say I left Wimbledon with mixed feelings being unaware of what the hallowed surroundings of Regional HQ would bring.

Waterloo Station.
However before entering the building let us remind ourselves of what the station was then like. It still had 21 platforms divided into 'main' and 'Windsor line' sections, the division being an administrative office block between platforms 15 and 16 containing a florist's shop at platform level and station manager's offices above as well as train crew accommodation and clerical staff canteen of which more later. At the concourse end was located the main escalator down to the underground. The main concourse was then not too cluttered. There were three W.H Smith bookstalls, one against the barrier line on low numbered main suburban platforms, the biggest in a concourse central position and the third adjacent to Windsor line platforms - the high numbered ones. The news theatre had already closed by the time I arrived but together with the usual station outlets there was also a branch of Messrs Boots and a bank. There was also a handy sub-post office branch, but regrettably this was an early victim of the "Beechingisation" of such establishments which have become all too familiar in recent years. Three booking offices served the station, one each for main, suburban and Windsor lines, the offices being of bowed wooden construction extending out on to the concourse. The main line booking office was a rather grand high-ceilinged affair being part of the main office building structure. Mention must also be made of the two departure indicators, one for main line services and main suburban, the other devoted to Windsor line departures.

NON-STOP: SOUTHAMPTON CENTRAL TO WIMBLEDON AND THEN WATERLOO

There was one arrival indicator for main line services only. All were mechanically operated and seemingly thoroughly reliable. I refer to reliability because during my time at Waterloo they were replaced by Solari indicators which certainly seemed to fail far more often than their mechanical predecessors. As much of the station was built above ground level, beneath the concourse was a veritable catacomb of arches used for all sorts of purposes, one being the Plan Arch referred to by Peter Tatlow in his interesting article on Bevois Park Sidings (SW issue 23), another being devoted to muniments (stored files etc). At road level and facing Waterloo Road was The Colonnade used to load LTE Red Arrow buses during peak hours and also the Bill Office, from where such items as cheap day and excursion tickets handbills and WTTs were despatched to stations throughout the region. This whole area is now incorporated in the Jubilee Line underground entrance.

Over the years of working at Waterloo the concourse became more cluttered with retail outlets so reducing circulation, especially vital when large numbers of passengers had enforced waits for trains at times of service disruption. Later the three booking offices were swept away, the two of "bow type" being demolished and the main line office area used for other retail purposes. Notwithstanding this alternative use, the location of the main line office can still be discerned for on the outside wall of the road dividing the main station from Waterloo (East) there still remains a notice prohibiting barrows being pushed across the booking office floor. In place of the three booking offices one large office was created, which also replaced the much smaller office on the slope leading to what is now Waterloo (East), which in those days was still known simply as Waterloo. With that office's closure, the unsuspecting passenger heading for a train from Waterloo (East) and requiring to purchase a ticket could well walk up the slope, find no booking office and have to walk to the main station, locate the new office, book a ticket, then retrace his (or her) steps up the slope to the South Eastern platforms. In so doing they could miss their train. The Information Office remained on the main station although over the years it was moved about a bit. In recent years South West Trains has progressively closed separate station information offices, Waterloo only succumbing towards the end of 2012, when it was replaced by three separate windows in the main ticket office. Other station facilities, refreshment rooms and toilets etc were at concourse level or with access gained from steps going down.

TO BE CONTINUED

'Southern Interloper'. Type 1 No D8040 at Clapham Junction with the 10.00 SO Willesdon Junction to Norwood Junction, 24 July 1965.

All images by the Author.

THE SOLENT RAILWAY TUNNEL

Fred Turton

FOREWORD by BART RUSSELL, Ventnor, I. o. W.
This little brochure has been written by Fred Turton, of Sandown, whose enthusiasm for the provision of a Solent Tunnel is well-known throughout the Island. He has brought to his theme the results of much research, and deals with it in a factual and practical manner. Whether it would bring all the benefits he enumerates is left to the judgment and imagination of the reader, but no one can doubt the author's confidence and public spirit. Mr. Turton takes up the torch which was lit by the late Mr. Aman, of Totland, with the backing of Sir Blundell Maple, M.P., whose efforts seemed likely, at one time, to bring the scheme to fruition.

The illustrations are reproductions of pen-and-ink sketches by the author, and it is hoped that the booklet will revive and increase public interest in a project which would confer lasting advantage on the people of the Isle of Wight - particularly those who cater for visitors - and solve what have hitherto appeared to be insoluble problems concerning quicker and better communication with the Island, and transport generally.

Introduction

I have been prevailed upon by an old friend of mine to write a history of the ill-fated Solent Tunnel Scheme, a scheme which I personally believe in as being the only remedy for the appalling conditions of existence (one can't call it living) in the Isle of Wight, "between seasons."

The reason is not far to seek. We Islanders depend for our living (most of us, at any rate) on a short three months' season! We all bank on it; and if that Season fails by as much as a week or a fort-night, our stock of money peters out about February. What do we see then? Mortgages, loans, overdrafts, etc. A bank manager said to me once, "People grouse and grumble at the Banks, but we keep the seaside, I.W., towns on their legs." That is literally a fact.

We were recently passed a small booklet published by Stanley Wrath in 1945/6 on 'The History of the Solent Tunnel Scheme'.

Very much in keeping with the theme we try and present in 'SW', this booklet had us captivated from the first page and we can thus do no better than to share it here.

Very much in the style of the time and illustrated only with a few simple pen drawings, it nevertheless describes an idea perhaps even worthy of consideration today.

We are grateful to Nick Lerwill for finding the original item.

This, then, is the state of the Isle of Wight. Of course it would be wrong to say the Island has not progressed at all during the last 40 years; it has, but not to the same extent as watering-places on the mainland. It had at one time Royal visitors. At Cowes, for instance, when Queen Victoria was alive, and Osborne House was the centre of interest. In those days Royalty used to come here more often. The German Royal Family used to stay at the King's Head Hotel, at Sandown. Royalty do not come here much now – Osborne House is a nursing home and the residents get less every year.

The great and crying need, in normal times, is a good, permanent residential population. This will never be as long as we are cut off as we are. I knew of one case, personally. A good many years ago (when Ventnor was booming as a chest and lung-trouble resort), a doctor, whose wife was rather delicate, bought a big house on the South coast of the Island and spent his weekends at Ventnor. One year, when he was spending a fortnight's holiday on the Island, a telegram arrived from London, saying an operation on one of his patients was imperative at once, and, if he could not come within 24 hours, they must summon another surgeon. He packed up as quickly as he could, but when he got to Ryde - a thick fog, and no boats running! He rushed round and telegraphed at once to London, and another doctor performed the operation, and he lost his patient. That settled it; he sold his house, and went to Bournemouth, where he could easily get backwards and forwards as often as he liked. This was only one of many similar cases.

As the following pages will show, we are no nearer London (or anywhere else on the Mainland) now than we were 40 years ago, and, in some cases, 50 years ago. The little bit of prosperity which comes to a town on the north shore of the Isle of Wight in war-

THE SOLENT RAILWAY TUNNEL

A pen and ink drawing from the cover of the original book as an impression by Fred Turton of a train leaving the Solent Tunnel. The remaining drawings are of similar style and depict contemporary trains from c1945.

time, is no criterion of the general prosperity of the Isle of Wight. This fictitious prosperity begins (and ends) with War.

THE ORIGIN OF THE SCHEME
The Isle of Wight is a lovely island at the extreme southern point of England. It is, roughly, 26 miles long, 15 miles across, and 60 miles round - and it is so close to the mainland, that the first question a visitor (especially a foreign visitor), may well ask, is, "Why has not a tunnel, or a bridge, or, at least, something, to cut out the miserable delay, discomfort and uncertainty of the sea-passage, been provided?"

He (or she) may well ask it, seeing that to-day, in this year of (Dis)grace, 1942, it takes, roughly speaking, just as long to get from the Island to most places on the Mainland as it did 40 years ago. And while we admit freely and thankfully, all that the Southern Railway have done for us in the way of better rolling stock, better track and more trains, the fact remains that the speed, both on this side of the Solent and on the Mainland side, is not much better, in spite of all the Electrification, and so on, of the Southern Railway.

Up to the end of the Steam Era, the crack 'Dining' car trains from Waterloo to Portsmouth, did the journey in 1½ hours. The "Electrics" take 2 minutes less, with two intermediate stops. The boat takes the usual 35 minutes that it has taken for the last 50 years. Of course, the boats are bigger, more comfortable, and more frequent ; but that's all. It still takes 3 hours to get from Sandown to London (if you are lucky), if not, as is more often the case, 3¼ hours. On our side of the Solent, although one rolls luxuriously in the fine 57-feet bogie coaches from the Brighton Main Line, with spring-cushions and steam-heating, it still takes the same time to get from Ventnor to Ryde, or from Cowes to Newport, as it used to do, the only difference being comfort.

Then the crossing! When it's foggy or very stormy, the boats don't run at all. In summer you are often very crowded, and in winter cold and miserable - and all because of a paltry four and half miles across

the Solent!

And, moreover, this is not the shortest distance from the Mainland. The Solent varies in width: it is only two miles across at a point opposite Cowes Harbour; only 2¾, from Stokes Bay to Ryde ; and, shortest of all, just under a mile, from Hurst Castle to Colwell Bay, at the "back of the Wight." In fact, in some ways we are worse off than we were 50 years ago, for there are now only three main routes to the Island, viz., Portsmouth-Ryde, Southampton-Cowes, and Lymington-Yarmouth, against a former five, the two extra ones being Stokes Bay-Ryde, and Southsea Seaview and Bembridge (this last being very useful for the remote eastern end of the Island, viz., Bembridge, St. Helens, Lane End, and Whitcliff Bay and Forelands).

Trains ran alongside the boats at Ryde and Bernbridge on the Island, and at Portsmouth, Lymington, and Southampton, on the Mainland (and also at Stokes Bay when weather permitted). As a matter of fact, the Southampton-Cowes route, instead of improving, has deteriorated still more since the Great War, as, before 1914, the trains used to run on to the Royal Pier at Southampton, alongside the boats, by being hauled through the streets by a little steam-tram engine, from the (then) Southampton Docks and Town Station on to the pier (the express engine having been detached at the Town Station). Now the rails are torn up, the Pier Station closed, and the unfortunate passenger has to make his own way from the Royal Pier to the West Station (now called the "Central ") by motor-bus. This means three changes, viz., trains to boat at Cowes, boat to bus at Southampton Pier, bus to train at the "Central," before the passenger has taken his seat in the London Express, in the course of a journey, say, from Newport to London.

So it will be seen that people with vision and foresight, have held, for many years, that something to cut out the sea passage, or, at any rate, the irritating changes in the journey from London to the Island, was very much overdue. The only questions are: What? How? Where? A bridge? A train ferry? A causeway? or a tunnel.

The bridge can absolutely be ruled out, as navigation would be interrupted. The causeway would be

Haven Street pre1923.
Roger Simmonds collection.

the best of all, if practicable ; but it would have to be done by the Admiralty.

So we come to the remedy nearly everybody is agreed upon as the best way out of the trouble, viz.,

A SOLENT TUNNEL: THE RAILWAY POSITION

Before we begin to examine the Tunnel Scheme further, it will be necessary to examine the Railway's shortcomings of the late 1890's and early 1900's that led up to it. As will be seen all through this book, Portsmouth was principal "jumping off" place for the Island, and it was served by the London and South Western Railway Co., from Waterloo, and the London, Brighton and South Coast Railway, from London Bridge and Victoria.

The Brighton Co. arrived there by continuing its Coast line from Brighton through Worthing, Ford, Chichester and Havant, to Portsmouth Town, a distance of about 48 miles. The Portsmouth trains used to run to London, via Brighton, making with the 51 miles between Brighton and London, a distance of 99 miles. It was a dreary, long and uncomfortable journey.

The London and South Western Railway arrived at Portsmouth, via Basingstoke, Winchester, Bishopstoke (now Eastleigh) and Fareham. Here the Gosport and Stokes Bay line branches off. They arrived by the Guildford branch from Woking to Havant, under hectic conditions.

At first, the Brighton Co. refused to let them go beyond Havant. However, they eventually obtained running powers into Portsmouth.

The Brighton Co. had constructed their line through Arundel, Horsham, Dorking, and Sutton to London, this bringing the distance by this route to 86 miles. The London and South Western Railway, on their part, having finished their new branch, called their line, via Guildford, the "Portsmouth Direct," and brought down the distance from London, to 74 miles. The Brighton Co., on the other hand, called theirs the "Mid-Sussex Direct" - an entire misnomer. It may have been "direct" from Arundel, but certainly not from Portsmouth, as they had to run about 30 miles due East to Ford Junction, before turning Londonwards. Competition was hopeless with the South-Western shorter route, so they agreed to form a local alliance, in which all the receipts from the London and I.W. traffic, via Portsmouth and Ryde, would be pooled. So the Portsmouth lines were henceforth known as the "Joint Railway Cos."

The arrangement was notorious; if one Company tried to "ginger" things up a bit, they had to hand over half the proceeds to the other Company. On one occasion, the South-Western, with their 12 miles less to run, put on an experimental train, reaching Portsmouth in 1½ hours, instead of the usual 2¼ (and 2½ for the Brighton Co.). Result - people flocked to Waterloo, and the South Western had to shell out half the extra proceeds to the Brighton Co. So they discontinued it, and agreed to an (approx.) timing of 2 hours between London and Portsmouth. This meant an acceleration to 2 hours by the Brighton Co. and a deliberate slowing down to 2 hours by the South-Western. This seems an almost incredible story, but I had it from no less a person that the late Mr. H. K. Day himself, the Traffic Manager of the old Isle of Wight Railway, who was an intimate friend of mine, and who would have introduced many improvements on the Isle of Wight Railway if he had had a free hand (which, unfortunately, he hadn't).

So for many years the best trains were:
LONDON and SOUTH WESTERN RAILWAY
12.10 midday : Waterloo to Portsmouth, 2 hrs. 5 mins.
5 p.m.: ditto   2 hrs. 15 mins.

2.20 p.m.: Waterloo to Stokes Bay, 2 hrs. 39 mins. (terminating at Portsmouth when too rough for the boat at Stokes Bay)

LONDON, BRIGHTON and SOUTH COAST RAILWAY
11.35 a.m. (Pullman Car) and 1.35 p.m. : Victoria to Portsmouth, 2 hrs. 5 mins.
(Season only) 8.45 a.m. : Portsmouth to the City, 2 hrs. 5mins. (London Bridge)
4.55 p.m. : London Bridge to Portsmouth, 2 hrs. 5 mins.

The Joint Companies built two new lines, including the new high-level platforms at Portsmouth Town, and continued the railway to the new harbour railway pier; and continued the I.W. Rly. and the I.W.C. Rly. from St. John's Rd. Station at Ryde, through the Esplanade Tunnel, on to a new railway pier - an expensive structure a mile long, with an intermediate station at Ryde Esplanade. Thus, Ryde has three stations within a short 1¼ miles, rather reminding one of St. Paul's, Ludgate Hill and Holborn Viaduct, on the old Chatham and Dover Line in London, where the platforms are so close together that they almost seem to be touching.

These lines - which, by the way, were the only true "double-track" lines in the Island - and their counter -part at Portsmouth, were a final bid for the monopoly of the London-I.W. traffic, via Portsmouth.

There were also built, from plans emanating from Brighton, under the late Mr. William Stroudley's regime, two "double enders," i.e., Ferry-boats with a bow at both ends, and two rudders to enable them to get in and out of Portsmouth Harbour without turning. These new works were, in reality, the "Wedding Ring" that united the two companies.

"Now," thought people, "we shall see some deve-lopments." They did, but not the sort they expected; for, instead of improving the services, the Companies did all they could (or so it seemed) to stifle them. The South-Western kept all their best rolling-stock for Bournemouth and the West; and frequently some of the earliest flat-roofed, bogie-carriages - no corridors, no meals, and sometimes, no lavatories - were seen on their best Portsmouth trains. The Brighton Co. was even worse, harsh-running six-wheelers generally making up the trains to London Bridge and Victoria. A few bogie-carriages, however, began to make their appearance about 1900. All their best stuff was run to Brighton, Hastings, and Eastbourne.

The two companies, while being outwardly friends, were, really, deadly competitors. And how? By developing their own preserves outside of Portsmouth and the Isle of Wight. For instance, the Brighton Co. developed Brighton, Bognor, Hastings and Eastbourne, while the South Western developed Bournemouth, Ilfracombe, Southampton, and the West generally. For example, the London and South Western Railway spent an enormous amount on Bournemouth alone, fast and powerful 4-6-0 type express engines, of tremendous size and speed, being built by the late Mr. Drummond (the

Locomotive Super), to reduce the journey (over 100 miles) to two hours. The Brighton Co., at their end, spent some colossal sums on Pullman Car trains, such as the "Brighton Ltd.," "City Ltd.," "Southern Belle," etc. and all this time we never had a single named train for Portsmouth and the I.W. One would have thought that they would have had a "Vectis Ltd." or a "Southsea Belle" ! Not a bit of it; anything was good enough for the I.W.

At long last, exasperated at being easily the worst served of any big town of comparable size in England, by rail, Portsmouth struck, and struck hard, and was backed up by the Island. They sent a deputation to the "Joint Railways," and got, or rather forced, some concessions out of them. In a very short time corridor, dining and tea cars made their appearance on the South-Western trains, these doing the journey in one hour fifty minutes; and the Brighton Co. ran 1st and 3rd-Class Pullman Cars from Victoria and London Bridge, with meals.

The greatest improvement, however, was on the Brighton Line. Earl Marsh was the new "Boss" at Brighton, and he introduced some fine 57-ft. bogie stock, with high elliptical roofs, and "Atlantic" type express engines, similar to the G.N. Ry. "Atlantics." These handsome trains, in their new umber and cream Livery, took their part in the Portsmouth Services, and were much appreciated by the travelling public. So Ports-mouth and Southsea were "appeased" for the time being.

But what of the Island? There was no improvement here at all; the waits were long, boats no better than they had been for years and rolling-stock dating in some cases back to 1864.

The L.S.W. Ry. were, in the meantime, developing two other routes to the Island, viz., Southampton-Cowes and Lymington-Yarmouth. These were outside the "Combine." They had their own boats at Lymington, but had to rely on the boats of the Southampton, I. o. W. and South of England, Royal Mail Steam Packet Co. for their Cowes route. The Railway Co. had a railway pier at Lymington and Southampton ; but, unfortunately, on the Island side, neither Cowes nor Yarmouth had a railway pier, and passengers had to make their own way to and from the boats. At Cowes, the distance is a few hundred yards, and at Yarmouth a little over a quarter of a mile. However, the Cowes and Yarmouth routes are well patronised by people living at Totland and "the Back of the Wight."

Although the sea-passage from Cowes to Southampton is long, the trains for London are fast much faster, even to-day, than those from Portsmouth and nearly all the Cowes boats connect with a crack Bournemouth "flier." If the old railway pier at Southampton were in evidence today, it would be really a fine service, as things are, from Cowes to London. Both Lymington (via Brockenhurst) and Southampton

The road exterior of Newport station in early 1967. Within a few years all would be swept away - not by a new platform and connection for train from the 'Solent Tunnel' but instead by the 'Medina Motorway' - the name given to the original section of dual-carriageway at Newport and which would cause such consternation to drivers who had never ventured away from the island. Some would insist on treating it as two separate parallel roads...... .

are served by the crack "Bournemouth fliers."

As regards time taken between the Island and Portsmouth, the following facts should be fully digested, as it is here that delay occurs, and the need of a tunnel is so apparent.

Take a typical journey from Sandown to London. You get down to Ryde pier-head in about 20 mins. ; you wait 15 mins., to get under way "on the boat - which takes 35 mins. Another 35 mins. are taken by the boat to Portsmouth Harbour, making the total 70 mins.; and with another delay of 20 mins. before the London train starts, we have an hour and a half for getting clear of Portsmouth. The train, if an "express," takes an hour and a half to get to London ; and so the passenger has spent as much time in getting from Sandown to Portsmouth (11¾ miles), as he spends in getting from Portsmouth to London.

Then again, the connections were always uncertain. Before the Great War there was a case in point. The 4.55 p.m. "Brighton" train arrived at the Harbour at 7 p.m. - a fine run! - but one had then to wait for the 5 p.m., fast from Waterloo (L. & S. W. Ry.), to come in at 7.20, and afterwards proceed by boat - one being made do for the two trains - at 7.35. If there had been a boat at 7.10 p.m., 25 mins. would have been knocked off the journey from London Bridge to the Island, as the 4.55 was a really fast train.

Then another example of recent years. During the "Southern" regime, just before electrification, the

"Southern " had a fast train leaving London Bridge at 4.50 p.m., for Portsmouth, she ran non-stop to Horsham, via Three Bridges and Crawley, and a few other places (Arundel and Chichester). However, she made the Harbour at 7.15 - a good run, as it was a longer way round - to arrive just in time to miss the boat, which left at 7.10! That meant that one had to wait for the arrival, at about 8.30, of the "6.50 Diner" from Waterloo, before catching the Ryde boat that left at 8.45. One hour and a half to wait!

As regards the railways in the Island, the I.W. Ry. had, in connection with the 12.10 p.m. from Waterloo, a "down" Express from Ryde pier-head to Ventnor, called the "Ventnor Riviera Limited," which did the 13 miles in 20 minutes, non-stop. This was the fastest train ever run on the Island.

The I.W. C. Ry. had a fast train from Cowes to Ventnor Town (now the West), in connection with the 11.30 a.m. from Waterloo, via Southampton; and a 12.30 midday, fast, from Ventnor Town to Cowes, in connection with the 3 p.m. "up" Bournemouth Express from Southampton West. These trains were known as the Undercliff Specials. A through carriage was run from the Royal Pier at Southampton to the West Station, via Tunnel Junction, and was attached to the rear of the Bournemouth Express. This coach was for I.W. passengers only.

The Central also had the "Overland" from Ryde pier-head to Yarmouth and Freshwater, in connection with

There will be no more trains past Newport signal box to and from Cowes. Instead the sidings lie empty and the rails gather rust.

the Brighton Co.'s 11.35 a.m. Pullman Express from Victoria.

As to the "status" of the Island railways, the Central were nearly bankrupt - hence their desperate attempts at a progressive policy, to try to improve matters. The L. & S. W. Ry. tried to buy up the Island railways. The Central would have sold; but the I.W. R. did not want to - for obvious reasons!

The reader will see from the foregoing that, while other towns were going ahead by leaps and bounds, thanks to their being fostered by the railway companies, and to their having a through run to Town, the Island has been cut off by an absurd sea-passage of 4½ miles!

At one time, we all hoped the G.W.Ry. would "woo" the Island, as for many years before the "War to end Wars" (sic.) they ran a through train between Paddington and Southampton Town. But, of course, once there, you had to find your own way to the Royal Pier and I.W. boat. This train ran via Newbury and Winchester (Cheesehill-*sic*), but was discontinued just before the Great War.

So, with all these drawbacks, the Island, instead of being a famous residential resort all the year round, has to rely on a short 3-months' season, and for all the rest of the year, stagnation and debt.

THE " FIRST WARNINGS " OF A SOLENT TUNNEL

The first whispers of a possible Solent Tunnel came from the West of the Island - the " Back of the Wight," as it is called - a district that was developing fast, owing to the enterprise of the L. & S. W. Ry., via Lymington, and the L.B. and S. C. Ry. and I.W. C. Ry., with their "Overland" from Ryde to the West, in connection with the 11.35 a.m.,

Victoria to Portsmouth. The main idea of the Central was to attract people to Yarmouth, via Ryde; and a fine "overland" route, right across the Island, would provide them with an ideal way of seeing nearly all the historical places of interest en route - the Church and Castle at Carisbrooke, the run through the lovely woods to Whippingham, with magnificent views of the River Medina, and Newport, the capital, with its swing-bridge and shipping. These were baits the Central Co. held out, to offset the S. W. Ry., which ran direct to the West, without using the Island railways at all (the boats used to continue the journey from Yarmouth to Totland Bay).

But the main strength of the Tunnel Idea, was Mr. Frank Aman ("Bulldog" Aman), of Totland Bay, the "Queen of Watering-places" of the Western Wight. Sir Blundell Maple also began to take an interest in the scheme, and, too, the L. & S. W. Ry.

As the idea developed, Sir Sam Fay, of the Great Central, began to "sit up and take notice," with the idea, no doubt, of running through trains from the North and Midlands to the Island - so far, nearly all our visitors were from London.

Things began to get " hot." A Bill was sent through Parliament, authorizing the formation of the "SOUTH-WESTERN AND ISLE OF WIGHT JUNCTION RAILWAY," with powers to construct a line of railway to connect the L. & S. W. Ry., by means of a Tunnel under the Solent, between Keyhaven district and Freshwater, with the Freshwater, Yarmouth and Newport Railway (the Tunnel line would have left the Lymington branch on the west side, and come to surface on the Island, at a point between Yarmouth and Freshwater stations); and, at the same time, to continue the line to Totland Bay, with a spur line to connect the Tunnel with Yarmouth, Newport, and the Island generally.

The I.W. Ry. naturally took alarm at the prospect, as it had a complete monopoly of the East Wight passenger traffic especially as there were no buses in those days.

The I.W. Ry. was the "spoilt child" of the Island railways, and it had, so far, every advantage over the other lines. To begin with, it had only 12 miles of main line of its own, and about a mile and a half of the Joint Co.'s line at Ryde, to operate; and in that short 12 miles, it had Ryde, the biggest town in the Island (although not the capital), Sandown, Shanklin and Ventnor, and the "King's town" of Brading, of historical interest. It also owned a valuable branch line to St. Helens, with its coal and goods' jetty, and Bembridge, the fashionable yachting and residential centre of the East Wight. This Brading Harbour Branch was a valuable asset.

So it will be seen that the I.W. Ry. was a solid, conservative, prosperous concern, which, so far, safe and secure, did not like to be disturbed; and that quite naturally, therefore, the idea of a Tunnel at the "Back of the Wight," and challenging the East Wight, was something that took their breath away. Don't think, however, that I.W. Ry. Co. looked askance at the Tunnel as such; they did not; their attitude was merely that they wanted it at their end, viz., Portsmouth and Ryde. But the Joint Railway Co., having spent such a lot on Ryde Pier Extension, did not feel inclined to push a Tunnel scheme here, at any rate; and, moreover, a Tunnel at this end would have cost considerably more than at the other end, as the distance is nearly double.

In the opinion of many, this is where the L. & S. W. Ry. lost a glorious opportunity of grabbing the whole Isle of Wight for themselves, because if they had refrained from building Stokes Bay Pier, and built a tunnel from Stokes Bay to Ryde, a distance of only 2¾ miles, they would have "put paid" to any other scheme ever put forward.

They could have used their main line to London, via Eastleigh, Winchester and Basingstoke - that is, a line which, although longer than the "Direct" is splendidly laid out for speed, and includes the famous racing stretch between Basingstoke and London, that is second only to the old Brunel line of the G.W. Ry, from Bristol to London.

Ryde, itself, could have been served by a Town Station on the Esplanade, and a Goods and a Suburban Station where the Tunnel came into the open, near the present St. John's Road Station.

Later, they could have rebuilt the Meon Valley Line, for main line traffic, and got a short cut to London, via Fareham and Alton, if required at any time.

They would have cut out all maintenance costs of steam-packets, piers (these are always a nightmare for under-water maintenance) and associated expenses; and although the initial cost would have been heavy, no further trouble would have been met, except, of course, periodical inspection of the Tunnel.

The Tunnel would have been run by electricity. The "Express" engine would have been detached at Fort Brockhurst - or wherever the Tunnel commenced and local electric plant would have come into operation, the train being hauled through the Tunnel by an electric locomotive, which would be detached at Ryde. Tank engines of the I.W. Rys. would have operated in the Island, as they still do now - only, of course, larger and more powerful ones, for hauling the mainland stock.

A handsome Pleasure Pier could have been built at Ryde, instead of the half-mile-long Railway Pier. As regards a Ryde-Portsmouth Tunnel, it is quite out of the question: it is too long (4½ miles).

On the Stokes Bay route, the 2.20 p.m. from Waterloo was always a popular train. A longer route was, of course, in question, but the fast, smooth running of the old S. W. Ry. main line through Basingstoke and Winchester, was in sharp contrast to the "Portsmouth Direct," which abounded with heavy gradients and sharp curves. The handsome "Adams" 7-feet 4-4-0 type, used to run these trains to Stokes Bay, and very fast and powerful locomotives they were, in their heyday. The Stokes Bay route was discontinued some time before the First World War of 1914.

In our next chapter, we will examine the various sites for the Tunnel. Experimental borings took place at several points, to ascertain the nature of the Solent bed.

THE LOCATION FOR A TUNNEL
Three main ideas were put forward as possible sites for a Solent Tunnel: (1) Lymington-Yarmouth; (2) Fawley-Cowes; (3) Ryde-Stokes Bay.

(1) LYMINGTON-YARMOUTH ROUTE.
There is no doubt that the obvious route is the Western one, as being the shortest, and, owing to a thinly populated district, and flat country on both sides, very suitable for a tunnel to come to the surface. But it would serve the Western Wight first, and so Mr. Aman had a good many unpleasant hints hurled at him, to the effect that he wanted the Tunnel at his end, for business purposes, etc. They were right - he did ; it would, naturally, have benefited him; but what the public would not see, was, that what benefited the West would also benefit the East and the whole Island. Mr. Aman said, "Very Well! If you want a Tunnel at your end, or in the middle, or anywhere else on the Island, put the money up."

This is exactly what the Isle of Wight didn't do. It's a strange fact that, while everybody grumbled at the short seasons and lack of residents, the one thing that would have solved the problem, the Isle of Wight people turned down. So Mr. Aman told them in future to hold their peace, and give up their "Dog-in-the-Manger" attitude.

Where O2s once simmered, their Westinghouse pumps thumping away, all is still. This was to be the end at Ventnor: the dream even of a 'Ventnor Marine Terminus' as empty as the platforms.

(2) FAWLEY - COWES ROUTE

The distance between Cowes and the nearest point on the Mainland is about 2 miles. This idea did not come into prominence till the Southern Railway built their Fawley branch. This line leaves the Southampton-Bournemouth main line at Totton, and runs down the west side of Southampton Water, through Hythe to Fawley. It could be easily continued to form a tunnel to Cowes. This route will be dealt with in our last chapter, "A Peep into the Future."

(3) STOKES BAY - RYDE ROUTE-

This was, for obvious reasons, too late, as pointed out before. We come now to the crisis in the history of the Tunnel, viz., the death of Sir Blundell Maple, the breaking off of relations between the Freshwater line and the Central Railway, and the possibility of the Freshwater, Yarmouth, and Newport Railway of becoming the Gateway to the Island, if the Tunnel at the West materialised. Then the crash came, and, with it, went all hopes of a Tunnel : Sir Blundell Maple died; and in the year 1914, when we expected big Tunnel developments, Great Britain declared war on Germany.

THE FRESHWATER, YARMOUTH AND NEWPORT RAILWAY

I have purposely refrained from giving actual dates of the various Railway happenings in previous chapters, as these only weary the reader, and serve no useful purpose in a short treatise like this one. I have dealt so far with periods, and not actual dates of events leading up to the Tunnel idea; that era was, from a broad, historical standpoint, from the late 1890s to the first World War in 1914.

There is one line in the Island, however, which must be dealt with in a much more detailed manner, and that one is the Freshwater, Yarmouth and Newport Railway, as it would have been the line associated with the "South-Western and Isle of Wight Junction (Tunnel) Railway."

This line would have risen from being the most obscure line in the Island, to being the most important one, as, had the Western Tunnel Scheme gone through, it would have been the one line to connect up direct with the Mainland. So far, the line was semi-bankrupt, and was run by the "Central" Company, not having any rolling-stock of its own; in fact, it was a mystery how the line existed at all. This line runs from Newport to Freshwater, in an almost westerly direction to Yarmouth, where it takes a sharp turn to the south-west and runs over flat marshes by the east bank of the River Yar. It was opened for goods traffic in 1888, and passenger traffic in 1889. It was a failure from the start, financially. It only had one big town (Newport) in 12 miles of main line, plus a small port at Yarmouth. Freshwater was only a village then, and Totland was not reached by the line at all. There were four intermediate stations en route - Carisbrooke, Watchingwell (private - a family station), Calbourne and Ningwood, with " loops " for crossing trains at Carisbrooke, Ningwood and

Yarmouth. (The "Southern" have abolished the Carisbrooke and Yarmouth "loops," but have retained the Ningwood one). This is interesting, as it shows the promoters evidently thought there was a possibility of future developments.

What strikes the visitor, first, about this line, is that it was neither begun nor finished properly. For example, there is no direct approach to Newport, the train, after having crossed the viaduct, across Town Gate Gap, Newport, takes a sharp turn to the left, goes right past Newport Station, and actually faces Cowes. Three plans are, therefore, in operation to bring the train into the station: (1) to keep a spare engine at Newport, to run up to the train and bring it in; (2) to run the train engine round and pull the train in; (3) simply to back into the West Bay at Newport, and prepare the train for a fresh departure at leisure. The two former means are used when it is a "through' train to Sandown or Ryde, and the third way when the train is running a "shuttle" service, and terminates at Newport.

The line, therefore, made a bad start. It also made a bad finish, as it neither serves Freshwater Bay nor Totland Bay. It terminates by the R. Yar, near Freshwater Church ; whereas, had it been taken through to the Bay, it could have been pushed through Freshwater town, and on to Totland, via Middleton - all of these places being easy of access in those days, and with no 'bus competition. As it is, it gets you nowhere; you have a mile walk to the Bay, about two miles to Totland, and still further to Alum Bay, Colwell Bay and other "show" places in the Western Wight. You are turned out into a sort of "No Man's Land."

Mercifully, there is an excellent service of motor-buses to all parts from the station. The line was expensive to build, and laborious to run. The Town Gate Viaduct at Newport was a big job for a small line, and there is a small viaduct at Ningwood. The line switches and turns about with short, sharp curves and gradients, with only one or two places where the driver can " get on with it."

In 1890 the Isle of Wight Central Railway placed an order for three pieces of brand-new rolling-stock -a fine 4-4-0 Type Bogie-Tank engine, with 5ft. 3in. driving -wheels, weighing 40 tons (No. 6), with Messrs. Black, Hawthorn & Co., and two 8-wheeled bogie-composite (1st and 2nd Class) coaches from the Metro-politan Carriage Co., Birmingham. With this stock, the "Central " ran through trains between Ryde and Freshwater, including the "Overland" 4¼ - hours service, Victoria to Freshwater, introduced by the General Manager of the "Central," Charles L. Conacher (" Connie of the Central)". This gentleman did really try to co-operate and make the Freshwater, Yarmouth and Newport Railway pay, but it didn't ; the long winters killed it.

In 1913, the Freshwater, Yarmouth and Newport Railway complained of the onerous terms on which the "Central" ran their line, and gave them notice that in future they wanted to run their own line. The Central retaliated by telling them to quit Newport Station, and so they were forced to build a small terminus of their own in the cutting adjoining the coal-yard at Newport, making the passengers walk a very exposed, and also congested, stretch between the two stations. People said they were mad to break away from the "Central," etc ; where was the money coming from for rolling-stock? One prominent Newport man said to me, "Ah, we shall soon see the end of the old Freshwater line! "But - there was method in their madness; they thought they could see a tunnel coming, and wanted their line in their own hands.

About this time Mr. Russell Wilmot succeeded Mr. Conacher at Newport. "Ruthlessness" was his motto. He introduced 3rd-class fares; cut down train services which showed no profit; bought up a lot of old Great Eastern Railway four-wheelers; and sub-stituted a black livery for the locomotives and a plain varnish for the coaches, instead of the handsome red of the "Central" under Conacher's regime.

Economy was the order of the day, and the "Central" became the dingiest line in the Island. Through services between Ryde and Freshwater were stopped. They were in such haste to put these old coaches to work, that they forgot to take the Great Eastern Railway advertisements out of the compartments, and photographs of Cromer, Lowestoft, etc., were exhibited ; not Carisbrooke Castle, Sandown Bay, and other Island places. A rather amusing incident occurred in this direction. One evening, a man who had had "one over the eight" got in at Sandown to go to Newport, and he was seen to be looking at these photographs intently. When we pulled up at Newport, he leaned out of the window and shouted to the guard, "I shay, (hic) old chappie, ish thish station Newport or (hic) Liv'pool Street ? "

So great were the complaints about the drastic cur-tailments of trains, that the "Central" were compelled to reinstate several. However, it did one good thing, it forced the Isle of Wight Railway to have 3rd-class fares as well, and they acquired a set of fine "Metro-politan" 8-wheelers, with radial axle-boxes (not bogies). These were released from the "Met." when the line was electrified, and were a great advance on any coaches the Isle of Wight Railway had had before. Their great fault was noise; they had iron-spoked wheels, and used to rattle on the rail joints in a most marked degree. They were well lighted with electric light.

Time went on, and in 1913 came a surprise, and in 1914, a disaster, which "put paid" to the Tunnel Scheme; and all hopes of its sponsors were dashed to the ground for the next decade, at least. Things were changing; motors, and, later, motor-'buses, were going to challenge the railways of this country, and the latter just began to see that they would have to cease fighting among themselves, and combine against a common foe.

A SURPRISE AND A DISASTER

It was supposed, as stated previously, that the Freshwater, Yarmouth and Newport Railway, having severed its connection with the Central Co., would come a cropper; and the opening of the new terminus at Newport, and the line fending for itself, created a lot of speculation and curiosity. And as we all flocked down to the little terminus, what did we expect to see? I think most of us expected a motley collection of old coaches, begged or borrowed from either the South Western Railway or South Coast Railway, and perhaps a wheezy old tank-engine, ramshackle and decrepit! But what a surprise! What we saw was about the neatest and the most well-appointed little train that ever made its appearance on the Island (with the one exception of the Central's fine engine, No. 6, and her two 8-wheeled bogie-coaches). This little train was composed of smart 4-wheelers, all in perfect alignment and of a type never seen in the Island before with slightly elliptical roof, long wheel bases, and fine upholstery on comfortable sprung seats, nice and low. They all looked spotless in their new paint, with "F. Y.N." in *gold lettering*.

An old farmer who was standing near me said, in the raw Isle of Wight dialect, "I allows this 'ere train cums from Furrin Parts. Leastways, she be an Overnur' " i.e., " over on the Mainland "—" of some sart. But where the 'ell does 'er come from ? Up narth, I'll bet."

At the head of the train was a smart little 0-6-0 type saddle tank-engine, of 1902 vintage (incidentally, the newest engine on the Island), painted Great Central green, numbered 1, and lettered F.Y.N. Ry.

They had one more - No. 2. This was an ex-Brighton "Terrier " (0-6-0) side tank. This engine was also painted in Great Central Railway green, adopted by the F.Y.N. In fact, the whole line, such as rolling-stock. station names, etc., had a decided Great Central atmosphere about it.

There was a rumour (which, by the way, I must say I cannot confirm) that the stock, station names, etc., had a decided Great Central Railway look, almost as it the latter had bought the line. Whether this was true or not, they got a smart turn-out ready in a very short time; someone, or some company, with capital was behind it; and, with generous good nature, the Isle of Wight folk did all they could to encourage the little railway's plucky attempt to struggle along on its own.

And I also heard the persistent rumours - that Sir Sam Fay of the Great Central was interested in it. If that was really the case, it meant one thing, and one thing only, viz., that he was interested in a Solent Tunnel.

The newly-conditioned F.Y.N. Ry. also took care, that none of its mainland passengers got stranded at Yarmouth. Sometimes, after a tiring journey to Lymington, and a cold crossing to Yarmouth, passengers would walk up the quarter-mile to Yarmouth Station, to find the last train to Newport or Freshwater gone. The new F.Y.N. Ry. management put an end to this by the purchase of a rail charabanc – a 12 h.p. rail motor, to

The end for the O2s (although fortunately with one exception), in the scrapyard at Newport in 1967. Ironically also, so far as the accompanying article is concerned, the scrapyard was on the route of the former Freshwater line.

carry 12 passengers. This could be telephoned for in any emergency, from Yarmouth Station, and would soon be on the road to convey mainland passengers to any station required, as it was for boat passengers only. It was a miniature "Boat Special."

Even then they were getting people to travel via the West, no doubt having a tunnel in mind. Very few people now travelled from the West Wight to Victoria, going "Overland" on the Isle of Wight side, owing to through trains being taken off, and the irritating break at Newport; they went to Waterloo, via Yarmouth and Lymington.

So much for the "surprise" the plucky little F.Y.N. sprung on us. Now for the disaster. Sir Blundell Maple died; and in August, of course, the War which we declared on Germany, automatically pushed the Tunnel Scheme into cold storage for at least a decade. The railways were forthwith controlled by the Government, and locomotives were taken away for foreign service; and all competition ended for the time being, at any rate.

When the Tunnel Scheme came up again during the middle of the 20 years' Armistice in the "War to end War" (about 1935), it came back under vastly different conditions. Competition was eliminated between the Southern Companies, the London and South Western Railway, the London, Brighton, and South Coast Railway, and the South Eastern and Chatham Railway, having been ordered to form one big company; and this included the Island railways. This was 1921. This gigantic combination (and not altogether a willing one) was called the "Southern" Railway, and controlled the most varied and opposite types of railways in England. It was not without its humorous side. The idea of the rich, prosperous and proud London and South-Western Ry. and the spick and span Brighton Line - not without its touch of the unconventional, dating from the Stroudley regime, with its "hind-part-in-front" express engines (they had the big coupled wheels in front, and the small carrying wheels behind) painted yellow (which used to complete the harmony of hue with the seasick passengers on a rough day in the Solent), right down to their almost isolated practice of using 4-6-4 tank engines of enormous size for Express work on long runs – - the idea of amalgamation of these two with the poor, old South Eastern and Chatham, most abused of any of them, was really very funny. However, this concludes the history of the first attempt for a Solent Tunnel.

IF !

It will be interesting in this chapter to ponder awhile on what might have been the development in 1914, if the Tunnel Scheme had materialised in the Western Wight.

The Tunnel would have been, no doubt, a double-track "Tube" tunnel, and would have been run by electricity—not that the Isle of Wight railways, or even the London and South-Western Railway, would have been wholly electrified ; they would have had an electric locomotive for use on the tunnel section, at first.

Newport would have been the "clearing centre for the rest of the Island - hence the importance of the Freshwater, Yarmouth and Newport Railway, as before pointed out. This line would have had to be completely rebuilt, on the lines of the "Southern," when they took it over. It would have been continued to Totland Bay for a certainty; and it would have been doubled (with the exception, perhaps, of the "Town Gate" Viaduct at Newport, which, no doubt, would not have been doubled at first) and relaid with "chair" rails, instead of the light "flange" rails of the original F.Y.N. Ry., to take the weight of Mainland stock. This the "Southern" has done (with the exception of doubling the line, of course).

At the present, 1942, and for several years, the F.Y.N. section of the "Southern" has accommodated the heaviest non-corridor bogie stock (57ft.) of the late Brighton line; and the recent "Tourist" Express (the 9.55 a.m. from Ventnor, high level, to Freshwater, via Sandown) was made up of two 57ft. "bogie" Brighton coaches, a corridor Observation Saloon, a composite 1st, and 3rd-Class open Saloon Car (bogie, length 57ft.), and two more "Brighton" 8-wheelers, to make up the very heavy train, for the Island, of six 8-wheelers. This train, which had the longest continuous trip in the Island (29 miles), was also the heaviest that ever ran on the "Central" and Freshwater section; and it will be seen that the Freshwater line could now carry any stock sent over via a tunnel.

The L. & S.W. Ry. would probably also have bought up the whole of the "Central." In that case they would have built a new station at Newport, a few hundred yards to the north of the present station, just by Newport (North Junc.) Signal Box, and this would have done away with the irritating "trailing connection at Newport.

Freshwater, Totland Bay, Colwell Bay, and Alum Bay, would have become one big Watering-Place, with attractions such as the coloured sands at Alum Bay, Tennyson's Land, the fine views of the Western Passage of the Solent, the Needles, the caves and Arch Rock at Freshwater Bay - all these would have competed heavily with the East Wight. They had all the undeveloped South Coast of the Island at their disposal a district, even to this day, without any railway facilities, and, in those early days, with no 'buses: The "villages" were simply crying out for a line from Yarmouth to Ventnor, via Chale.

A scheme, by the way, was actually proposed in 1874, called the "Yarmouth and Ventnor Railway," to run from Yarmouth, with a station at Freshwater Bay, and, by means of a short tunnel under Freshwater Down, to Brooke, via Compton Bay. There it would have struck the old "Military" Road between here and Chale, taking in Brixton, Shorwell, Atherfield and Lower Chale, without much trouble. Then, engineering difficulties would have meant an expensive job, as the line pushed its way on to Ventnor, via the Undercliff; but what a glorious run it would have been, if they had had a tunnel down at the West to give it a start! Anybody who has travelled from Whitwell to Ventnor West, on a clear day, and has seen the grand views on emerging from the St. Lawrence Tunnel, can well imagine 8 miles of it from Lower Chale to Ventnor. The late Dr. Dabbs, of Shanklin, always said that Chale had the finest air in the Island, and that the Sanatorium at Ventnor ought to have been built there instead.

A Western tunnel scheme would have opened up endless possibilities in the Island. The London and South Western Railway would certainly have developed a new traffic from the North and Midlands; and the persistent rumours of the Great Central Railway having acquired an interest in the Freshwater, Yarmouth and Newport Railway, leads one to suppose that it would have run through trains from the North and Midlands, in close collaboration with the South Western and Isle of Wight Junction Railway.

Where the Great Central Railway would have joined the L. & S. W. Railway, is a rather debatable point; but one thing is certain, that, wherever the Great Central wanted to get, they got! Witness their London extension! As most people know, the Great Central was originally a big cross-country line known as the "Manchester, Sheffield and Lincolnshire Railway"; and its dive into London, via the Metropolitan extension, was quite a mild sensation at the time; and it would never have surprised me if they had "picked up" the South Western Railway somewhere, and ran the Island for all it was worth.

Lymington is a peculiar place to get at. It is on a branch from Brockenhurst Junction something very similar to the Bognor branch from Barnham Junction - but through coaches are not run to the main line the same as the "Southern" does at Bognor, I believe there have been isolated cases in the past where a through coach from Lymington Pier to London has been run in the "up" Bournemouth Express, and vice versa; but not for many years now, since the main traffic centres on Portsmouth. So trains from the north would have had to come down to the Solent Tunnel, either via Bath and Broadstone (Somerset and Dorset Railway), or, by the late M. & S. W. Junction Ry., from Birmingham to Southampton, via Cheltenham and Andover (G.W. Ry.).

Then there is the popular Great Western Railway route via Reading, Basingtoke and Southampton, and also the picturesque Great Western Railway route via Reading, Didcot, Newbury, Winchester (Cheesehill) and Southampton. All these routes to the Island from the North, via the "South Western Junction Railway" would have centred on Brockenhurst Junction, which would have become a very important place.

Further, there is no doubt that the trains of the Midland Railway, London and North Western Railway, Great Central, Lancashire and Yorkshire, and others, would have given the Island a look up, the same as they do at Deal, Brighton, Bournemouth, etc., as the traffic developed; and it can be stated as a certainty, that, having spent about £3,000,000 on a tunnel, and this by highly competitive Private Enterprise, the promoters would have run the Tunnel line for all it was worth, to the mutual benefit of the whole Island as well as themselves.

The "boom" in land in the Western Wight would have been colossal and it would have spread like wildfire all over the Island - at least, that is what the promoters thought; and no doubt they had good reason to believe it, as long as railway companies competed with railway companies.

Now, since the amalgamation of the railways of Britain, no railway competition exists in the South, as the "Southern Railway" controls the whole of the South, from Plymouth to Dover.

The estimated cost of the Tunnel was about £3,000,000.

The second "if" concerns the original Island railways. As is well-known here, only two lines ever really "paid" in the Island, viz., the "Pioneer" line (the little 4-mile "Cowes and Newport," opened in 1862) and the Isle of Wight Railway (Ryde to Shanklin, opened in 1864, and continued to Ventnor later).

The first line prospered because it connected the capital of the Island (Newport) with the aristocratic town and International Yachting Centre of Cowes, and because it was, in the main, an easy line to build. It had its terminus in the present Coal Yard at Newport Station, and the first 3¾ miles are practically level along the west bank of the Medina River. The line rises to its summit at Cowes suburban station (Mill Hill), and then drops through the short Mill Hill tunnel to Cowes Town Station, on a very sharp gradient – so sharp, in fact, that the "Southern" uses gravitation marshalling of the trains back into the terminus. It possessed the valuable Medina Wharf at Cowes, and paid its way from the start.

The Isle of Wight Railway was a paying concern also, for reasons fully explained in a previous chapter.

The success of these two lines led to the most crazy "Railway Mania" in the Island, people seeming to think that wherever "two or three were gathered together," there should be a railway. And the consequence? The I.W. (Newport Junction) Railway was a failure. The Ryde and Newport Ry. was a failure. The Freshwater, Yarmouth and Newport Railway was a failure; and, lastly, the Newport, Godshill and St. Lawrence line was the most pitiful failure of all, financially.

All told, before amalgamation, the Island has had no less than ten railway companies in its history from 1862, viz :—

Cowes and Newport. 1862.
Isle of Wight. 1864.
Isle of Wight (Newport Junction Rly.). 1875.
Freshwater, Yarmouth and Newport Railway. 1888.
Ryde and Newport Railway. 1875.
Newport, Godshill and St. Lawrence. 1897.

London and South Western Joint Rly
London, Brighton and South Coast 1880.
Brading Harbour Railway. 1882.
Nos. 1, 3, 5 and 6 were formed into Isle of Wight Central Railway; and Nos. 2 and 9 were known as one line. viz., I.W. Rly.

Why all this pitiful waste of good money on railways? One reason only: they put the cart before the horse. They should, after the two successful lines had run a year or two, have built a Solent Tunnel in conjunction with L. & S. W. Rly., and thus assured free access to the Island, first. "If" they had done this, we could have planned our lines differently, and had a big railway company behind us. "If," in those early days, they had had to run steam-engines through the Tunnel, they would only have been doing what was being done in other places, by means of condensing apparatus, such as the Mersey Railway and Metropolitan used. And the Severn Tunnel is even to-day run by steam. So the difficulties *could* have been overcome. It would have been a pioneering venture, of course! But the Island would have grown to the tunnel; and there are precedents by the score. People laughed at the late London, Brighton and South Coast Railway, when they built their splendid terminus at Bognor, at a time when it was a small, obscure seaside town. Look at it now! Did they do right? Of course they did. Bognor to-day is "Bognor Regis," the King's Watering Place, world renowned, and second only to Worthing and Brighton in this particular district. Same thing applies to the Isle of Wight. Had we been given a tunnel 45 years ago, we should, with our lovely climate, mild and yet bracing, and the beautiful Island scenery and short distance from London (90 miles, approx., Ventnor to London) have held our own with the best.

THE SECOND ATTEMPT
The "War to end War" ended for the time being in 1918. In 1921 the railways were ordered by the Government to form themselves into four big groups, viz., London, Midland and Scottish; London and North Eastern; Great Western; and Southern. As the period between 1918 and the present war was really an uneasy "armistice," the Government had an eye to future events, deciding that if "Nationalised" railways ever came, four groups would be easier to "absorb" than a host of smaller lines. I, for one, really thought that the Great Western Railway would have come in with the London and South Western Railway as the "Southern" and "Great Western" group, because they are so inter-connected, and left the South-Eastern and Chatham and the London, Brighton and South Coast to form a "London and South Eastern Rly."; but I suppose they had their reasons for not doing so. One thing stands out clearly, the G.W.Ry. is the only line which has been allowed to retain its original name, and also its original livery, viz., its own distinctive shade of

Hooker's Green for the engines, and chocolate and cream for the coaches.

When the "Southern" was formed, they took over the Island railways. The Isle of Wight Railway and the Isle of Wight Central Railway joined up at once; but the Freshwater, Yarmouth and Newport Railway had negotiations for a time, and did not come in till August 1st, 1923, the others having come in on January 1st of the same year. They had concluded an "Armistice" with the Central in 1920, and were allowed to use their old terminus at Newport (Central) Station, viz., the West Bay.

After "Grouping," the Southern Railway spent a lot of money developing the Ryde-Portsmouth Route. They re-built the Island railways, doubling the track in places, and brought over a large quantity of Mainland bogie carriages from the old L.C. & D. Railway, L. & S. W. Railway and L.B. & S.C. Railway, some of it being quite modern, and only released from service on the Mainland owing to "Electrification of the Southern Railway."

Ryde Pier Head Station was re-built, new boats put into service, and a fine fleet of ex-L.S.W. Railway 0-4-4 Tank engines sent over to deal with the passenger traffic, and a set of three 0-6-0T Brighton medium Goods Tank engines to deal with goods traffic. With all these improvements, however, we are very little quicker now than we were 40 years ago, to London - a matter of a few minutes, that is all.

Then came the revival of the Channel Tunnel Scheme, which was turned down by the Government on strategical grounds; and, as events proved, alas! they were right.

When this controversy was raging, up pops the "Bulldog" again, and got busy on the Solent Tunnel idea. Mr. Aman tried to persuade the "Southern" to move in the matter: nothing doing, the railways now having no incentive in the shape of competition. Then he tried the Isle of Wight Chamber of Commerce: again, nothing doing.

Mr. Aman then instituted a postcard "Gallup" Poll, and got favourable answers. The poll was a straight question -

"ARE YOU IN FAVOUR OF A SOLENT TUNNEL - YES or NO?"

He had a majority of *Ayes;* but when it came to putting their hands in their pockets for an increased rate for an "all-Island Tunnel," people put them in their pockets and kept them there!

Mr. Aman wrote to me and said, "This time they can't blame me for wanting a tunnel in the West for my own private interest. I want it for everybody's interest as well as my own, as once the tunnel is built, the whole Island will benefit," which was quite true.

But, sad to relate, the second attempt also failed.

THE SOLENT RAILWAY TUNNEL

We had, however, one consolation - our big comrade, the Channel Tunnel Scheme, was also turned down.
We tried to get the Government to take an interest in the matter, with a view to relieving the terrible and disgraceful unemployment then obtaining; and we thought it would be useful from a military standpoint: but no, nothing doing!

Then the final, sad end to the Solent Tunnel Scheme's best friend - Mr. Frank Aman died. Yes, the "Bulldog" and "Father of the Tunnel" fought for a thing which has always been lacking in the Island, viz., VISION.

Another reason of the Isle of Wight natives' opposition to the tunnel, was their rooted objection to "Overnurs" (people from "Over" the other side). However, the old native element is rapidly dying out, and as a good percentage of important business in the Island is conducted by "Overnurs," this is not so dangerous to progress as years ago.

One thing, I believe to be certain: the TUNNEL WILL COME, either in the near or distant future.

This little work will conclude with a prophetic Vision of a Solent Tunnel in being, and the experiences of two travellers from Ventnor to Waterloo, in the "Solent Tunnel Express," in 19 ? It is reprinted by kind permission of the Editor of the "Isle of Wight Mercury." In this article, I saw a vision of the "Southern" and "Great Western Railway" formed into one group, and the present Ventnor West line continued right into Ventnor, to complete the original scheme, which never materialized for want of capital, so that the line had, perforce, to terminate where it does now, viz., Ventnor West.

A PEEP INTO THE FUTURE

It was a bitterly cold morning in December, 19— when I strolled down to the railway station to meet an old friend who had bought a big estate at Ventnor, now that we had the tunnel to the Mainland. We were going to have a day's trip to London on the, "Solent Tunnel Express." I was in high spirits, as a trip to London in winter now was a pleasure, instead of the misery it was in former days.

Ah! here he is - standing under the Clock Tower of the magnificent Ventnor Marine Terminus, erected by the London, Great Western and Southern Railway. (Since the G.W. and S. Railway combined, they have extended the line from Ventnor West Station into the centre of the town, and built the Ventnor Marine Station and Hotel).

Hello, Harry! I see you are in good time."
"Yes, old man. I was just thinking of the difference between the old days, when we were cut off by fog and bad weather, and now, when we jump into a train in Ventnor and get out in London. By the bye, how did you succeed in getting the tunnel eventually? You had one or two abortive attempts, did you not? "

"Yes," I said. "We nearly got it just before the 1914 War, when the late L. & S. W. R. Co. and the Freshwater Railway Co. got together, and passed a Bill in Parliament, for the "South Western and Isle of Wight Junction Railway" to connect the Island with the Mainland by a tunnel at the Western end of the Isle of Wight. There were good men behind it, too - Sir Blundell Maple, Mr. Aman of Totland, and 'Sammy' Fay of the Great Central."
"Why did it fail?"
"Sir Blundell Maple died, and then came the Great War; so that was that."
"Indeed ! Why did the second attempt fail?"
"It was turned down on financial grounds, just after the big depression."
"Then how did you succeed at last?"
"We must go back to 1936-7. At that time several things in favour of the tunnel all turned up at once. First, we had an alarmingly short season in 1936. Secondly, we had a very progressive Council in 1936-7, and they at last 'put their finger on the spot,' so to speak, and that was the supreme and definite necessity of a through carriage to London, without all the annoyance and delay of the boat journey. Then, lastly, we had the military people behind the scheme. They wanted the tunnel for strategic purposes; and also, with modern warfare, we Islanders would be completely cut off from the Mainland in certain eventualities."
"In fact, I gather that Public Opinion demanded the Tunnel what?
"Exactly. Ah ! here is the train !"

A fine train of six corridor coaches and dining-car backed into No. 3 platform, in charge of a very capable-looking Express tank-locomotive of ex-G.W.R. origin. The porters called, "Newport and London only. Fast train to Waterloo." We take our seats, and, after admiring the lovely scenery past St. Lawrence, settle down.

Eventually we pull up at Newport (Central), after a smart run of 22 minutes. Here the tank-locomotive is detached, and through carriages from Freshwater and Sandown are attached to the rear of the train. As we looked, a long, wicked-looking streamlined electric Express locomotive backed on to our train. She looked like a monster from another world. She was painted (like the rest of the train) in the handsome purple-lake livery of the L.G.W. and S.R. Co., and was built for speed - and looked it.

The whistle blows, and we are off. Our train, now composed of ten bogies with dining-car, swings gently over the points, and pulls out on to the main line of the old Cowes and Newport Railway, which has been doubled and electrified from Tunnel Junction to Newport. We gather speed, slow to 35 m.p.h. for Tunnel Junction, and then begin the drop of 1 in 80 to the tunnel. The tunnel is dead straight, except for about a quarter of a mile where it emerges on the Mainland. Here it curves sharply to the right. In a

49

few minutes we were descending at speeds which quickly rise from 35 to 40, 55, 60 to 65; and then a gradual upward lift is experienced as the express climbs the long 1 in 80 out of the tunnel. Here speed drops to 30. We emerge near Fawley, this useful branch line having been electrified and used to complete the tunnel route to the Island.

We are now gathering speed, having just passed Fawley and Hy'the, with fine views of Southampton Water on our right. With commendable caution, our driver slows round the curves at Totton and Redbridge Junctions, and presently we are roaring through Southampton Central, and so on towards London.

As we were passing through Brookwood, we both got up and looked out of the window. " What is that streamlined greyhound doing now?"

Harry coolly lights another cigar, and, sinking back in his luxurious pneumatic cushion, says, with a twinkle in his eye, 103 miles per hour."

As we quietly slide along the last part of the trip, from Vauxhall to Waterloo, I cannot help thinking, what a contrast! In the old days, what with rough weather and the waiting about at Portsmouth and Ryde, is it any wonder that we got no residents? The Solent Tunnel has put the I.W. on the map, and we can now compete on equal terms with Bournemouth, Brighton and other places. Land is at a premium. Ventnor and the Undercliff is full up all the year round. Rich residents are buying up all the big houses there. Shanklin, Sandown, Freshwater are booming; in fact, the whole Island is booming all the year round.

APPENDIX

NOTE ON ST. LAWRENCE AND VENTNOR WEST LINE
Reprinted from Ventnor "Mercury," June 18th, 1892; The Bill for the extension of the St. Lawrence Railway to Ventnor was passed by the Commons, ... The I.W. Ry. has thus been taught a lesson. Since they drove the Stage Coach off the road, their exorbitant fares have done more to injure Ventnor's prosperity than all other adverse influences put together. In a letter to the "Pall Mall Gazette," Mr. A. Ball, C.C., says, "The Railway Monopoly is simply starving Ventnor out of existence."

ELECTRIFICATION OF I.W. RYS.
The "Southern" has given us the finest steam-operated service in the world, for an island of a size comparable to that of the Isle of Wight. Completely cut off from the Mainland, by sea, as the Island is, an electric-train service would only pay for about 3 months in the year; but if we were connected to the main "Southern" system by a tunnel, then electric working would become a certainty.

OTHER MEANS OF REACHING THE ISLAND

Several other means have been suggested to connect the Island to the Mainland, including

A SOLENT BRIDGE
This would have had to be of the "Forth Bridge type, on the cantilever principle, between Hurst Beach and Colwell lay. It would have been a colossal undertaking, and would never have paid, as the terrific currents through the Western Passage" would have made Navigation dangerous, and the upkeep would have been tremendous.

A TRAIN FERRY
This was proposed, and one of the big ferries operating between here and France in the last war suggested. But it would not cut out the sea passage, and such ferries are far too clumsy to operate in the close confines of the Solent.

A ROAD FLOATING BRIDGE
This is already in operation between Yarmouth Slipway and Lymington Pier. There is another Motor-car Ferry between Fishbourne (I.W.) and Portsmouth.

A SOLENT CAUSEWAY
As this comes under the Defence of the Realm Act, the details cannot be discussed here. The idea was, apparently, to close up the Solent, with just a "gate" for shipping to pass. It never came to anything, however.

AN "ATMOSPHERIC" RAILWAY UNDER THE SOLENT
Mr. Dendy-Marshall (author of "The History of the Southern Ry.") gave a rough outline of an Atmospheric Ry. under the Solent, in the "Engineer" for 31st May, 1932.

"NAMED" TRAINS IN THE ISLAND SERVICE (OFFICIAL) THE "TOURIST."
The only "officially" named train in the Island was the pre-war "Tourist" (9.55 a.m. Ventnor to Freshwater Express, via. Sandown).
(NON-OFFICIAL) THE "OCEAN HOTEL" EXPRESS, **L. & S. W. RY.**
This was the 12.10 p.m. Express, Waterloo to Portsmouth and Isle of Wight, named by Herr Lowell-felt in his "Ocean Hotel" Sandown Guide. The L. & S.-W. Ry. had no objection.

The "Ventnor Riviera Limited" was a limited train consisting of 3 First-class saloons (with a few "2nd" compartments) and brake-van, for the invalids to Ventnor, to avoid all the irritating stops which wearied the patients. It left the Pier Head at 3.18 p.m., two minutes ahead of the Slow, and ran non-stop to Ventnor - originally in 18 minutes, but 2 more minutes were added later. It carried the "Express" code discs in front, and everything was very "posh."

After a year or two, the treatment for consumption changed, and Ventnor felt a draught; so the Riviera stopped at Shanklin as well. This made Sandown very wild; so it was decided to stop the train altogether, which was done before the Great War. A full description of the "Undercliff Specials" and the "Overland" trains of the "Central" will be found in this book.

The 'new' order (well 'second-hand' order), at Shanklin and Ryde St Johns in 1967. Clearly some old-fashioned habits die hard: headcode discs and paraffin oil tail-lamp.

LANCING PICTORIAL
Ian Nolan

Issues 6 and 9 of 'SW' carried two articles on the Southern Railway carriage works at Lancing. We have been wanting to continue this theme for some time and with the arrival of these views from Ian Nolan that is now possible. Recorded at the works open days mainly in 1961, 1963 and 1965, the latter views especially showing the run-down of the site which had started in 1962. Post 1965 work was moved to Eastleigh. Closure may well have been as much about politics as economics as to the then Conservative government Lancing was within a safe Conservative area whilst Eastleigh was considered marginal. At the time Lancing was inspected prior to a decision being made, staff recall a swarm of 'suits and brief-cases' making what was literally a flying visit, not stopping even to discuss the situation with management or works representatives. To be fair, with the accelerating run-down of steam Eastleigh was likely to run out of work at some stage so an amalgamation of resources did make sense. But it was the way it was done that was injurious - however were not so many closures of that time proceeded with in like fashion?

Above - Viewed from the Western Road bridge at Lancing in June 1965 on what may well have been the final day of working. (Lancing station is in the distance.) The siding on the right on which the vehicles are standing led to the works which are off camera to the right.

Opposite top - Two former LSWR vehicles in the works yard, seen on the occasion of the works open-day, 21 August 1963. Left to right: a six-compartment first, and a luggage van.

Opposite bottom - On the same occasion, the south end of the works (looking WNW) with larger items of stores in the open. Some of the buildings still remain today as part of the Churchill industrial estate.

Opposite top - A few hundred yards away, Ian Nolan recorded E4 No 32468 in the down yard at Lancing on 12 June 1962. The gate was just off South Street, the buildings behind the wall are the old telephone exchange. The notice referred to a walking path to the works and displayed the following notice: 'STAFF MUST KEEP TO THE PATH AND NOT PASS THROUGH THE GOODS YARD. ANY PERSON IGNORING THIS INSTRUCTION WILL BE SUSPENDED FROM DUTY'.

Opposite bottom - The 'Lancing Belle' about to pass Lancing Station, 21 Aug 1963. Two LMS 2-6-2Ts 41325 (leading) and possibly No 41312 hauling the workers' train having just gained the main line. The leading coach is Ironclad brake/2nd DS70068 (compartments 91-94 + Guard).

Top - Lancing Belle coach DS70063 at Lancing Works, 21 Aug 1963. This was LSWR Lavatory 2nd No 329 (re-bodied by the SR) and formed the 5th coach of the current daily workmen's train. It contained compartments 39-47. The plate gives dimensions as length 61'7", width 9'0".

Right - End view of the 1st coach, seen this time at Lancing Works on 21 Aug 1963. DS70080, an ex-SECR Brake 2nd 3473. This contained allocated compartments 1-8.

Opposite top - EMU motor-coach on the traverser at the works, 21 August 1963.

Opposite bottom - Detail of the Lancing Works traverser, 21 August 1963.

Top - A1 No DS680 at Lancing Works, 23 August 1961. At the time this was the allotted works shunter. The engine was later withdrawn by BR and restored to pseudo-Stroudley condition (the word 'pseudo' is used as it is an A1 but with an A1X boiler). As No. 54 'Waddon', it was shipped to Canada in August 1963 and is preserved at the Montreal Railway Museum.

Right - A1X DS681 (the former 'Cheam') at the works on 23 Aug 1961. Lancing station may just be made out in the background.

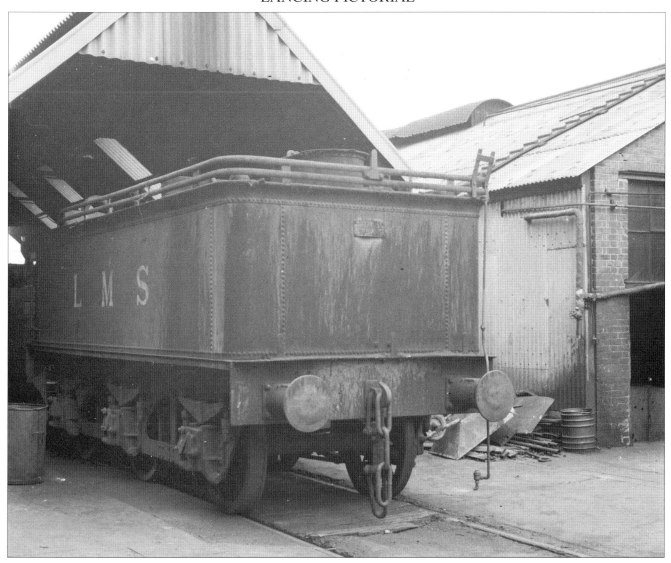

Opposite - The small ex-SR carriage works petrol shunter, No. DS499, 23 Aug 1961.

Top - A former LMS tender at Lancing, 21 Aug 1963. The purpose this vehicle served is not clear but it must certainly have been some form of water / chemical tank. Notice any pipework and hoses have been removed. (Two LMS liveried tenders were at Eastleigh for some time in the 1950s, so it is possible one at least had by this time migrated to Lancing.)

Right - USA No DS236 (the former BR No. 30074) as the works shunter at Lancing Works on 21 Aug 1963. Following closure of the works, the engine did not survive long and was withdrawn in August 1965.

Left - One thing that could be guaranteed at Lancing was the gathering of old vehicles scattered around the yard and used for a variety of purposes. (A modern-day preservationists goldmine if only they had survived.) This is a former LSWR vehicle once used in the Lancing Belle train. Possibly a former composite containing compartments numbered 30-36. Dimensions were quoted as: length 51'10, width 8'10, tare 25 tons. With a workforce of something like 1,500 men, many of whom came from Brighton, there was allocated seating in the 'Lancing Belle'. 23 August 1961.

Bottom - A former luggage / post office van at the works, 21 Aug 1963

Top - A former SECR / Post Office Van seen at the open day of 21 Aug 1963.

Right - An unusual vehicle in the form of a Waterloo & City match-truck, No. DS1665. This had started its life as an LBSCR 5-plank open.

Opposite page - Birdcage & Maunsell? coaches at Lancing, 21 Aug 1963

Top - An unidentified vehicle but with LSWR type bogies - the 'clerestory' was definitely not part of the original vehicle! The two-tone livery will be noted.

Bottom - Ex SECR Birdcage brake at Lancing Works, 23 Aug 1961. Dimensions were quoted as: overall length 63'10, width 8'10, tare 30 tons.

Right - Paul Nolan at the open day of 31 August 1961. He is seen climbing into an EMU brake compartment.

Hellingly Hospital

We have recently been fortunate to acquire the b/w collection of negatives from Roger Thornton. Apart from locomotives and trains there are some fascinating views of other subjects including these three of the Hellingly Hospital Railway.

This 1¼ mile light-railway was owned and operated by East Sussex County Council and used to transport passengers and stores from Hellingly station to Hellingly Hospital, then referred to as a 'lunatic asylum'.

The railway was in use from 1903 to 1959, motive power being provided by a small 500v dc electric locomotive. This machine was used to haul coal and other wagons, passengers being conveyed in a 12-seat railcar also operating by means of electricity. Passenger services ceased in 1931 and the railcar body was later used as a sports pavilion at the hospital (seen above).

One of the best references on this quaint system is Peter Harding's book, 'The Hellingly Hospital Railway'. Some colour views of this railway also appear in our new publication, 'Industrial Railways of Southern England in Colour'.

1864 Key

1 - No evidence of coal sidings at this time.

2 - 1863 flat junction for the Kingston line, signal post but no signal box.

3 - Cottages, engine shed and turntable all sandwiched between UP platform and the brewery.

4 - Field or orchards where the Albany pub is to be built.

5 - Evidence of sidings and installation of goods yard.

1894 Key

1 - Firmston sidings in place and the 1884 flyover.

2 - Relocated turntable and loco servicing facilities.

3 - Newly established Twickenham West signal box.

4 - Engine shed still in use but UP passenger loop in place of turntable.

5 - The station now has three platforms and a footbridge

6 - Iron footbridge in place.

7 - Goods yard track layout in place.

1934 Key

1 - Headshunt for Power Station.

2 - Total of five sidings in the vicinity of Twickenham Junction.

3 - Turntable and engine shed now removed.

4 - Sub station building, circa 1915, now erected.

5 - 1897 and 1934 goods yard extension.

6 - Good shed.

7 - Coal staithes - Twickenham Coal Company (possibly).

Twickenham station circa 1864

Twickenham station circa 1894

Twickenham station circa 1934

Here we see a flat junction becoming a mature railway grade-separated junction while the station also evolves. Though the locomotive servicing facility is lost, by 1934 the site is at its fullest extent and remains as such until the relocation and rationalisation that followed in the 1950s.

The Twickenham Timeline - *take 2*

Further stories of Twickenham Station

Nicholas Lewin

Following-on from the first part of this story published in Southern Way 25, this is the article that you have all been waiting for. It may not complete the picture but, as they say in railway parlance, *we're getting there*. Thanks to revelations and discoveries uncovered during further research, the history of the goods facilities at Twickenham station can now emerge from the mists of time. Expect more information regarding the unusual layout of this otherwise unremarkable site in a quiet corner of southwest London together with the correction of some previously published inaccuracies along with more detail on some aspects not covered so fully before.

The series of maps opposite helps us to trace the evolution of the station in both a historical and a geographical context. The maps were not fully developed for the first article and are included here as a better illustration of the original article and also to show, along with the photographs, the development of the sidings and local facilities.

Our Editor, Kevin Robertson, made the point to me that the goods side of railway business remains rather neglected and its history is rarely supported with much photographic or even written evidence. Luckily, I gained access to some pictures of Twickenham's goods yard (and shed built later) which have not been published before. Some are reproduced here and my research has led me to piece together more of the story behind this curious location. I hope to convince you that this is not just an exercise in dry-as-dust railway archaeology, that my sidings are not just metal rails, and that there is life beyond the buffers. Do read on!

Twickenham's sidings and goods facilities

Twickenham effectively had four areas of sidings which can be grouped as follows:

Up sidings: relating to the former engine shed and subsequent substation, with a sinuous head shunt that moved towards Marsh Farm Lane sandwiched between the up Strawberry Hill line and the River Crane.

Five long sidings: of varying length in front of Twickenham West signal box, three of which extended under the up Strawberry Hill line flyover towards Whitton.

Down sidings: in the vicinity of the flyover.

The goods yard: itself which was on the down side roughly halfway between St Margarets station and Twickenham.

Use of these sidings is debatable and over the years practice changed. For example, we know that Twickenham had locomotive servicing facilities up to the end of the

nineteenth century and that vestiges of that regime remained until the 1930s. I think that we may assume that the sidings in the vicinity of the substation had a *locomotive bias* in their use.

1.   Up sidings

The siding which extended around the back of the up flyover line sandwiched in between the embankment and the canalised River Crane was not fully in place in 1884 (when the engine shed and facilities were still in use). I say *fully* because its beginnings related to the locomotive servicing facilities at Twickenham. Once these were relocated to Strawberry Hill in 1897, the siding's purpose changed. In 1899, the siding was listed (on the lever index for West signal box) as *Turntable Siding*. Indeed as the centre road of three, it included the relocated locomotive turntable and was skirted by two other lines, alongside one of which coaling facilities were provided. By 1915 the siding had been extended almost to Marsh Farm Lane and ended in a group of buildings, rail access to which was controlled by gates. By then the emphasis was on serving a local business rather than servicing the products of Messrs. Drummond, Adams and Beattie; indeed one wonders just how much use Twickenham's turntable saw from 1897 to 1930. Marsh Farm itself has a reasonably well-documented history (see bibliography). The allotments around the North end of the current footbridge are a vestige of the farm itself and are in the location of the buildings which this long siding served (see also the section on level crossings below).

In 1899, the single siding which went past the substation through the water tank (in front of the cottages) was still labelled as *Loco Shed* on West 'box's lever index despite the removal of that double track structure. The single siding was one of the original pair of shed roads. The last remains of these sidings were taken out of use in 1980.

The rotary converter station (substation) was also rail-connected. Electrification of the LSWR had occurred when the railways relied on rail to transport anything and everything; the rotary converters themselves and other equipment within the shed are likely to have been delivered by rail and it is reasonable to assume that deliveries for repair or maintenance would also have been undertaken by rail, certainly for the first twenty or so years of its existence.

2. Five long sidings

According to Ordnance Survey, the long sidings were in existence in the 1860s. I believe that they were originally carriage sidings used in conjunction with the locomotive facilities and semi-terminal nature of the station. Minimal photographic and observed evidence suggests that in BR days these sidings were used for carriage storage, some train formation activity and holding cripples or defective vehicles. They were taken out of use in October 1967 and then partly reinstated to store civil engineering wagons and equipment when the 1974 Feltham Area Signalling Scheme passed a death-sentence on Twickenham's signal boxes. The reinstated sidings disappeared in September 1984.

3. Down sidings

A loop siding (points at both ends) off the down Windsor line appears on the 1864 OS map roughly where *Firmston Sidings* and the *Twickenham & Teddington Electricity Supply Co Siding* were installed later. This loop became separate facilities serving these two customers because, I suspect, as railway operation developed and greater emphasis was placed on safety, it was safer to install trailing points on a running line than to use facing points. Both sidings became conventional head-shunted, trailing-accessed sidings.

Firmston Sidings (as labelled on West 'Box's lever index) were clearly the domain of Firmston's the coal merchant who also featured in Shepperton and Richmond. As mentioned previously, the name still appears on a building in South Worple Way, Mortlake. The sidings were certainly operational by 1915 and taken out of use in July 1964.

At the beginning of the C20th a siding also existed through a trailing connection off the *down Kingston line -* the *uphill* line towards Strawberry Hill (see item 1 on the 1894 map). The area underneath the south end of the flyover had sidings accessed from both down running lines. [I highlight the location of this siding as it was a potential peril since it ended at right angles to the Windsor running lines and was laid entirely on a considerable gradient!]

The Hamilton Road power station appears to have had its own siding until June 1938. Referred to as the *Twickenham & Teddington Electric Supply Co Siding* and installed in 1915, it was on the down side of the line accessed conventionally through trailing pointwork controlled by ground frame B (itself controlled by Twickenham West signal box).

This installation of a siding during a world war was prioritised in order to deliver coal to a power station supplying electricity to the Pelabon Works in Cleveden Road, Twickenham, amongst other customers. This establishment was the brainchild of Charles Pelabon a Belgian industrialist, and was staffed by refugees and wounded Belgian soldiers. The factory made hand-grenades and had been converted from a roller-skating rink by Collinsons of Teddington in 1914-15. Pelabon's works were expanded in 1915-16 and it was the production of munitions as well as the more benevolent function of the factory which generated the urgency to install the new siding. After hostilities ceased, the Pelabon Works was converted into the famous Richmond Ice Rink.

Our last down sidings are the vestiges of the 1863 flat junction at Twickenham. The present single set of rails

climbing to Strawberry Hill follows the course of the original line to Kingston, though at some point it was slewed to ease the curve; given left-hand running in the UK, the original line was the inner of the two curved lines and was uphill for trains towards Kingston. By compounding the curve as it climbed away from the junction, the drag on wheel treads and flanges would be reduced making the job of getting to Strawberry Hill, and beyond, easier. Once the flyover for the up line was built in 1883, the new track made the original up line rails redundant for any purpose other than a long siding. I can find no specific reference to this facility but it seems likely that it is an example of the classic railway economy where a line is retained as a siding for occasional convenience rather than a specific purpose.

No photos of the down side sidings are included here as I cannot find any of the coal facilities themselves. There are images which show buffers, or other bits and pieces but they are neither helpful nor worthy of reproduction for our purposes.

4 The goods yard

As I am sure many readers will know, research based on Ordnance Survey maps can be problematic for a host of reasons. A key problem is an updated map which displays only one date at the bottom some years later than its original publication, and so it can be difficult to know what elements have been updated. One 1890s map showed orchards and another showed the genesis of Twickenham's goods yard...

I believe that the goods yard did not exist during the 1840s/'50s and probably came into being in the 1860s, when the branch to Kingston opened. The 1894 OS map

Opposite bottom - In the 1960s, the goods shed (background-right) is seen from platform 4/5 of the current station on the London side of the iron footbridge. If you were waiting for a fast train to London looking towards St Margarets, this is what you would have seen...

This page, top - This photograph of the goods shed is taken from a train drawing into Twickenham from St Margarets in the 1960s. The facility is still in use with the rail-line doors closed

This page, bottom - Moments later, we see the other end of the shed and catch a glimpse of 69/71 Amyand Park Road, the Victorian semi obscured by the SR van and mineral wagon

shows the yard tracks but no shed; it shows a loading ramp roughly where the shed was to stand and it shows staithes or something similar where staithes were to be found rather later.

Once constructed, the shed itself was fairly generic in terms of design: a pitched slate-roof brick structure with doors at each end for rail access, two weather-protected loading bays on the road side of the structure and a small office at its London end.

The first photograph presented isn't the best quality, but I hope it helps the reader locate the facility with reference to present-day structures.

The goods yard was fairly conventional in its layout although it does not appear to have included a separate raised ramp (at the same time as the shed) for handling livestock, heavy goods and wheeled items. Such loading presumably took place within the goods shed (once it had replaced the original ramp). It is also likely that the passenger station itself handled goods in its early years as partly suggested by the presence of the level crossing and gates at the London end of the platforms (see level crossings below).

I also conjecture that the Twickenham Coal Co had

their facilities in the goods yard. Certainly the 1934 OS map indicates coal staithes, and the photo overleaf gives a further clue (see caption).

Road access to the goods yard was from Amyand Park Road via the cobbled road seen in the photographs below. Nos. 65/67 & 69/71 Amyand Park Road remain as the two houses either side of the access road. Candler Mews now occupies the site of the goods yard (see recent photos on pages 70 & 71 for comparison) with not one clue as to the previous use of the land. The coal staithes were to the left of the tree in the left foreground.

In the general run-down of BR local freight facilities in the late 1960s, the goods yard closed in January 1967 and was taken out of use in June 1969.

The iron footbridge seen in the distance on page 71 links Cole Park Road and Beauchamp Road. It was probably installed in 1883 when the station expanded from two to three platforms, prior to the subsequent extension of the up passenger loop line to St Margarets. It remains in use to this day and has just been treated to a Network Rail wash and brush-up.

East signal-box controlled the goods yard and London end of the station throat and was closed in 1938.

This page, top - *This 2014 view looking towards Amyand Park Road from Candler Mews (similar direction to the 1960s photo). No. 69/71 on the right is the link between 2014 and the 1960s...*

This page, bottom - *Sometime in the 1930s, Adams T1 No.5 accelerates past the front of Mary's Terrace, west of the entrance to the goods yard and east of London Road Bridge. The shot suggests that the wagons are being sorted for the goods yard. The 8-plank open wagon belonging to the Twickenham Coal Co poses the question; were they tenants at the goods yard?*

Opposite, top - *Looking towards the back (road side) of the goods shed about 1968/9 with very little sign of this facility being rail-served! Discernible on the left is the local pedestrian footbridge still in use in 2014. Candler Mews retains a cobbled access road as shown in the next photograph.*

Opposite, bottom right - *Early in 2014, looking into Candler Mews from Amyand Park Road; the cobbled access road is a link to the past as well as the Victorian semi (no. 67) on the right (just out of view in the 1960s shot above). Centre-frame, the 3-storey mansard-roofed building stands almost exactly where the goods shed had previously stood.*

Opposite, bottom left - *Feltham Driver Bill Feaver alongside Drummond 700 30688 in front of Twickenham East signal-box in the late 1950s. The engine appears to be alongside platform 1 of the 1954 (current) station.*

The signal box was replaced with a non-standard, temporary, wooden Southern Railway structure which was so *temporary* that it endured for 36 years, being subsumed by the Feltham Area Signalling Scheme in 1974. Seen behind the driver in the photograph below, is the long-life temporary 'box.

Coles Brewery

The brewery in Brewery Lane (née Staten Road) has an interesting history. Thomas Cole began brewing in Twickenham in 1604 and established a brewery by the river Crane in 1635. The building we know as Coles Brewery is likely to date from the mid-1700s. By 1890 it had become Burrows and Coles Brewery. Brandon's of Putney took over Cole & Co in 1892 and brewing ceased in 1906. Closed in 1927, the buildings were later bought by the borough for use as a depot and offices despite objections from a newly formed Ratepayers Association. Developers' whims dominated the site in the 1960s and the site was eventually taken over by the GPO. History takes the circular route, and, as I write, the Post Office development is being redeveloped by St James's; their marketing suite (for which, read 'office') has appeared where once Beattie locomotives were turned prior to service. Where the long-gone the brewery buildings once stood, there are plans for houses and flats. The future of the two semi-detached

cottages is soundly assured, all as part of the brave new world of Brewery Wharf, a reminder of a highly mythical past when the Crane was a navigable river.

Level crossings

In my previous article I reported the scene of death and destruction at the level crossing at Marsh Farm Lane during the nineteenth-century. Further research has led me to take-on the mantle of pseudo-detective. By 1915, a footbridge had been installed though the crossing remained in place. As Holmes might have done, I deduced that, at that time, pedestrians were expected to cross the line in safety using the bridge; wheeled vehicles were able to cross the line possibly with prior agreement with the signalman at West 'box or at their own risk. Marsh Farm's historian refers to produce from the farm being taken by horse and cart over the crossing to the station for delivery to London. This raises two questions: by station did the writer mean *station* or did he mean the goods yard?

As the produce was fresh and perishable, I think it more likely that it was sent at the earliest opportunity by passenger train occupying space in the Guard's van. It is possible that this traffic belonged to an earlier time, perhaps between the 1840s and the development of the goods yard. As any good detective would, I found that I considered the matter further and asked yet another question. If the farm

comments on the potential level crossing at the London end of the station abutting London Road bridge. The crossing certainly existed in 1883/4 but what purpose did it serve?

What becomes clearer by studying the map sequence at the beginning of this article is just how awkwardly the railway cut through Staten Road. In the 1864 map, the railway line severs Staten Road roughly where West signal box was later located; Staten Road made a level T-junction with old London Road. When the railway was built and London Road bridged the railway, Staten Road became a road to nowhere with access at neither end. At some point the road (which we now know as Brewery Lane) was relinked to London Road and access restored [could this be related to the removal of the toll arrangements on London Road and (to my relief) beyond the scope of this research?] Deprived of hindsight, Twickenham had acquired an unlikely level crossing which unexpectedly lasted in some form until the demise of the Victorian station.

Sandwiched between the platform ramps and

had a rail connection via the siding mentioned on page 73, why bother to take the produce to the station? The answer is the same. The passenger train would be quicker and the key is to get the perishable produce to market in as fresh a condition as possible.

The original 1883 LSWR plans for Twickenham are in parlous condition at the National Archives at Kew *but they are there*! You may recall from the earlier article my

This photograph from around 1897-1900 shows a wide 6-bar gate (bottom right of the image) at the end of the platforms clearly designed for vehicular access. Other later photographs of this end of the station show infill in the four- and six-foot to enable a vehicle to cross the line on the level. (To aid comparison with the following image, London Road Bridge is behind the viewer in this shot)

London Road bridge, the roadway crossed the running rails at a slightly oblique angle. The 1883 plan shows levers (11 & 14) in West signal box dedicated to its safe operation, interlocked with the Up platform starting signals. There was also a structure marked *crossing box* on the diagram sited on the down platform. It is not clear by then just how often the level crossing was used (see below), but the gates and facility certainly existed.

I have pointed out that some data is patchy regarding the history of the LSWR. In terms of modern railway lore, Twickenham is a relatively early station (1848). It is highly likely that the location of the goods yard and the station (being separate) are partly due to geography, but more likely the result of the concept and purpose of railways, in general, maturing through *modus-operandi*. Looking at Twickenham with hindsight, and surely Poirot would also have done so, I considered a few further questions:

Why are the main station buildings on the down side of the line and not the up?

Given the unusual duplicate location of the level crossing, why did it endure so long?

Was the separate goods yard a result of growing traffic at a constrained site or insufficient foresight?

In other words, the design, layout and operation of the station make sense at the time that each aspect was altered or introduced, but as time passes, some aspects of the facilities and layout make less sense as a whole - a judgement which is not limited to Twickenham!

To answer those questions:

Given there was room for the locomotive facilities on the up side, the station could have been located here and the shed where the station was; the answer lies, I think, in the position of Twickenham town centre. Access to the station was easier on the down side. The station also *flattered* the town by facing it rather than being located more logically in terms of passenger traffic; this would have resulted in the station having its metaphorical back to the town.

Everything suggests that the level crossing at Twickenham was initially provided to maintain access to Staten Road, but it also gave level(ish) access to the London-bound platforms. For some time that I cannot define (but at least from 1848 to, say, 1915, when Marsh Farm was rail-connected), the crossing may have had a role to play in accessing trains bound for the Capital, [a declining traffic I suspect].

Similarly, the goods yard, being physically remote from the station and visually barred by London Road Bridge, required at least two signal boxes and the slow communication that must have arisen in the pre-telephone era was hardly ideal. But how could the SWR of the 1840s

*This 1954 photograph, taken from the new station looking thru' London Road Bridge toward the old station, clearly shows the foot crossings which connected the platforms abutting the bridge itself (the crossing visible **through** the bridge, not the wooden one in the foreground!) Looking at other photos which show glimpses of the crossing, it was clearly not for vehicular use by this time as it was too narrow and angular.*

envisage the explosion in demand for railway services that occurred in the latter part of the C19th? What alternative did they have, given the 1883 construction of the flyover and the constraints imposed by the town itself, the river Crane and, crucially, London Road?

These are rhetorical questions and I now relinquish the rather fun role of detective.

Station footbridge

The station footbridge was installed in connection with the creation of the up loop line and new platform 3 in 1883; whether it was second hand or not is less certain. Its design was without question unconventional and perhaps a reflection of the cramped location of the station rather than anything else.

Early history

Having browsed the Windsor, Staines & South Western Railway Board meeting minutes for the period 1846 -'50, Joseph Locke was indeed the Company's Chief Engineer and construction of the line to Windsor was contracted to Thomas Brassey. William Tite Esq. was referred to as the Company's Land Valuer. Later to gain fame as a distinguished architect, he clearly had some level of influence on architectural style and application and would nowadays perhaps be referred to as Company Surveyor.

The Board minutes are brief and lack the detail of discussion. Certainly there are references to Twickenham's suitability as a *semi-terminal* station rather than Richmond with its even more constrained site. This leads to the Board instructing Locke and Tite to prepare plans with costs for moving the locomotive facilities from Richmond to Twickenham. An 1847 Board resolution also instructs Tite to buy land enabling road access to Twickenham station, but to take no immediate action [was this a reference to the London end, the bridge and level crossing perhaps or to something more prosaic?]

Those in need of a bit of a wet after the torrent of drought I may have inflicted might enjoy the following glimpse of News-of-the-Worldesque human interest discovered during my research; the snippet refers to a driver allocated to Twickenham Shed:

'...these findings clearly suggest that for the most part the LSWR's drivers and firemen were, while at work at least, a temperate group of employees...as for the fourteen drivers and firemen found to be under the influence while at work, it is probable that most never got as far as being in control of a train. Usually the 'Black Book' recorded that they came 'to duty the worse for drink' or they were 'under the influence of drink whilst on duty', and only in two cases was it explicitly stated that a driver had been 'under the

A close-up of a section of the barrow crossing, possibly just after the war.

influence of drink whilst in charge of an engine': J. Appleton of the Nine Elms Shed was caught in May 1896, while R. Reid., who was based at Twickenham, was found driving a passenger train while drunk in August 1889.'

I hope that you have enjoyed reading this further potted history of Twickenham station. The 1960s photographs of the goods yard were taken by David Curtis whose collection of prints and negatives are now with the South Western Circle and provide a rich source of previously unavailable/unpublished information relating to the Southern Railway *and* the LSWR. Twickenham & District MRC's re-creation of Twickenham in miniature is progressing well. It may be ready for exhibition in 2016. A later development might add an additional 5' board to accommodate a compressed Mary's Terrace and the goods yard. Interested modellers are very welcome to join us in creating what will be an impressive display.

If there is anything else *you* can provide, please do get in touch either via Kevin Robertson of Noodle Books or directly to me at nrgl@btinternet.com. Thanks in anticipation!

Bibliography, as before with the following additions:

Inreach at the National Railway Museum

National Archives, Kew

Goods yard photographs credited to David Curtis (© South Western Circle)

Photo of Driver Bill Feaver – his own collection

The history of Marsh Farm, Twickenham from 1635 to its closure in 1933. D. Rose, 2003

Map chronology is an amalgam based on OS maps

http://postcardsthenandnow.blogspot.co.uk/2011/04/twickenham-middlesex-pelabon-works-1914.html

http://www.mulehouse.myzen.co.uk/stations/index.htm

Present day photographs (both articles), Nick Lewin

http://turniprail.blogspot.co.uk/2013/11/how-drunk-were-late-victorian-train.html

REMEMBER THE 'HORNBYS?'

We are delighted to announce 'Southern Way Special No 11', to be released in April (concurrent with 'SW No 30'), will deal specifically with the history, operation and technicalities of what are more accurately known as the 'Booster' locomotives, CC1/CC2/20003.

'REBUILT' - THE LETTERS AND COMMENTS PAGES

A further bumper selection of comments and feedback from friends old and new. We start with 'Windy' Gale

"Hi Kevin, In case nobody has pointed it out before, the phone on page 31 (SW Issue No 24) at a "suburban location" has bothered me for weeks but today I have managed to locate a similar photo from a Middleton Press book and also the photo on page 79 of SW 27. The station concerned is Streatham and the train must then be on the Victoria to Holborn Viaduct via Croydon service. I originally thought that it must be on the Bromley North branch because of the headcode but I knew that many of the headcodes were common to more than one Sector of the SR. Please keep up the good work and although I only read the SWs in batches, I soon get carried away in a 'Southern World of my own' each time I start to read a new batch."
Windy Gale, SLS Bromley Centre Secretary

Now from one of our regular contributors Jeremy Clarke: "Hi Kevin. May I add a snippet to this very interesting article? The presence of the LSWR still exists a little further south of Shepherds Bush in the form of the embankment/viaduct that brought this line down to the existing level of the Piccadilly and District lines rising from Hammersmith towards Ravenscourt Park station. A survey of Cambridge Grove W6 by the helpful yellow man on Google Maps shows there are two closely aligned railway bridges - carrying respectively up and down trains on the two TfL lines - with quite architectural brick retaining walls between them where the original LSWR line once had been. I recall passing these then very dilapidated remnants on almost daily journeys to and from Turnham Green in the early 1960s. They appear to have been rather tarted up since those days."

On a different tack this from Chris Duffell re SW27, "Dear Kevin, thanks for another excellent Southern Way. The frontispiece of the Worting Flyover is superb, many a happy hour was spent there watching trains, when we went to visit my Aunt who lived in Worting." (Hope you approve of the others that appear in this issue as well - Ed.) "Just a small point, I think that the photo on Page 76 should be captioned Tooting Bec Common and not Wandsworth common. The line in the background curves to the left as it does on Tooting Bec Common on its approach to the junction at Balham. The Lido would be behind the photographer on the left. I seem to remember that there were the remains of a signal cabin somewhere on the RHS which presumably disappeared during the resignalling."

One image that has created a lot of interest was that on page 91 of SW27. (This showed the 'open day' at Eastleigh.) David Cox has noted the following, "Looking closely at this picture I would submit the following observations which make me think the picture dates about December 1945.

1) The Navy personel are not wearing white summer cap covers.

2) The Bulleid Pacific is one of the first series denoted by the tender "raves" smooth continuous curve up to the roof line, also is one of the first 2 having a cast ownership plate on Tender.

3) If caption to picture is correct about the Bulleid Pacific's first coat of Malachite Green post war then the engine could be 21C1, repainted December 1945 whilst in works on an unclassified repair (New Cylinders) being released on the 12th of December 1945.

4) 21C2 which also had a cast Tender ownership plate did not receive Malachite until July 1946."

We are also grateful to Eric Youldon who wrote in on the same subject as follows, "Re-'Moments Eastleigh Works.' Very interesting photograph on p91 of SW27, but your comment: 'clearly this must be soon after 1945', is frankly nonsense. The MN tender displays Southern on a plate so this can only be 21C1 or 21C2. The engine has yet to receive smoke-deflectors which were duly fitted in 12/43 and 6/44 respectively when the locos were also painted black. Q1 No C6 was built in June 1942 so the view has therefore been taken sometime between that date and early 1944.

"As I have detailed for you before, Merchant Navies from 21C1 to 21C6 were turned out in malachite green, in fact black for SR top link locos was not introduced until May 1942. Return to the splendid malachite green for the MNs commenced with 21C12 in March 1945 and was completed with 21C8 in August 1947. As a matter of interest a small number of Nelsons, Arthurs and Schools continued to display 'old' malachite green until the mid 1940s.

"Just what the occasion was that's illustrated – goodness knows! At a guess I'd say it depicted a treat for families of Work's employees who collectively had reached a commendable target set for a salvage drive. It is unlikely that an Open Day would have been held during war years."

Now to a point which I definitely should have known (and did when it was pointed out to me). The fact in question referred to the illustration on p36 of SW27 reference the blank colour light attached to the semaphore arm (not the new multiple-aspect head with the 'X' awaiting commission). The below is from Pawel Nowak - and from his profession he should know...!

"Dear Sir, I refer to the letters and comments pages in Issue No. 27 and particularly the photograph of the signals at the London end of Shortlands station on Page 36. Subject to confirmation from someone who actually worked in or drove through the area in 1959 or thereabouts, I can suggest the following explanation: The signalling here is 'in transition' in two senses of the word: firstly, the tracks are being remodelled in connection with the Kent Coast Electrification and associated resignalling and a new colour light signal with junction indicator is ready for commissioning on what will become the Up Chatham Slow line. Secondly, the signalling on the 'T' shaped structure is typical of installations on the fringe of a colour light area in Southern territory, the stop signals all being semaphore, but the taller signals leading towards Beckenham Junction

A cropped version of the Shortlands image as originally appeared in SW27.

having a two-aspect colour light below. Presumably, by this time colour light Track Circuit Block signalling had already reached Beckenham Junction from the west, and if the next signal after the semaphores in the picture was a colour light, a corresponding colour light 'distant' would be installed under the platform starters applicable to both Up platforms at Shortlands. This would be capable of exhibiting either a yellow or a green, but unlike its semaphore counterpart would show nothing if the semaphore above it was at danger as in the photograph. I suggest that the green aspect of the semaphore stop signal was blanked out (Tony Logan suggests this blanking out was by using an opaque metal plate - Ed.) to avoid showing a relatively ineffective oil-lit green above the much stronger green or yellow of the colour light distant and to avoid confusion on entering a colour light area, where the second green aspect would be superfluous. In the case of the shorter post applicable to the Catford Loop direction, presumably the next box at Ravensbourne was still operational under Absolute Block at that date, so the conventional semaphore distant appears below the platform starter and the lamp indications would be the normal ones under that system, reflecting the state of the block instrument and the signals controlled from Ravensbourne. Similar, but 3-aspect, colour light distants on semaphore gantries figure in photographs of Hampton Court Junction." We are grateful also to Ted White, retired signalman from Mount Pleasant and Eastleigh panel who mentioned there was a similar arrangement on the up starting signal at St Denys at the time when this was the fringe to Eastleigh panel. (The example I was personally aware of but had forgotten was the down home signal at Winchester Junction for trains coming off the Alton line. Here a colour light distant was mounted part way down the post of a mechanical stop signal. The colour light only appearing if the semaphore was in the 'off' position. I

cannot be certain if like at Shortlands the green glass of the semaphore was similarly blanked out.)

Now from Peter Clark, "Further to previous issues of SW concerning 'Britannias' on the Southern and particularly in Kent, I was idly browsing yesterday (when I should have been doing something more important but less interesting) and came across a photograph of No 70030 *William Wordsworth* on the up 'Night Ferry" near Shortlands Jct. in May 1953. As so often, 'The Railway Observer' provides a fuller explanation. "When the 'Merchant Navy' Pacifics were temporarily withdrawn following the driving axle fracture on No 35020 in April 1953, seven 'Britannia's were loaned to the SR on 13 May: Nos 70017/23/4/8/9 from the WR and Nos 70030/4 from the LMR. The first five apparently went to Salisbury and Exmouth Jct. and Nos 70030 and 70034 *Thomas Hardy* to Dover and Stewarts Lane respectively for boat trains. No 70030 is reported to have worked Dover duty 430 which covered the 'Night Ferry' in both directions. However, neither was seen after 20 June when No 70034 worked the Ramsgate-Nottingham train as far as London on 20 June. No 70030 had been replaced on the "Night Ferry" by Nos 35029/30 and the Eastern Section MNs, Nos 35026-30, had returned to traffic. No 70034 was reported at Willesden shed on 21 June and the LMR then loaned Nos 70030/4 to the ER (though why and for how long is not a matter for SW)." (Peter also commented in similar fashion on the Shortlands signalling query.)

Again the subject of the Britannia class, Tony Francis forwarded this rather delighted comment, "Dear Kevin, My thanks to both Bob Radcliffe and Peter Clark for their replies concerning the subject of 'Britannias' on the Kent Coast lines in Southern Way Issue 27. It really goes to demonstrate the value of a forum such as Southern Way in resolving those questions you have pondered for years. The down side is that I now feel compelled to buy my Dad his favourite tipple of a half bottle of Lamb's Navy rum for doubting his memory! Regards, Tony Francis. Fleet Standards Engineer, Southern Railway.

On a totally different topic from one of our regular subscribers, Tony Logan, who signed himself 'Ian Allan Locospotter Club No 800'. Tony kindly contributed comments on Shortlands and the Eastleigh Open Day query, plus the following (referring back to SW22 "The Portsmouth express unit 3064 is a 4 Res.... Sturt Lane Junction. There were a few timetabled electric trains between Brookwood and Frimley. The third rail extended on the main local lines as far as the bridge over the Farnborough North line. The west loop at Sturt Lane was also electrified but could not have seen any electric services.

"Finally a question. Can anyone confirm a memory I have of a report in the *Railway Observer* of a 'Remembrance' N15X working to Exeter. It came about through a locomotive failure on a down West of England train. The 'Remembrance' came on at Basingstoke with the intention of taking the train as far as Salisbury. In the event it stayed on to Exeter. True or false ? (Any thoughts would be appreciated - Ed).

From John Burgess, "I don't know how you manage it, but there is always something interesting and new in every issue of The Southern Way, and Issue No 27 is no exception. Firstly 'David Williams' images. "I saw some of David William's beautiful work published a short while ago, and subsequently read some of the reactions that the images provoked, some suggesting that original photographs should never be tampered with in this way. I was really surprised by this response, as it seems to me that what David is doing is essentially artistic, in much the same way that I would pick up a paint brush and attempt to illustrate some long lost scene, all of which I think assists us in understanding what the railways used to be like. I also rely on the efforts of photographers, sometimes going right back to the dawn of railway photography, but I rarely simply copy the work, always making changes, perhaps changing the period or the locomotive/stock or attempting to create a different atmosphere, or maybe attempting to recreate a unique scene. Sometimes, I fail to find enough useful reference material, and may have to resort to a degree of conjecture, particularly with Victorian scenes or closed lines where everything has been demolished.

"The question of colour is an interesting one. By and large, railway locomotives and stock of all eras were photographed in their day to day work, sometimes looking pristine, sometimes weathered or dirty, and towards the end of steam in downright disgraceful conditions of rust and muck. Even with stock in pristine condition, gloss paint finishes are highly reflective, and will pick up the colour of the sky and areas of highlights, as well as areas of deep shadow, all of which can significantly alter the look and colour of the object. If you want to see this, take a look in the street and see how reflective today's motor vehicles are. To depict them without taking account the reflections would render them dull and flat. A layer of grime can significantly alter appearances, and bright colours have to be toned down to create the correct effect. I have never attempted digital work on photographs, but imagine that exactly the same problems are posed as those for the traditional artist.

"There is a potential issue of deception if these images were in some way to be passed off as originals, but that is not what David is doing, and for me honesty of approach is key in this. Carry on producing these beautiful images, David. I for one think that they are stunning.".

(This subject of colour manipulation has, I will admit, divided opinion amongst readers. Most are in favour, but we must also respect those who hold a different view. I will admit to being in the 'aye' camp. To my mind what David is doing is producing something which I wish I had been around to see in person. Subjective opinion as to colours will always prevail and similarly we will have personal choices. I will not expand further: suffice to say look at some of the exquisite models we see produced in the various scales and gauges. Who is to say the colour scheme on a model locomotive, item of rolling stock or station is inaccurate, or should we only have models made in black/white/grey?

Co-incidentally David has sent me an unsolicited copy of a calendar he has produced for 2015. I can do no more than reproduce below that for November 2015. In my mind this is exactly where colouration can score, the image represents precisely what could have been seen at the time,

1955. (Two other Southern related views also appear, a 'Well Tank' and a LBSCR 'Baltic' tank in Brighton colours.) I should also add that David has allowed us to use another of his images as the front of the current Noodle Books catalogue and 'SW30'

Copies of his calendar are available at £7.99 post free from D P Williams at 41 Mansewood Road, Glasgow, G43 1TN. See also **www.railphotoprints.co.uk**. David has asked me to point out that those with views on his work regardless of opinion might care to visit the LNER forum at http://www.lner.info/forums/viewforum.php?f=15 where they would find what is fast becoming a hugely popular thread dealing with computer coloured monochrome and averaging over 1000 visits per month with a current score of over 11,000. There are some very complimentary views being expressed here (as well as critical comments).

John Burgess has also contributed to our respective pieces on the Chessington Branch (issues 24 and 26). "The Chessington Branch under Construction. I had always felt that there must be some images somewhere of the construction of this line, so it was fascinating to see that you have uncovered some. I have lived in Chessington since the 1980s but this is the first time I have seen so many images of the work in progress. The four photographs of the work at Bridge Road are particularly interesting as they show the bridge before it was encased in concrete, probably one of the less attractive features of Southern Railway engineering and architecture. I have always assumed that Bridge Road was named after the bridge, but felt it might be time to check this out, and trawling through a selection of local history books, I found a picture of the street in 'Chessington Remembered' by Mark Davison, probably dating from the late 1930s, in which he tells us that "Bridge Road was laid out in 1937 and named after Councillor Clement H Bridge, a prominent member of Surbiton Urban District Council who lived at Chessington Grange". So never assume anything! Incidentally, the Southern Railway originally intended that Chessington South be called Chessington Grange. As the house was demolished many years ago, the name no longer means anything to the ordinary man in the Chessington street.

"It was also interesting to see pictures of the contractor's locomotives. I think that 'Ashendon' is a product of the Manning Wardle factory, very similar in looks to the preserved Matthew Murray on the Middleton Railway. Because of its name I wonder if it had some earlier role in the construction of the GCR line, which was undertaken by Pauling and Co, but have been unable to find anything definitive. The older looking saddle tank to its left looks like a Hudswell Clarke product. Looking forward to the next issue."

Peter Clarke (different spelling and who I know is an expert on the railway in the Micheldever area, has added some most interesting information on the photographs and railway stamps that appeared in SW27. "Dear Kevin, I thought you might like to know my views about the two photographs relating to Micheldever on page 33 of Southern Way No. 27.

"First with regard to the stamp. I believe that this design for the 10/- stamp was introduced on 1st April 1884

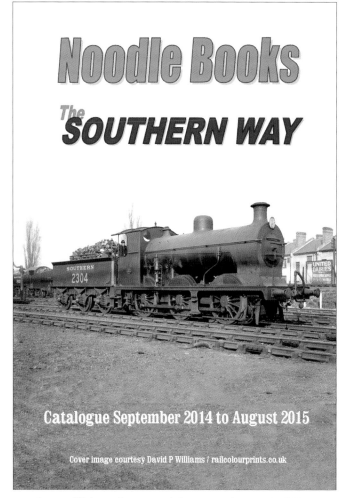

and so will have been used between then and 1902. The value of the stamp is very high and I therefore think it was probably not used for postage purposes. My guess is that it would have been used to pay stamp duty due on a deed, contract or other document as postage stamps could be used for this purpose at this time – you will no doubt remember the old practice of sticking a 2d. stamp on receipts. (But Peter, surely none of us is old enough to recall signing over a stamp on a document - Ed!) A fixed rate of 10/- was very common for many types of document and so it is not surprising that the GPO issued postage stamps of this denomination even though postage rates would hardly justify this.

"If I am right, why you may ask, has it been franked by Micheldever Station? The answer to this is, I think, that at that time Micheldever Station Post Office enjoyed the status of being a head post office and could therefore handle a wide range of services, including revenue collection, in addition to offering postal facilities. The office was probably established shortly after the arrival of the electric telegraph on the Southampton main line in 1845. Mail (and passengers) used to be distributed by mail coach from Micheldever to a wide area around which included Andover and Whitchurch until sometime after the L&SWR opened the line to Andover in 1854. Sutton Scotney was also served from Micheldever even after the Didcot Newbury & Southampton line opened in 1885, presumably because of its direct connection with London.

"Turning now to the photograph of the station staff, I think this must have been taken shortly after 1905 when the lines through Micheldever were quadrupled. The signal box was located on what used to be the down platform but became an island platform when the extra tracks were laid. This platform fell out of use then until electrification took place in 1965. Unfortunately, I have not been able to identify any of the people shown in the photo but if any of your readers can do so, I would be interested to hear from them." (I seem to recall also, on a recent edition of I think BBC 'Antiques Roadshow', there was reference to the first motor car ever brought to the UK. This was on 6 July 1895 when The Hon. Evelyn Ellis had a motor car transported from Paris to Micheldever by train. Upon arrival at Micheldever, Ellis and his friend Frederick Simms drove the vehicle to Datchet. This was without the then legal requirement of a man having a flag preceeding the vehicle. He was not stopped and the law in question was repealed in 1896. As an aside a delightful contemporary account is available on the Datchet history website reproduced below, *"We set forth at exactly 9.26 am and made good progress on the well-made old London coaching road; it was delightful travelling on that fine summer morning. We were not without anxiety as to how the horses we might meet would behave towards their new rivals, but they took it very well and out of 133 horses we passed only two little ponies who did not seem to appreciate the innovation. On our way we passed a great many vehicles of of all kinds* (ie horse-drawn)*, as well as cyclists. It was a very pleasing sensation to go along the delightful roads towards Virginia Water at speeds varying from three to twenty miles per hour, and our iron horse behaved splendidly. There we took our luncheon and fed our engine with a little oil. Going down the steep hill leading to Windsor we passed through Datchet and arrived right in front of the entrance hall of Mr Ellis's house at Datchet at 5.40, thus completing our most enjoyable journey of 56 miles, the first ever made by a petroleum motor carriage in this country in 5 hours 32 minutes, exclusive of stoppages and at an average speed of 9.84 mph.*

"In every place we passed through we were not unnaturally the objects of a great deal of curiosity. Whole villages turned out to behold, open mouthed, the new marvel of locomotion. The departure of coaches was delayed to enable their passengers to have a look at our horseless vehicle, while cyclists would stop to gaze enviously at us as we surmounted with ease some long hill. Mr Ellis's motor carriage is a neat and compact four-wheeled dog-cart with accommodation for four persons and two portmanteaus. The consumption of petroleum is little over a halfpenny per mile and there is no smoke, heat or smell, the carriage running smoothly and without any vibration.

Finally for this issue and again from Peter Clark, "Good morning Kevin, I have only just obtained issues 26 and 27 and am enjoying reading them when I should be doing other things of a more domestic nature! With regard to page 51, SW 26, the answer may be in the September 1952 issue of *The Railway Observer*. On Wednesday 20 August 1952 No 34008 worked a Pullman excursion which left Waterloo at 9.45 a.m. for Wimborne via Ringwood. It was due to arrive at 12.18 p.m. but did so three minutes

early. It left at 1.45 p.m. for Dorchester via Broadstone Jct. and Hamworthy Jct. On arrival at Dorchester at 2.30 p.m., passengers were taken on a coach tour to Wareham via Bovington and Lulworth while the train went empty to Weymouth for servicing. The return journey left Wareham at 5.45 p.m. direct to Waterloo. The train was formed of Pullman cars 27, 171, *Cassandra, Rosemary*, 60, 208 and observation car 13."

"With regard to page 35, SW 27, Merchant Navies certainly worked east of Swanley. My childhood memories (thank you for publishing them) recall that No 35029 *Ellerman Lines* was a regular on boat trains via the Canterbury East line in the early to mid-1950s. According to the 1952 Ian Allan locoshed book, Nos 35026-8 were at Stewarts Lane and Nos 35029/30 were at Dover. In the spring of 1959 just prior to electrification I saw No 35001 *Channel Packet* come through Canterbury East on an up morning train. No 35015 was also allocated to Stewarts Lane for a period after rebuilding. I don't remember seeing it on the LCDR but rebuilt No 35014 *Nederland Line* appeared one morning on the 9.20 a.m. Dover Priory-Victoria which was the best up train of the day. It left Canterbury East at 9.52 and only called at Chatham afterwards.

The return working was the 2.35 p.m. Victoria-Dover Priory which detached a Ramsgate portion at Faversham. I do not have the precise date but think it was in the summer of 1958. I must have been on holiday again because I was not at school. I made a point of looking out for the down train in the afternoon but No 35014 did not come back. I have photographs of No 35030 *Elder Dempster Lines* at Canterbury East on 20 October 1949 with its nameplates covered and 35001 there on 14 May 1959. They were taken by my good friend the late Arthur G. Wells. Copyright passed to his widow, but I lost touch with her some years ago and believe that she too has died. Arthur's collection passed to the care of the RCTS and I think Bob Ratcliffe has custody of it. He would probably know if you can reproduce them if you wished to."

Just as we were completing this section (and with a small piece of space I was wondering how to fill up - Ed.), this from Richard Bell re SW27, "The illustration on p72, of Longhedge Junction. The leftmost pair of tracks, coming from Factory Junction, were not LBSCR but London Chatham and Dover Railway property. They pass under the former LBSCR and LSWR main lines. Ownership changed to LSWR where they emerge on the north side of the latter (the boundary point was named Lavender Hill Junction), and they join the Windsor lines at what was named Ludgate Junction.

Since December 2012 these tracks have been used by the London Overground trains between Highbury and Clapham Junction via the North-, East- and South London Lines. The last predecessors of these were SECR trains between Moorgate or Ludgate Hill and Clapham Junction, withdrawn in 1914, and LSWR trains between Ludgate Hill and Richmond via Kensington and Hammersmith (diverging onto the West London Line at Longhedge Junction), which faded away in 1916."

The Southern Railway from Inception to Nationalisation and beyond

Part 7: The completion of Sir Herbert's work and the Southern at War

Alan Blackburn (continuing the series started by Tony Goodyear)

Sir Herbert Walker KCB was followed as General Manager (GM) by Gilbert Szlumper CBE, son of Alfred Szlumper the Southern's first Engineer. Gilbert was also an Engineer by training, but by 1925 he was Assistant to Sir Herbert, and like his chief he was before all else a well-rounded manager. Incidentally, when a railwayman speaks of the Engineer, it is always the Civil Engineer that he is referring to. The Mechanical Engineer is someone else. (The Civils are senior to the 'rude' Mechanicals and like to remind them from time to time).

A little scheme I should perhaps have mentioned before, and of which I've not been able to find out very much, was the re-arrangement and extension of the Romney branch in Kent. This ran originally from Appledore to Dungeness where it was intended to build a ferry terminal, with a later branch from Lydd, about half way, to New Romney. Needless to say the ferry terminal was never built. The Southern found it worthwhile to close Dungeness to passenger traffic and lay a new line from a point approximately a mile beyond Lydd to join up with the New Romney line about one mile outside that station. The new alignment took the line parallel to the 15 inch Romney Hythe and Dymchurch Railway (opened in 1928 after consultation with the Southern) and was provided with new stations at Lydd-on-Sea and Greatstone-on-Sea. The former had a signalled loop but I cannot imagine that it was much used, if indeed at all? Someone described this area as the land God forgot to finish; at the time there was little there except shingle, a few old shacks and some interesting carriage bodies. Anyway this deviation opened on the 4th of July 1937. At a guess the track of the original route was coming up for renewal and the land required was probably very cheap.

Back to the home counties. Outstanding business was the extension of electrification to Gillingham and Maidstone, to Reading and Guildford via Ascot and

Southern built electric stock at Waterloo East in 1955. From left to right, at Platform 'D' is an ex-LSWR bodied 4 SUB, at 'B' is a 1939 HAL on a Gillingham working and over at 'A', a Bulleid 4 SUB 'all stations to Dartford'. The EPB type was yet to arrive on the scene.   *Alan A Jackson*

Aldershot, and the construction of the Chessington branch: more of the latter later...

A scheme that was not progressed, to Sir Herbert's regret, was the electrification of the Tonbridge to Hastings line. He proposed it twice but the Board felt there was insufficient traffic potential to justify the cost of the work. Incidentally the Southern Board never passed a proposal unless it was unanimously agreed. (Some Heritage Railways take note.)

We will look at the 'Medway' scheme first as it spawned a new type of train, the 2-HAL. The electrics and underframe etc. were as the later 2-BILs but the bodywork was new, and Bulleid's influence was immediately apparent. The Driving Trailer Composite was similar in layout to that of the BIL but the Driving Motor Third lacked a toilet and side corridor. What the whole unit lacked was any degree of comfort; and unfortunately the same type of train was provided for the Reading scheme although here they ran mixed up with the BILs and the regular commuters quickly spotted the differences!

The Medway scheme called for a further platform to be electrified and two others extended at Holborn Viaduct and two more at Cannon Street where all seven platforms were now electrified. Elsewhere considerable civil engineering work was undertaken at Strood and Swanley, and the Halt at New Hythe was completely rebuilt as a station.

At Swanley a new four-platform station was provided on the London side of the junction. This station is notable as being the last example of a major Southern Railway-designed station. Unfortunately it had to be provided with a temporary booking office as the local authorities had not decided on the alignment of a new road scheme. The road was never built and Swanley still has a very basic booking office at street level on the up side whilst a 'Passimeter' office intended for the down side entrance was never built.

Another major structure required for this scheme was a four-road car-shed at Gillingham and this was also the last SR designed car-shed to be built. It's a small point, but in the Southern's world, steam stock was kept in 'carriage sheds' but electric stock was 'berthed in car-sheds'. The electric train service commenced to Gillingham, Maidstone East and West on the 2nd of July 1939.

The Reading and Ascot to Guildford schemes were very straightforward although they did call for a new track layout and signal box at Ascot, whilst the spur between Frimley Junction and Ash Vale provided the rare example of an electrified single line. One could also run from Frimley Junction up to the main line at Sturt Lane Junction. These routes opened on the 1st of January 1939.

In connection with the opening of the electric services to Gillingham and Maidstone The Railway Gazette published an excellent Supplement including a very interesting table giving the main details of all the SR Electrification schemes to date. Unfortunately it does not lend itself to reproduction but to quote some figures-

Prior to 1932, (Suburban) Route Mileage Electrified 300,
Track Mileage Electrified 800,

Approx. Cost £7m,
Number of Sub-Stations 46: capacity of SS, 201,500 kW.
Number of Vehicles 1813.

7 Major schemes 1932-9. Route Mileage Electrified 402,
Track Mileage Electrified 946.
Approx. Cost £13.5m,
Number of Sub-Stations 112, Capacity of SS 282,500 kW,
Number of Vehicles 1376.

It also paid a handsome tribute to the main characters involved namely Sir Herbert Walker, Alfred Raworth, George Ellson, REL Maunsell and since 1937 Mr. O V S Bulleid.

The Chessington line was not included in the above details unfortunately and if the RG published a Supplement covering this line I have not found it. Anyway it was intended to form a connection with Leatherhead, and like the Wimbledon-Sutton line before it, it was brand new and proved similarly expensive and difficult to build, with lengthy embankments and several large bridges as Mike King's article in the last SW illustrated very well. Construction started in 1936 but the Green Belt Act was published in 1938 and that effectively put a stop to any further building in the area, essential to the line's success as a loop. As it was, the line opened to Tolworth on the 29th May 1938 and to Chessington South on the 28th May 1939.and there it stopped until finally killed off by the Town & Country Planning Act of 1947. Goods yards were provided at Tolworth and Chessington South, the latter being some distance beyond the station. The whole route was fenced and in fact some rubble was tipped beyond Chessington South during the war but that was only as a matter of convenience. The gradients were uphill all the way to Chessington so it was not surprising when one early morning some coal wagons ran away from Chessington South. The Signalman there sent "Vehicles Running Away" and this in due course was passed right back to Raynes Park. No one was too concerned as there was a heavy upgrade to Raynes Park and this was confidently expected to stop the wagons. It did, but they then rolled back to knock down the gates at West Barnes just as the crossing keeper there judged it was safe to open them! Such incidents were part and parcel of everyday railway life and many a minor mishap was "squared up" if it was not witnessed by officialdom, especially if it occurred in the dark hours.

On an altogether much more serious scale was a collision that occurred at Battersea Park on the 2nd of April 1937 killing ten and injuring many more. It happened in the middle of the morning business traffic and was caused by the signalman becoming confused and improperly releasing the Sykes' block instrument under the impression that it had failed. Now much of the Southern's inner suburban area was controlled by the Sykes' Lock and Block system and speaking from experience it could become very complicated at junctions and it was not beyond failure, the more so in its later years. Anyway, the outcome of this incident was the accelerated re-signalling of the Victoria area with the usual track circuits and colour-light signals. In detail the work was very similar to that at Waterloo.

Over on the Chatham side the 1919- built 'A' cabin with its 200-lever American frame was retained; but on the Brighton side a new cabin at Victoria with a 225-lever frame was brought into use on June 4th 1939. (Note that the South Western had 'boxes', the Brighton and I believe the South Eastern people spoke of 'cabins').
All the Southern's London termini were now provided with colour-light signalling. The Victoria box itself was constructed to withstand bomb damage and reflected the railway industry's general preparations for war at this time.

Another important scheme carried out in 1939-40 was the re-construction of the Waterloo and City line and the replacement of its rolling stock. As opened in 1898 the line was electrified with a centre live rail carrying 500 volts d c, the power being supplied by a small power station alongside the W&C sidings at Waterloo. The line was built to a reduced 'tube' line loading gauge with curves down to five chains radius, and that is very sharp indeed. The rolling stock was made up of five 4-car saloon trains built in the USA. Later came five single saloon motor cars built by Dick Kerr for use in the off-peak periods.

There was nothing to be done about the loading gauge of course but the Southern did all it could to improve the line generally. New 95lb BS running rails with a 100lb juice rail were laid in the normal position. The 660-volt power supply was now taken from 'upstairs' but the power station was retained for some years for non-traction use. New colour-light signals were installed but the box at Waterloo was retained much as before. That at the Bank was little more than a panel on the wall and could be operated automatically. Incidentally it was said that the signalman at the Bank occupied a unique position in the City of London. He was the only person in the City to sit on an "Elsan" toilet (For those perhaps not familiar with the term, this was a portable chemical toilet, the modern-day equivalent would be the type used in cubicles at open-air festivals.) If you are interested the contents were conveyed to Waterloo on the last train of the day, officially an empty working! The toilet in the W&C yard at Waterloo was unusually situated on top of a short tower, this being necessary to elevate it above the local sewers.

The new trains consisted of twelve double-ended saloon motors that could run on their own in the off-peak and 16 saloon trailers. They normally ran as five 5-car sets with a motor car each end of three trailers. English Electric built the trains and the motors might best be described as a double-ended version of a LPTB standard stock motor car with a modern body, It was not possible to follow the latest LPTB 1938 design as these trains required train-length inspection pits for which there was no room at Waterloo. The livery was a light green (malachite) body with silver ends which uniquely showed two red lights back and front.

The seating was not too bad, but despite efforts to do something about it the noise level was high. There was a long history of rough riding on this line and it was not until 1990 that yours truly discovered 'officially' that the tunnel rails were laid vertically. In truth I could hardly believe what I had found, so I phoned the line's former ganger whom I knew, by then at Hither Green, and asked him what was unusual about the track in the W&C? Back came the answer straight away, "the tunnel rails stand vertical; not many people know that". He was certainly right about that. The standard chairs were carried on long timbers trimmed to offset their 1 in 20 inclination but it was not easy to see without taking a timber out. The wheels meanwhile had the normal 1 in 20 coning! Seemingly the rails had always been laid vertically to match the original American wheels and this was not picked up when the line was re-built. There was nothing to be done about it beyond grinding the rail heads as best we could with an Italian rail-grinding machine and not long after that LT took the line over and re-laid it.

An interesting story concerned the little electric shunting loco used to move wagons between the lift and the power station siding. This was a very weak machine that was only supposed to handle one loaded or two empty wagons at a time. One night someone decided to hurry things up a bit and attached two loaded coal wagons in the lift with the result that the wagons overpowered the engine and the whole lot finished up under the river!. There was nothing for it but to take two motor coaches wrong line to the Bank and so push the locomotive and its wagons back up into Waterloo yard. Needless to say it was a move not tried again.

Elsewhere, as mentioned briefly in the last article, Mr. Bulleid arrived on the 20th September 1937 to replace Maunsell as the Mechanical Engineer and in 1938, Alfred Raworth took over as Electrical Engineer following the retirement of Herbert Jones.

As you might guess from my closing comments in part 6 about Oliver Bulleid, I have my reservations about this gentleman. I am no mechanical engineer myself and all I know about Bulleid is what I have read or been told about him by those who worked for him or worked with the engines and rolling stock he built. With the exception of drivers and firemen their collective comments were not very complimentary. I get the impression of a very clever man with great energy, brimming over with ideas he could not wait to try out. Unfortunately it seems he did not always know when to stop and with all Maunsell's Assistants retired or sidetracked, there was no one left senior enough to influence him.

So far as his LNER days go I can only conclude that Gresley had kept him on a very tight reign and I guess that when Bulleid left Kings Cross there were those there who were more than a little interested to see what he would do on the Southern. They did not have long to wait.

We have already touched on the Mid-Sussex Buffet cars and with their interiors there seems to be a connection with the carriages built for the Coronation and Silver Link trains: his 2-HAL units likewise. They might have looked quite smart on the outside, but their interiors were austere to the point of being uncomfortable and so too I guess were the two 4-LAVs he had to build although I

Milk empties passing Byfleet Junction behind No 21C7 'Aberdeen Commonwealth' on 7 August 1947. The tanks might have been empty but they were still a fair weight. Note there is one road tank in the middle of the train. Incidentally, those tanks might have carried colourful liveries at one time but I never saw one that was not completely covered in brake-block dust, a comment that might well be applied to the average utility van as well.

never rode in one. Worse still were his first 4-SUBs, the so-called 'Queen of Shebas'. Mind you, you have only to ride in the preserved Gresley articulated set to see where he got the thin sides/maximum width at shoulder height from. Perhaps he designed those too, but beyond that were the LNER passengers smaller than their cousins south of the river? One is reminded of the old saying "16 inches to the bum, 16 bums to the ton" - but I think that applied to tramcars.

So far as locomotives went he rode on the Nelsons and decided that they did not steam too well and as a result he gave them a new front end. I have read and heard it said that the only thing wrong with the Nelsons was that there were not enough of them and as a result only a comparatively few top link enginemen were used to them. One has only to see what the LMS did with the very similar Royal Scots to learn what a good re-build could do for such an engine. You may not agree, but I would guess the re-built Scots were the most capable 4-6-0s in the country and something similar could probably have done anything the Southern ever required.

Now here is a question. Did the Southern at that time need any new express passenger locomotives? It was

the CME's job to build and repair locomotives but running them on the Southern was the Operating Superintendent's responsibility. That at the time was Eustace Missenden. Yes, the SR locomotive stock was getting old but electrification was the name of the game at the time and has any one ever seen anything in writing requesting a new express passenger engine, and yet here was Bulleid complete with an ex-LNER locomotive draughtsman all ready from day one ready to design one? The answer may go back to Bulleid's interview with Walker. It is quite possible that it was he who told Bulleid they were needed. We will probably never know but we do know that Missenden and Bulleid got on very well together and on the 30th June 1938 Bulleid was granted authority to build twenty 4-6-2 Express passenger locomotives. Having said that, it has been reported that a diagram existed dated the 7th June 1938 for a 2-8-2, and an even later one for a 4-8-2 so the decision to go for a Pacific must have been a very late one.

The result was a three-cylinder engine with a very good boiler mounted on a sound set of frames but provided with a most unconventional valve gear that was destined to give many years of expensive trouble. The idea of an enclosed valve gear was laudable and yes, the chains were not originally intended, but the fact of the matter was that the oil bath leaked badly, the drive chains stretched, the reverser was unreliable and the whole lot was only accessible with great difficulty, who ever heard of a steam engine that caught fire and if all that were not enough they were seriously overweight. Yes, they were powerful and the enginemen liked them but they did not have to maintain them.

When the immensely experienced senior staff at Salisbury and Exmouth Junction complained of their problems with these engines Mr. Bulleid blamed the people. That tells us much about the man; he was never wrong. Better to have built a couple and when their serious problems emerged, finish the others off with conventional valve gear, but that was left to wiser men eleven years later by which time a vast sum of money must have been wasted.

21C1-10, built Eastleigh 2/41-7/42l; 2IC11-20, built Eastleigh 12/44-6/45; and 35021-30, built Eastleigh 5/48-4/49   The first twenty were described at first as Express Passenger engines, then when this was questioned they became Mixed Traffic engines, and finally with the war over all thirty became Express Passenger engines. They did in fact do a fair amount of freight train work in their early years but only because they were not reliable enough to be used in passenger service.

While all this was evolving, war had broken out and by the time these engines were being built things were not going well for our country and that's to put it mildly.

The most immediate effect of the war was that the Government took control of the country's railways; and as in the first war a Railway Executive Committee (REC) was appointed and the Southern's GM, Sir Gilbert Szlumper, was appointed to chair it.

His successor as GM was Eustace Missenden who we have already met, a former SECR Traffic man. He had come up through the ranks and was as sound a railwayman as the Company could hope for; but it was said that he did not get on too well with people. That aside, he was a fine railwayman and he was knighted in 1944 for his war efforts.

It has been said that the country was unprepared for war and this was so in many ways but the writing had been on the wall for at least five years and behind the scenes the nation was desperately preparing for war even if many did not recognise it. Unfortunately much of the military equipment produced in the run up to war was to be lost in France in 1940 but that is to jump ahead a little.

So far as the railway industry was concerned the engineering departments commenced in 1937 to prepare for

Loading 'funnies' - bridging tanks in this instance. Axminster, 3 October 1943. Note the Lyme Regis 2-set over in the bay in full malachite livery.

Bomb (crater) damage on the main line at Malden 10 November 1940. Filling in of such craters was easy: train loads of open wagons full of rubble were kept at strategic places and worked to site as required. The contents were then shovelled out, ballast and sleepers placed on top and the whole could be running again in a comparatively short space of time. Decades later the legacy of such infill is causing difficulties for the modern day network as they invariably result in wet spots. Dealing with craters on viaducts was a different matter but then bridge beams were often used to restore working. Much of this work would also be accomplished within hours or days at the most, the priority being to keep traffic going - a slightly different timescale would probably apply in peacetime 2015... . (For a wide selection of images featuring the Southern at War, see the three 'Wartime Southern' volumes in our 'Southern Way Special' series.)

a war that it was widely thought would be fought in the air. Windows in strategic buildings such as signal boxes and workshops were bricked up, blast walls erected, strategic materials stockpiled, and emergency bridge beams constructed. Additional break-down and permanent way cranes were ordered, largely with bridge work in mind. These, incidentally, carried Southern lettering and numbers but were never owned by the Southern. They were eventually purchased from the Government by BR in 1952.

In other directions the scrapping of old but otherwise useful engines was stopped and thought given to the possibility of the widespread transfer of engines from one company to another. The best example of this was the earmarking of former GER Westinghouse-braked tank engines for possible use on the Southern in the event of the company losing its electric power supply. In 1940 Durnford Road power house was indeed seriously damaged and lost 50% of its power output but this was largely made up by an emergency power line connection from Deptford power station and the running of trains at reduced speed. As for damage to the conductor rails generally. it was soon found that was not a serious problem, the ETM men could replace the rails before much else was ready. Bridges, viaducts and unsafe buildings alongside the railway were another matter, as were unexploded bombs.

Another precaution was the dispersing of the company's London offices to Deepdene House in Dorking and the setting up of the Divisional Control Offices at Orpington, Redhill, Woking, Southampton and Exeter. This was a wise move as the Company's offices at London Bridge and Waterloo were both seriously damaged and many records were lost, or so it was said later.

The Special Traffic Sections, those people responsible for the pre-planned arrangement of special trains, were to play a very important part in the war years starting with the planning for the evacuation of children and other vulnerable people from London and other locations likely to be bombed. The first of several such evacuations actually took place a few days before war was declared. This was followed by moving the British Expeditionary Force (BEF) to France via Southampton and the Channel ports; again much planning, and altogether a lot of work, but the Southern was very good at this sort of thing and all went well.

I am not going to repeat in any great detail a blow by blow account of what followed in the war as it has all been dealt with by several publications recently and one could still write another book on the subject. Rather I will try to put a more personal touch to things a I remember them as a child and as told to me by my older colleagues when I first started work.

First: Dunkirk. Well, Redhill was the key station involved. Not all the special trains involved passed through Redhill by any means but many did, and most of these needed to reverse there and change engines for their onward journeys to the south west where much of the army normally lived. I've read and heard it said that Redhill became so congested that locomotives could not reach the Loco Shed. Water would not have been too much of a problem as there were several columns scattered about the station but engines were being re-coaled by a process of taking coal from other engines standing adjacent. Fires were cleaned wherever the engines stood and what about turning? Did some of those trains leave with their engines running tender first? I think they must have. Again I've not seen it recorded but many of those trains must have left Redhill behind GWR locomotives, their men were not used to cleaning their fires; that was a shed labourer's work on their railway. Having, from personal experience, a less than high opinion of the Western's Traffic people I am bound to say that it was a good job that the Southern served the Channel ports and not the GWR, but to give those Western train crews their credit there can be no doubt that they pulled their weight alongside our men.

We all know the story of the 'little ships' and some of you may remember the brass plaques to be found on some of the Island paddlers that recorded their participation at Dunkirk. What they did not tell you was that they would never have got there were it not for the Royal Navy who had to man them. This was not a case of the Southern crews refusing duty but was due to a misunderstanding as to what Articles (terms and conditions of service) they were to serve under, compounded by the Navy's refusal to explain what was actually required. I do not know the full story but I would expect that some at least of the senior officers and engineers did go with their ships although there were many RN Reserve men who knew how to handle a paddle steamer. For the record the SR owned 42 ships in 1939 and by the end of the war it had lost 12 of them to enemy action.

One evacuation that I have not seen reported in the railway press was that of sheep (!) from Romney Marsh to safer areas in the south west. It had long been the practice for west country farmers to send their cattle to the south east for final fattening before slaughter but this was a move in the opposite direction.

Dunkirk was followed in due course by the Battle of Britain and with that started the heavy daily and latterly nightly bombing raids. Redbridge works was the first SR installation to be bombed, as early as June 1940, when a large number of sleepers was lost, but Portsmouth Harbour station was the first SR station to be seriously damaged by enemy action on the night of 12th August 1940. Most of the damage was caused by fire, the platform awnings were largely destroyed as were a 4-BIL and three coaches of a 4-COR. Later it was said that the main water supply was

damaged and so it might have been. However more to the point was the fact that when the raid first started there was only one member of platform staff available to tackle the numerous fires that were breaking out all over the place, everyone else on duty was across on the 'Hard' in the pubs! Reality was not always what you might think if you have read *War on the Line*.

The Home Guard was a sore point. Yes, many railwaymen did join voluntarily but as things became more organised and better equipped, so the training became compulsory and more physically demanding. Some of those involved were young men but most were middle-aged to elderly, and many had served in the "the last lot" and knew what war was all about. As one put it to me, "We were 'past it' and would have been no match for fit young men well equipped and highly motivated."

Mind you, if you will allow me an aside, not all the Germans involved were highly motivated or convinced of what they were doing. My wife's uncle, then a young man, was serving in the German Navy at the time and training on the French coast with converted river barges for the invasion we all expected. As he recalled, the barges when loaded lacked any reasonable freeboard and were seriously underpowered. As he said "Your navy would not have needed a gun to sink us, the wash of a passing ship would have been sufficient!" He and many others were much relieved when it was all called off. Sorry about that, but I thought you might be interested, back to the Southern Railway!

The damage done by the Luftwaffe was very serious, and at one time or another all the London termini were closed and on more than one occasion five out of the six at the same time. Being on long brick arched viaducts made many of the approach tracks particularly vulnerable. Normally a brick arch is very strong but they are easily damaged by high explosive bombs falling from a great height. Some of these arches were simply filled in with brick rubble as were many bomb craters. Quite a few track 'wet spots' in later years owed their origin to starting life as hurriedly-filled-in bomb craters.

The Engineer set up emergency depots at Hither Green, Knockholt, Ashford, Faversham, New Cross Gate, Beddington Lane, Salfords, Three Bridges, Brighton, Mitcham, Woking, Fratton, Eastleigh, Yeovil Junction and Broad Clyst. These held emergency bridging and p-way materials including in many cases whole trains of old open wagons loaded with brick rubble for filling in bomb craters. Other depots were also set up to hold the department's 'Dispersed Stores'. Many of these depots were later to become Pre-assembly Depots (PADs) for pre-fabricated track construction and indeed, the pre-fabricating of track panels might well have started in the war years in a small way: does anyone know?

Still thinking of fires, we must not forget the old Stroudley D1 tanks converted into 'fire engines' each with their own train of water tank wagons (not tenders). They got a lot of publicity at the time but sadly it was found that a locomotive boiler was not really suitable for serving a fire

An official photograph taken on 31 July 1942 of C18 on a goods train but without giving the location. One can tell it is on the South Western section from the near track but where exactly? The headcode of 'one top left and one over the hook' gives us three possible routes: 'Brent to Feltham', 'Nine Elms to Guildford via the new line', or Guildford to Godalming'. The trouble is I know (or knew) all three very well yet I cannot be certain it is any of them. One can well imagine what the Southern enthusiast of the day felt about the appearance of these engines but happily they soon proved themselves to be very fine machines. Not only were they the most powerful 0-6-0 in the country, they were probably the fastest!

pump: they could not sustain a jet of water for long enough to have any real effect, and they were quietly relegated to shunting and storage and one or two went to the army at Longmoor. Something that now seems largely forgotten these days was the construction of additional connections to the GWR to provide alternative routes in the event of the more normal ones being damaged. These were provided at St Budeaux, Lydford, Red Post Junction, Winchester Junction and Staines Moor, the latter with the object of keeping traffic out of London. There was also a new very sharp curve put in at Crayford, presumably to turn trains back if Dartford was seriously damaged.

It was a toss-up as to whether being a p-way man or shunter was the most dangerous job on the railway. Personally I would say shunting was the worst, especially so when you were on your own in the dark and without any overhead lighting. Just you, a shunting pole and a hand oil lamp. The army did not believe in lighting and I had some experience of that at Longmoor in the mid-fifties: it was not funny. It goes without saying that during the war years such overhead lighting as existed was reduced to the point where it was next to useless.

Signalmen were not supposed to leave their boxes during a raid and surrounded as they were by glass and not much else they were provided with a sort of metal box in which to take refuge if things became too hot. One of my old signalmen told how he was working Chapel Crossing in Southampton one night. As you might expect these metal boxes, coffins people called them, were not very popular. but this night things were becoming very unhealthy and Jack took to his 'coffin'. The next thing he remembered was regaining conscious and finding himself in a nearby graveyard. Bizarre indeed but at least he was still alive; the upperworks of the box was a wreck. (Incidentally, Jack had fought the Afghans in the 1920s on the North West frontier; nothing is new.)

After the battle of Britain and the night raids that followed, things quietened down a lot as the Luftwaffe turned its attention to Russia, but there were still nuisance raids as they were called, usually a single plane flying in low under the radar. One of these came in over Havant one day. The air-raid siren had gone but nothing had developed as was frequently the case. My father was out in front of the house and spotted the plane approaching, he ran back into the house shouting "Get down - he has dropped three". He had, the first two killed two cows and injured a horse in a field alongside the Hayling Billy - but Jerry got lucky with the third, and a large lump of switch and crossing work came down in our garden. It must have gone up to a great height as there was a screen of tall trees between where it landed and the railway. Much to my regret the local gang came round a few days later to recover the material. Why were we not in our air-raid shelter? By this time most people had given up on air-raid shelters, they were altogether too unpleasant and frequently nothing happened.

It was about this time that the first of Bulleid's 'Charlies' appeared; No. C1. It is well recorded that Bulleid did not like the Q class and regretted not being able to stop their construction. What is not so well known is that Maunsell had gained authority to build 20 more in March 1937 and Bulleid used this, together with another dated April 1940 to build the Q1s. With possibly the most unconventional appearance of any locomotive ever built they were without doubt very fine machines. It has been said that they lacked brake power: well, that could be said of most 0-6-0 goods engines. The answer of course was a fitted head, not a great problem, even the driver of the very fine 'A' class goods (S15s) might ask for one on a wet day. I worked at Feltham for three years and there they were very popular and only once did I witness one have trouble stopping its train and that was on a wet day and he had 65 on. (Note the 'he': one is referring to the driver not the engine; if one spoke of the 1.15 man it was the driver (and engine) for the 1.15 train.)

Not only were these engines strong but they were also capable of being driven very fast. When I worked at Chiswick there used to be an early morning van train down to Reading. Normally, it was a T9 turn but it was not uncommon for a Charlie to appear. To see one of those at speed was a sight never to be forgotten. How fast? I do not know; around 70, I would guess. Beyond that with a light load they also had an incredible rate of acceleration and this made them ideal for working with the early Track Relaying Machines. One remembers the weekly Special Traffic book peppered with the note "Q1 class locomotive to be provided". CI-16 were built at Brighton 3-11/42; C17-36, Ashford 5-12/42, and C37-40, built Brighton 12/42. There was, by the way, a diagram for a 0-6-4T version but of course it never came to anything.

At the time the Q1s were built it was said that one of their uses would be to put a stop to the double heading of goods trains: now this practice was very unusual on the Southern but Guildford shed still had an active allocation of Adams A12 0-4-2s. and they were used in pairs on heavy trains out of Aldershot Government sidings. To quote an old Guildford driver I once knew, "Two of them could pull anything". Guildford was one of the first sheds to receive an allocation of Q1s and I guess this was to counter the double heading referred to.

In July 1941 the first of the 'Hornbys' appeared; No. CC1. This and its sister CC2 had been authorised way back in October 1936, possibly with electrification to Hastings in mind as their bodywork complied with that line's restricted loading gauge. Presumably there were design problems before the onset of the war delayed their completion. The construction of both had started at Ashford

but they were moved to Brighton for completion, even so CC2 had to wait until 1945 before it could be finished.

CC1 was a very successful engine that spent most of its life hauling Central Section freight trains which it did very well: the only problem seems to have been that there was not much else for it to do. Nevertheless it was joined in 1945 by its sister which must have been welcome because I remember that when one was not available, the number of steam engine duties that had to be altered to cover for one electric was quite amazing. In 1948 a third, No. 20003 appeared from Eastleigh and spent much of its time on the Newhaven Boat trains.

Way out of sequence, but of some interest I hope. For a short period in the summer of 1953 or 4. one of the first two used to work a Central Division Freight train into Fratton on a Saturday morning. Now only the 'Goods loop' between Fratton East and Fratton West was electrified so that was the road it arrived on. The engine then came off its train and ran down to Blackfriars bridge near to Portsmouth Town. In the meantime the road would be set up the non-electrified Reception Road and when the signalman at Fratton East was ready he would clear back to West box who would then pull off his signals and the Co-Co would then start back. He would pass Fratton West doing about twenty miles an hour and coast up the Reception road and out on to the juice at Fratton East and away back to Chichester. No problem, as people would say today.

Sorry about that, back to the war! Trains, of course, made a very attractive target for the hit-and-run raiders and in 1943 it was decided that certain trains in Kent, probably those running across Romney Marsh, should be provided with anti-aircraft gun protection. To this end six of the newest 5-plank open wagons were provided with vacuum brakes and a Bofors gun. This was mounted in the middle of the wagon and some sort of canvas shelter was erected at each end for the protection of the gun crew. Having gone to all this trouble it was then decided that it was not such a good idea after all and the guns were then emplaced around Ashford works and the wagons returned to normal use. A pity - they would have made a fine model!

George Ellson, CBE, MICE, the Southern's Chief Engineer retired at the end of 1943 and he was followed by "VAM" Robertson, MC and bar, MICE, MIME,MIEE, M InsT, (the MC was awarded for building bridges under fire). He was a very experienced engineer and came to the Southern from London Transport via the LNER and GER. But he had begun his railway career with the SE&CR so he was familiar with at least a third of his new railway. On the LNER he was a District Engineer so it is unlikely that he had met Bulleid before but you can be sure that Mr. Ellson would have included some mention of him when he briefed Mr. Robertson as to his new responsibilities. Something he would not have been used to was to find himself responsible for the Plant &Machinery Department. This was a CME responsibility on the other railways and became so on the Southern in 1948.

The war dragged on and the hit-and-run raids continued but the tide was changing and the Southern was

Above - Mr Bulleid's drawing office staff were no doubt hard at work at the time this photo was taken but this old Drummond S11 was still coping quite well in the meantime on a train from Redhill to Reading. The Southern was rather short of medium size engines at this time. (Later quite a few Drummond 4-4-0s were converted to oil burning when the scheme was aborted. The small number of larger engines involved were quickly reconverted to burn coal but the Drummonds lay around in store until they were scrapped.)

Left - 'Top right and right buffer' = 'Down main goods terminating at Woking', passing Byfleet Junction hauled by 'Black Motor' No 316. Why they were so called no one seems to know. I asked several drivers and they would all agree they were good engines but with one annoying drawback. As 'second string' goods engines it followed that they did a fair amount of shunting. This was all right so long as the engine faced the direction of shunt, but if the shunt was tender first then one had to hang out over the side rather more than was convenient to see past the tender coal rails. Another few inches on the cab width when they were built would have been very welcome.

Above - 'King Arthur' No 789 'Sir Guy' with a Boat Train headed for Dover or Folkestone via the No 1 Boat Train route - Victoria-Orpington-Tonbridge, seen here coming up on to the South Eastern main line at Petts Wood Junction. (There were no less than six recognised Boat train routes.) There is no date on the photograph but is possible post-war, I also cannot be certain if the engine is green or black.

Right - A look back to happier times. T9 No 114 in immaculate condition with a train of LMS stock leaving Woking on the Down main (local), August 1938. Note the wooden lineside cable trunking that characterised all the pre-war main line electrification schemes, one side carried the power cable and the other the control cables.

preparing to serve the needs of invading France. Initially this showed itself in the extension of goods yards, the strengthening of end loading docks and the provision of more sidings for holding traffic under load. The additional traffic at this time was mostly stores and material for building temporary camps. As many of the country goods yards concerned were now seeing more traffic than at any time since they were built, they frequently lacked any cranes. so this deficit had to be made good by the construction of additional rail-mounted hand cranes. Like the cranes already mentioned, the Ministry of War Transport owned them and all four main line railway companies received some. The Southern had eight, four of 10 tons and four of 6.5 tons capacity. Like the breakdown and p-way cranes before them they had SR numbers etc. but they were never owned by the Southern and eventually passed to BR in1952.

A very important part of the preparations for D-day was the reconstruction of the GWR line from Newbury to Winchester as a part of which scheme the Southern improved the connections at Shawford Junction and Allbrook. Eastleigh, and converted the up and down local lines between the two to 'Permissive Working', a very unusual practice on the Southern.

By the time of D-day much of the South of England was packed with men and material and Southampton and Portsmouth were at the centre of it all. I was well placed to watch all this and from what I saw the troops and equipment destined for the actual landing reached our area by road. I do remember just two Churchill tanks arriving at Havant but they were destined for an Engineer training camp. Rail really came into its own later in feeding Southampton Docks with vast amounts of every type of war materiel. I particularly remember trains of American wagons coming down from Longmoor where I now know they had been assembled from 'flat-pack' kits.

Tanks and heavy guns did of course travel by train. There was much movement of English tanks around the country for training purposes and these travelled on 'Warflats'. However most of the much more common and higher America 'Sherman' tanks needed 'Warwell' wagons to carry them safely in gauge and there were not so many of those wagons, so I guess that was one of the reasons that many of the Shermans reached the coast on their own tracks. Having said that it is on record that many tanks were unloaded at Winchester, Botley and Droxford *en route* to the various 'Hards'.around the Hampshire coast.

Opposite page - *Passengers, that is what the Southern was about. This picture of Waterloo concourse was taken in 1946 and was typical of the scene there on any Summer Saturday around the mid-1950s. Thereafter and the car plus cheap package holidays would cut such numbers significantly. The view might look a bit chaotic but all was under control (more or less) behind those chalk boards. Passengers destined for Southsea and the Isle of Wight would have been wise to have visited those cavenous underground toilets whilst waiting as they might otherwise spend the whole journey in a 4SUB without any! Notice even then the clock has the '24' hour face.*

This page, top - *Ampress Halt (Lymington Branch), the last to be built by the Southern, opened on 1 October 1956 to serve a nearby factory. It still exists today but it is many years since a train stopped there. I presume Exmouth Junction supplied the concrete platform units, but if they did they are unlike those being produced in the 1930s and which would replace or extend the wooden pre-group designs.*

This page, bottom - *An H16, No. 30519, passing Woking in 1953 with a train for Guildford. Much of that coal is likely destined for Tongham gas works. He has about 30 on, but that is no problem for an H16: they often worked into Feltham with 60.*

No sooner had the invasion of Normandy taken place than the Germans started to send over their V-1 'Flying Bombs'. These were launched at London and Southampton, but where they came down was another matter. They might not have been too accurate but collectively they did do a lot of damage and of course they led to a massive increase in the number of air-raid alerts. Mind you, the one I remember most clearly passed my bedroom window one morning going west without any warning. Again, there was some evacuation movement but not on the scale of the earlier ones. No one liked the things but so long as they kept going you were all right and they gave you time to take cover. The V-2 Rockets were another matter altogether. At first the Government tried to keep quiet about them but the public soon got wise to their existence and I can tell you, those things seriously frightened people. My Grandmother, living alone in London, had lived through the blitz and the V-1s - they did not worry her, but one of the first V-2s came down near her home in Cricklewood and that had her down to Havant in double quick time, and believe me she was a tough old lady!

The V2 gave no warning of its arrival and when they landed they did a lot of damage, The Southern got off quite lightly with some damage to Peckham Rye Repair Shops and elsewhere, but at Deptford a block of the Company's flats were hit and eleven people were killed.

Perhaps not of great interest to readers, but for the record the railways were among the largest owners of

Almost exactly what the Southern needed, a modern simple and very capable Class 4 tank engine. No 42080 is seen at Horsham on a test train from Brighton, 4 September 1951. I say 'almost', because Brighton built 41 of these fine engines, they were constructed strictly to LMS drawings and the result was two pages of annoying restrictions as to where they could not work. Mostly, as I remember it, this concerned crossover roads and goods sheds. The BR version addressed these issues and in due course the Southern Region got the BR (80xxx) type and the LMS engines went north.

J B Heyman

property in the country, and as Rule 1 of the Rule Book stated, "All employees must reside at whatever places may be appointed". Many of these were cottages in remote locations but there were also many houses and large blocks of flats in the towns.

During the war the Ministry of Housing took control of the railways' housing and thereafter started to fill up any empty property with non-railway people. They never altered Rule 1 but after the war the railway was no longer able to enforce it and many railwaymen commuted long distances. In pre-war days much of this housing was tied to specific jobs and the Southern rarely promoted a man to a senior post locally. You were expected to move and never mind the domestic problems. Plymouth to Portsmouth and Portsmouth to Dover - that could be the price of promotion for a more senior man.

It is time to look again at locomotives and rolling stock. After the 'Charlies' it was nearly a year before the the Southern built any more locomotives but on the 6th February 1942 the REC placed orders with the Southern for the construction of 105 Stanier 8Fs for the LMS and later, a further 25 for the LNER. These were built in 1943-4: 103 were erected at Brighton, 23 at Eastleigh, and 14 at Ashford. I say erected, rather than built, as I feel sure individual parts were made at other works or even supplied by the LMS.

As the war slowly came to its conclusion the railways began to look to the future and Mr, Bulleid had his drawing office staff hard at it designing all manner of things. A new lightweight passenger locomotive was seen as a definite requirement especially for use in the West of England to replace the ageing Drummond 4-4-0s. Early proposals included designs for 2-6-0 and 2-6-2 engines but, as we all know I am sure, what was built was a scaled down MN 4-6-2, the 'West Country/ Battle of Britain' class. All were more or less identical except that the first 70, 2IC101-170, were 8ft 6ins wide, the later ones 9ft. From 21C164

onwards a 'V'-fronted cab was used and in due course the earlier ones were so altered.

Authority to build the first of these engines went back to "30 passenger engines" with no further details, agreed on the 17th of April 1940. After that Bulleid obtained further authority to build various numbers of engines of a type usually unspecified. He would never have got away with this in Herbert Walker's time and one must query the GM's wisdom in allowing him such latitude.

What the Southern got of course was a locomotive far too large for much of the work it was called upon to do but it had the saving grace of a superb boiler that would burn almost anything and still make steam, and that was very important at the time when they were built as good quality steam coal was virtually non-existent, engines on most duties having to make do with slack and various kinds of briquettes. Even with an experienced fireman the older engines would not steam well on this rubbish but a WC or a 'Merchant' could.

I have briefly mentioned the 4-SUB 'Queen of Shebas'. Up until the appearance of this unit, the standard SR suburban train was a 3-SUB augmented in the business periods by a further 3-SUB and a two-car trailer set. This was seen as an economic answer to the differing traffic needs of the day at the time, but it gave rise to a lot of potentially dangerous propelled shunt moves and in 1939 it was decided that the future lay with four-car units. There was little that could be done in the war years but a start was made in disbanding the two-car trailer units in 1942 and incorporating the best of these vehicles in 3-SUBs, thus making them into 4-SUBs. However it would not be until September 1948 that the last of the trailer sets were eventually withdrawn. The story of the suburban stock post-war is interesting, but far too complicated to go into here; so I will simply say that the outstanding nine 'Queen of Shebas' were completed at the end of 1944 and the beginning of 1945. These trains were followed by a large number of new Bulleid trailer cars that were used to augment many of the existing 3-SUBs.

The result looked rather peculiar but 'needs must' and the plan was that in due course most of the old 3-SUB bodies would be replaced by new ones matching the new trailers. In April1946 there appeared what might be called the typical Bulleid 4-SUB. To simplify construction the front end now became vertical and much use was made of welding and that went hand-in-hand with jig construction. The dreadful 5ft 6in compartment of the 'Queen of Shebas' was replaced by a minimum of 6ft and the comfort of the seating greatly improved. The Southern completed 35 of these units, and BR a further 175, all built at Eastleigh.

Alongside the production of suburban stock, new main line steam stock was also being built. Lynes was still nominally in charge of the C&W Drawing office but much detail was seen to come from Bulleid. First came twenty 3-sets built on the old standard 58ft underframes that had been built prior to the war, putting a stop to their completion (in the meantime many were used as flat wagons). There is not much to be said for these vehicles as they are best described as 'Austerity coaches' and they were certainly no advance on the best Maunsell stock. However just because the war was over did not mean all was back to normal; far from it, and so far as basic materials and indeed everyday household goods were concerned, the late forties and early fifties were in many ways even worse for supplies than the war years. In my opinion Bulleid's greatest achievement was to get built as much as he did in the face of very severe shortages of almost everything a railway needed. In 1947 came the first of what I consider to be the real Bulleid carriages built on a new standard 63ft 5in underframe. The body had the now familiar Bulleid profile with wide windows and really comfortable seats. Mind you, if you have had anything to do

with them in preservation you will know that whilst any two may belong to the same diagram, that is no guarantee that they are identical in anything other than their general appearance, there might well be endless minor variations of thickness of materials etc, as Eastleigh built with whatever it could get hold of. The result though was a fine carriage, better in many ways than a BR Mk 1 but not, it must be admitted, having such a strong underframe..

One might expect that Bulleid would have his hands full, especially as he so frequently got involved in detail but no, he found time to design and patent jointly with Lynes at least two types of entirely new steel wagon underframes, one of which is best described as triangulated.

The inspiration for this work was a weakness in the standard 1923 RCH wagon underframe design with continuous draw-gear which gave rise to bent headstocks, a difficult and expensive member to repair. The official RCH answer to this problem was the 1939 RCH underframe which had additional longitudinal members behind the headstock and non-continuous draw. The Southern used this but it put the weight up and set Bulleid and Lynes thinking. The first new design of underframe they came up was used under a plastic-bodied version of the familiar 'utility van' and might be described as a spine with the wheels carried on a sub-assembly. We will return to this subject in the next part.

On a general note the Southern announced in 1946 its intention to electrify all the remaining non-electrified main lines in Kent, and to work all the remaining lines to the East of the Portsmouth Direct by diesel traction. This sounded good but the Labour Government had won a massive majority in the 1945 General Election and they were intent on nationalizing the nation's railways and where would that take the Southern Railway? We will see in the next part.

You can read that the Billinton moguls were not so suited to passenger work as the Maunsell ones, but try telling that to a Brighton driver! Here is No 32346 passing Shoreham-by-Sea on the daily express from Bristol to Brighton sometime in April 1960 - one may wonder what has happened to the booked Bulleid Pacific? It was not unusual to see one of these engines on this or the similar Bournemouth duty. Another substitute sometimes was a Class 4 tank, which I was told resulted in the longest tank engine working in the country.

Terry Cole's Rolling Stock File No. 29
Ex SECR Coaches on the Isle of Wight

At the end of World War 2 the ex-London, Chatham and Dover stock on the Island was in urgent need of replacement. It was decided that 54ft long ex-South Eastern and Chatham stock currently in use on outer suburban services met the requirements although substantial alterations would need to be made. A pool of vehicles was created using twenty 3-coach 'birdcage' sets built around 1910/11. These sets comprised a Brake Composite, Lavatory Composite and Lavatory Brake Composite. The conversion work (with the exception of three composites) was carried out at Lancing prior to shipment to the Island. Air brake equipment largely salvaged from the LCD coaches was also fitted.

Above - Sixteen 4-compartment Brake Thirds Nos. 4134 – 4149 [Diagram 171] were created from the Brake Compos by removing the birdcage lookouts, (too high for the Island loading gauge), and stripping out three compartments, the space created being used to extend the guards compartment to provide luggage space. Additional double doors were also fitted. Here is No S4145 at Sandown in 1966 unusually marshalled at the south end of the train. This coach was originally SEC No 1122 built in June 1911. It became SR No 3390, was transferred to the IOW in 1949 and withdrawn at the end of steam in January 1967. Fortunately this vehicle has survived, preserved on the IOW steam railway.

Opposite top - Eighteen lavatory Brake Composites had the guard's and luggage area replaced by two additional compartments whilst at the other end of the coach the toilets were stripped out and the space converted into a 'half' compartment. This produced 8½ compartment thirds Nos. 2438 - 2455 to Diagram 40 and seating 83 passengers. No S2447 is seen here at Shanklin. Notice the right angle bend in the handrails and the different roof profile in contrast to the LBSC coach behind. No S2447 was originally SEC 1120, built June 1911. It became SR No 3375, was transferred to the IOW in May 1948 and withdrawn in January 1967 to be cut up later that year.

Bottom - Fifteen Lavatory Composites had the toilets removed and the space incorporated into the adjacent compartments to form a saloon. The resulting composite coaches to Diagrams 376-8 had numbers 6364-6365 and 6368-6380. A further three lav. compos were similarly modified but designated thirds Nos. 2456-8. Although the number is not visible in this view at Shanklin on the last day of services, this is S6375, the last survivor. Built in December 1911 as SEC No 1133 it became SR No 5412 and was transferred to the IOW in April 1949. Withdrawn in January 1967 it escaped cutting up and is preserved at the IOW steam railway. *All photos Terry Cole.*

SOUTHERN RAILWAY PORTSMOUTH LINE CORRIDOR STOCK

4-RES / 4-BUF / 4-COR / 4-GRI / 4-PUL / 4-COR(N) Corridor Units (Part 1)

John Atkinson with contributions from Colin Watts

Electrification to Portsmouth

Following the success of the main line electrification of the Central Section lines, the Southern Railway pressed ahead with plans to extend the system on both the main routes to Portsmouth. These schemes came to fruition as follows:

1. The Portsmouth No. 1 Electrification in July 1937 covering the lines from Hampton Court Jct. to Portsmouth Harbour via Woking and Guildford also the lines from Woking to Alton and from Weybridge to Staines.

2. The Portsmouth No. 2 Electrification in July 1938 covering the lines from Dorking North to Havant, Three Bridges to Horsham, West Worthing to Ford and the branches to Littlehampton and Bognor Regis.

Portsmouth No.1 Electrification Scheme

The Portsmouth No. 1 scheme was estimated to cost about £3,000,000, covered 242 track miles and involved quite a number of other works to improve capacity and facilities. Major works (which commenced from October 1935) included the rebuilding of stations at Woking and Havant to provide platforms 820' in length in order to accommodate 12-car electric trains. Other stations also had platforms extended to this length, these being Guildford, Haslemere and both Portsmouth stations at Southsea (High Level and Harbour).

Track layouts were altered at Haslemere (the Up line was made available to Down trains when required), Havant (new platforms were located outside of new centre

Through lines) and the installation of a Down Relief line between Fratton and Portsmouth & Southsea. There were also numerous smaller changes at other stations.

To accommodate the new rolling stock, new carriage sheds were built at Wimbledon Park, whilst other sheds there were also enlarged, and at Farnham (5 roads) and Fratton (4 roads) all these sheds being capable of holding 12 coach trains except those at Fratton which only took 8 coaches. Carriage washing machines were also installed at Wimbledon and Fratton.

Resignalling work was also extensive with colour light signals being installed between Woking and Guildford (from 27th June 1937), at Haslemere (from 18th July 1937), from Havant to Farlington Jct. (from 27th June 1937) and between Portsmouth & Southsea and Portsmouth Harbour (from 20th June 1937). Other sections were split with new intermediate signals installed (both semaphore and colour light).

Power was supplied for this extension taken from the CEGB at both Portsmouth and Woking, with electrical control rooms located at both Woking (controlling 19 substations) and Havant (controlling 7 substations). All the new substations followed the now standard pattern of unmanned rectifier substations; Guildford's rotary converter being replaced. The capacity of the Durnsford Road Power Station was also increased to cope with extra demand in the suburban area.

Trial running of electric trains commenced as far as Woking from 1st November 1936, and between Weybridge and Virginia Water from 30th November, with

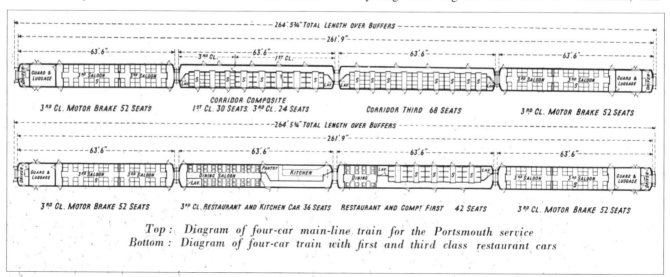

Top: Diagram of four-car main-line train for the Portsmouth service
Bottom: Diagram of four-car train with first and third class restaurant cars

the full service on this section starting from 3rd January 1937, with some electric trains also reaching Guildford and Farnham from this date. Through working to Portsmouth began on 11th April 1937 and the full service was inaugurated from 4th July 1937.

Like the previous main line extensions, the new train service was generous with two stopping trains each hour leaving Waterloo and running fast to Surbiton then calling at all stations, splitting at Woking into Portsmouth and Alton portions. Fast trains (most with restaurant cars) ran each hour calling only at Guildford, Haslemere and Portsmouth & Southsea. The Weybridge to Staines section was served half hourly by portions off the Waterloo to Windsor trains which divided at Staines. The usual business extra services operated during the rush hours, when the Weybridge - Staines line also had through services via Surbiton and the Alton line had some complete trains formed with the corridor stock.

Portsmouth No. 2 Electrification Scheme

Work on the Portsmouth No. 2 electrification scheme commenced before the completion of the Portsmouth No.1 electrification scheme. Estimated to cost about £2,750,000 it covered 165 track miles.

As part of this scheme a new station was provided at Horsham (with two 820' island platforms) whilst platforms were extended at Sutton, Dorking North, Pulborough, Arundel, Littlehampton, Barnham, Bognor Regis and Chichester. Platform extensions also took place at Shoreham-by-Sea and Worthing Central with the coastal Halts being lengthened to mostly accommodate 6-car trains as well as provision being made for them to be staffed. Carriage sheds were provided at Littlehampton (3 roads) and Streatham Hill (8 roads, four for 12 coaches, the remainder for 8 coaches). Littlehampton also had a carriage washer installed. Extra electrified sidings were provided at New Cross Gate, Streatham Hill, Littlehampton, Barnham and Bognor Regis. A centre reversing siding was provided at West Worthing to allow reversal of local trains from Brighton clear of the running lines, and a Down Bay was provided at Chichester.

Signalling alterations were less extensive than the Portsmouth No.1 electrification scheme but colour light signals were installed controlled by new signalboxes at Dorking North (from 15th May 1938) and Horsham (from 24th April 1938); new boxes were also built at Arundel and Bognor.

Power for the new scheme was taken from three existing CEGB locations at Portsmouth, Leatherhead and Fishersgate; there were 20 rectifier substations all supervised by a much extended control room at Havant. Existing rotary converter equipment was replaced at Leatherhead and Dorking with the recovered equipment being reused to uprate the power supply in the London area. Trial running of electric stock began from 3rd April 1938 and the full service was introduced from 3rd July 1938. The first through electric train reached Portsmouth on 11th April 1938, whilst the first public trains ran on 19th May 1938

when an 8 COR was used as a relief train to 11.50am and 3.50pm from Waterloo and the 1.40pm and 7.57pm from Portsmouth Harbour.

As customary, the new services were an improvement of existing frequencies with regular interval interconnecting services. An hourly fast train ran from Victoria (most with buffet cars) calling at Sutton, Dorking North, Horsham, Pulborough, Arundel and Barnham where they divided for Portsmouth Harbour and Bognor, the Portsmouth portion calling at Chichester, Havant and Portsmouth & Southsea. However, a few trains ran via Three Bridges to Horsham calling at East Croydon, Redhill and Three Bridges, then forward as those via Sutton.

The existing Victoria to West Worthing fast trains were extended to Littlehampton. A half hourly stopping train ran from Three Bridges via Horsham to Littlehampton, alternate trains continuing to Bognor, whilst a shuttle from Arundel to Littlehampton connected out of the fast Victoria via Sutton trains.

Two trains each hour from Waterloo to Dorking were extended, one to Holmwood, the other to Horsham. Six trains each hour left Brighton westwards, ½ hourly all stations to West Worthing, ½ hourly to Portsmouth calling at Hove, Shoreham, Worthing, one then all stations to Portsmouth Harbour the other a semi-fast stopping only at Barnham, Chichester, Fratton and Portsmouth & Southsea, this train having a connection from Chichester calling at all stations to Portsmouth & Southsea.

The final pair from Brighton, again at ½ hourly intervals consisted of a further West Worthing local and a Brighton to Bognor via Littlehampton local. The usual business enhancements were also provided, with some trains running to London Bridge which was not served in slack hours.

Portsmouth Electrification Rolling Stock

The additional rolling stock for the stopping services was in the form of further 2 BIL stock, units 2011 - 2048 being provided for the Portsmouth No. 1 electrification scheme, whilst 2049 - 2116 followed for the Portsmouth No. 2 electrification scheme and further 2-NOL units 1883 - 1890 were authorised for the No. 1 scheme to cover the Staines – Weybridge requirements. Some of the trains between Worthing and Littlehampton were covered by the existing Brighton line 6 coach units, both 6-PUL and 6-PAN units being used, and a few 4-LAV units now ventured to Bognor along the coast.

For the express workings, three new types of unit were constructed at Eastleigh works on frames built at Lancing, though some vehicles were constructed by Metro-Cammell and B.R.C.W. These were introduced in two batches, the first in 1937 for the Portsmouth No. 1 electrification scheme being nineteen four-car corridor units with restaurant cars (4-RES) and twenty nine four-car corridor units (4-COR). The second batch in 1938 comprised thirteen four-car corridor units with buffet car (4-BUF) and a further twenty-six 4-COR sets, these being intended for use on the lines electrified under the

Portsmouth No.2 electrification scheme. However, some of these units also saw use on the Brighton line from the outset.

Unit Ordering

The following table shows details of the vehicles ordered for the COR/RES/BUF units:

SR Official view of a Waterloo - Portsmouth service with what was referred to as, "...vestibule connection through driver's compartment", the date is either 6 May 1937 or 20 June 1937. The sweeping nature of the 'Portsmouth Direct' will be seen with the location believed to be south of Petersfield.

SOUTHERN RAILWAY PORTSMOUTH LINE CORRIDOR STOCK

Vehicle Nos.	Type	Weight		Seating			Builder	Date	Diag.	Elect. Code
		Tons	Cwt	1st	U	2nd				
10055-10109	TTK	32	13	-	-	52	Eastleigh	1937/8	2009	BB
11081-11254	MBT	46	10	-	-	68	Eastleigh	1937/8	2114	A (Even) A - 1A (Odd)
11791-11858	TCK	32	11	30	-	24	Eastleigh	1937/8	2309	BA
12232-12250	TFK	33	0	42	-	-	Met. Cammell	1937	2505	BD
12518-12530	Buffet	37	2	-	26	-	Eastleigh	1938	2601	BE
12601-12619	Dining	35	7	-	36	-	B.R.C.W.	1937	2571	BC

Orders were placed for these vehicles as follows:

(Note, only details for vehicles built by the SR are shown, separate contracts were let for the contractor built trailers in the 4 RES units).

1937 order (dated 14th May 1936)

Unit type	Vehicle type	Underframe HO No.	Bodywork order No.
4 RES	MBT	6173	924
4 COR	MBT	6173	924
	TCK	6240	925
	TTK	6240	926

1938 order (dated 6th November 1936)

Unit type	Vehicle type	Underframe HO No.	Bodywork order No.
4-BUF	MBT	6839	951
	TCK	6840	951
	Buffet	6840?	951
4-COR	MBT	6839	950
	TCK	6840	950
	TTK	6840	950

Two further HO numbers were issued to cover 'finishing work' at Eastleigh on the coaches delivered from contractors, these, dated 9th June 1936, being HO 931 for diner firsts 12232 - 12250 and HO 932 for kitchen diner thirds 12601 - 12619.

Each vehicle was 66' 3" long over buffers, 63' 6" over body with bogie centres at 44' 6" and were slightly wider than the standard width (9' 3") at 9' 4½". All units were 264' 6" long. Trailer bogies were 8' 0" wheelbase leaf sprung and weighed 5¾ tons whilst motor bogies were 9' 0" wheelbase and weighed 15 tons 17cwt complete with motors; these were to an improved 'equalising beam' type as fitted to the 6-PAN units.

Motor coaches had only one power bogie (at the driving end) fitted with EE 163 motors, these being to an improved design with extra ribbing on the motor case to improve heat dissipation and were nominally rated at 250hp, though often quoted as 225hp as with the earlier ones in the 6-car sets. This resulted in the 'Portsmouth' stock having a lower power-to-weight ratio than the earlier 6-car sets.

Anecdotal evidence suggests that the Southern Railway's Chief Mechanical Engineer Richard Maunsell may have sought to equip each motor coach with two power bogies but was overridden by a cost-conscious General Manager (Herbert Walker).

During the war, no less than twenty-five coaches were lost to enemy action and were replaced by newly built replacements to the original designs in 1945/6, though three dining cars were replaced as TTKs (nos. 10110 – 10112), two TFKs were replaced as TCKs (nos. 11859/60) and a damaged TFK (no. 12232) rebuilt as TCK 11861. Three of the 4 RES units were thus replaced as 4-COR units. These replacement coaches were ordered as follows:

Underframes for MBT vehicles HO 5734, for trailer vehicles HO 5736.
Bodywork numbers were MBT 3075, TTK 3078 and TCK 3079.

The replacement motor brake thirds were built at Eastleigh, and the trailers at Lancing. However, there is some doubt as

Portsmouth Units into Service

Units delivered for the Portsmouth No. 1 electrification scheme were similarly equipped on cab ends to the PUL/PAN/BEL sets with only a control jumper at high level under the offside cab window, with low level air pipes. However, early in their lives a further power jumper was provided under the window on the driver's side, this being done to facilitate coupling-up once the units began working on the Portsmouth No. 2 electrification scheme where regular splitting /joining of units took place at Barnham. The 4 BUF and second batch of 4=COR units were equipped with these from new. These units could run in multiple with the 6 car units.

Routine maintenance was undertaken at both Fratton and Wimbledon Park depots, with some also being dealt with at Lovers Walk, Brighton and Streatham Hill. Body overhauls were undertaken at Lancing until this works closed in 1963 when Eastleigh took over. Programmed electrical overhauls and bogie exchanges were done at Peckham Rye and occasionally at Slade Green; Selhurst taking over when Peckham Rye closed in 1963.

Third Class became Second Class from June 1956 and the vehicles were all reclassified at this time, a Motor Brake Third (MBT) becoming a Motor Brake Second (MBS).

As built, all MBTs were fitted with a motor generator and emergency batteries. However, following experience with the Kent Coast 4-CEP/BEP units, the 'Portsmouth' stock was modified from 1960 and one MBS had the MG removed; the other the emergency batteries reducing their overall weight. As a result, when electrical codes were allocated to these vehicles (around 1963) the MBSs were subdivided as type A or type A-1A, normally with even numbered vehicles becoming type A and odd numbers becoming type A-1A, though due to earlier reforms this did not apply in every case.

The extension of electrification into Kent allowed the units to expand their range on special workings, the first being a football special to Margate worked by 8-COR on 31st October 1959, though regular workings in this area were not scheduled. However regular special trains had worked at weekends between Portsmouth and Gillingham for naval requirements since before the war and 4-COR stock was used on some of these alongside 2-HAL units.

From March 1962 units began to be fitted with roller blind headcodes replacing the former stencil arrangement, this followed one cab of unit 3108 being fitted with this equipment in 1958 as an experiment. They also received air horns, starting bells and loudaphone equipment

Above - Taken at Selhurst I June 1937, the interior of the kitchen within the composite cars.

Right - Advertisement for the new service.

at this time and the heating in the cabs and guard's vans was uprated. The 4-COR and 4-RES units were done first, the 4 BUFs being completed about late 1964.

Motorbogies were of the equalising beam type, (trailer bogies were standard leaf sprung) and a number of the motorbogies began to be replaced with leaf sprung bogies from about 1969 though many units were withdrawn still in original condition.

In January 1964, a review of the Southern Region catering requirements led to the first large scale alteration of the units' duties, with the displacement of the 4-BUF units off the Victoria - Bognor route by 4-BEP units; the displaced 4-BUFs moving to the Waterloo - Portsmouth route, though a number still remained on the Central section for business trains.

Displaced 4-RES units had their restaurant cars withdrawn (except three converted to Griddle cars) and were reformed with 6-PUL/PAN trailers to create 4-PUL and 4-COR (N) units for use on Central Division services, mostly Victoria - Littlehampton during the transition from 6-PUL/PAN to new 4-CIG/BIG stock (units then being based at Lovers Walk depot).

Once all the 4-CIG/BIG fleet was delivered to the Central section, these 4-PUL and 4-COR (N) units were further reformed as standard 4 COR units.

A further batch of 4-CIG/BIG stock was ordered for the Waterloo - Portsmouth route and began to be delivered in 1970, the first entering traffic in June 1970 with the bulk displacing 4-COR/BUF/GRI units from October 1970 (a few lasted a short while longer). These new units were intended to be in use in time for the new timetable from 4th May 1970 when a ½ hourly fast service was introduced, but late delivery meant the 4-COR/BUF units had to be used instead, this more intensive use taking its toll with an increase in units suffering from hot axle-boxes and some other problems. Once the new units were in service, most of the 4-BUF units were withdrawn and displaced 4-COR units relegated to slow trains on the Portsmouth line and used to replace further 2-BIL/HAL units on the Waterloo - Reading and 'Coastway' services between Portsmouth and Ore.

Into Withdrawal

The first undamaged 4-COR units were withdrawn in

Approaching Woking from the Guildford line on 16 September 1946. The roofboard reads, Waterloo - Portsmouth - Isle of Wight.

B A Butt

September 1971 and main-line duties on the Brighton line ceased in October 1971; the last with catering facilities having gone in May 1971.

Further deliveries of new 4-VEP and 4-CIG units displaced the units from the Reading line from 3rd January 1972.

Units last worked on the West Coastway in August 1972 (though odd later trips did occur) and the final normal working by a 4-COR was on 30th September 1972, with a farewell railtour running 9th December 1972 using units 3116 /3123 /3142 retained specially after the others were withdrawn.

Withdrawn units were stored around the system and all worked to Selhurst for electrical stripping prior to sale and disposal to scrap dealers. During 1972 the 4-COR units were allocated Class No. 404/2 under the BR TOPS system though no unit ever carried it. Class 404/1 was intended for 4-BUF/GRI units but all had been withdrawn by this stage.

A number of vehicles had their bodywork scrapped and the underframes used as the basis of long-welded-rail carrying bogie flat wagons. These vehicles had their bodies removed at Hoo Jct. and were fitted out for their new roles at Stewarts Lane.

BR Liveries

Dates for SR livery changes are sought including painting into BR green livery. Certainly early units appeared in the current SR green with yellow and black lining. However, the yellow subsequently appeared to have been changed for orange possibly at the time units were still being constructed. With Richard Maunsell's retirement, his post was filled by Oliver Bulleid who introduced the buffet cars in the thirteen BUF units in a very different livery to the rest of the units; this being covered in the section on the 4-BUF units.

The 4-RES units 3054 to 3072, 4-PUL units 3054 to 3059 and 4-COR(N) units 3065 to 3071 never received blue livery (or green with full yellow ends) and are therefore not included in this table of liveries. Equally painting dates from SR to BR(S) are currently unknown for all units. Many individual dates for the application of small yellow warning panels on BR-green liveries are currently unknown (most of the dates come from Eastleigh records) although most probably date from 1964-on when there was a big push to add them to BR(S) units.

SOUTHERN RAILWAY PORTSMOUTH LINE CORRIDOR STOCK

Unit	BR(S) Green dates		BR Corporate blue livery dates		Notes
	Yellow warning panels 4 BUF	**Full yellow ends**	**Yellow warning panels**	**Full yellow ends**	
4-BUF					
3072	N/K	No	No	27-Mar-68	
3073	22-Mar-66	No	No	2-May-69	
3074	N/K	No	No	8-Nov-67	
3075	20-Dec-65	No	No	9-Aug-68	
3076	26-Apr-65	No	No	12-Aug-69	
3077	N/K	No	No	12-Nov-67	
3078	N/K	No	c.Jan-67	28-May-69	
3079	N/K	Withdrawn			
3080	10-Jun-66	No	No	24-Mar-69	
3081	4-Nov-65	No	No	13-Nov-68	
3082	11-Jun-64	No	No	24-Feb-69	
3083	N/K	No	No	By Aug 68	
3084	21-Jun-65	No	No	c.Jan-68	
3085	1-Mar-65	No	No	24-Jun-68	
4-GRI					
3086	23-Sep-66	No	No	26-Sep-69	
3087	N/K	No	No	31-Mar-67	
3088	17-Jan-67	No	No	30-Jan-69	
4-COR					
3101	4-Nov-65	No	No	15-May-68	
3102	N/K	No	No	18-Nov-68	
3103	N/K	No	4-Jan-67	9-Jun-70	*Last blue liveried unit with small yellow warning panel*
3104	21-Apr-65	No	No	Jul-67	
3105	30-Apr-66	No	No	9-Oct-67	
3106	4-Jan-67	No	No	30-Jun-69	
3107	Apr-64	No	No	By Oct-69	
3108	N/K	No	27-Jan-67	24-Feb-69	
3109	N/K	No	No	26-May-67	
3110	N/K	No	27-Sep-66	17-Jun-69	
3111	N/K	Aug-64	No	26-Aug-70	
3112	N/K	No	No	24-Jun-69	
3113	N/K	No	No	29-Aug-67	
3114	N/K	No	21-Jan-67	11-Mar-70	
3115	Feb-64	No	No	12-Sep-69	
3116	N/K	By Aug-64	No	27-Nov-70	*Last unit in green with full yellow ends.*
3117	25-Sep-65	No	No	8-May-68	
3118	11-Nov-66	No	No	25-Feb-70	
3119	29-Mar-66	No	No	17-Sep-68	
3120	Mar-64	No	No	27-Aug-68	
3121	N/K	No	14.Sep-66	4-May-69	
3122	Dec-63	No	No	5-Jun-67	
3123	13-May-65	31-May-67	No	13-Oct-70	
3124	N/K	No	12-Jun-66	25-Jul-68	

3125	N/K	No	No	22-Feb-67
3126	9-May-66	No	No	27-Aug-68
3127	N/K	No	No	10-May-67
3128	6-Jun-66	No	No	c.Jan-69
3129	2-Aug-65	No	No	21-Nov-67
3130	28-Jan-66	No	No	8-Oct-68
3131	30-Apr-65	14-Apr-67	No	30-Oct-70
3132	N/K	No	20-Dec-66	29-Jan-69
3133	N/K	No	2-Nov-66	24-Apr-70
3134	4-May-66	No	c.Dec-66	4-Sep-68
3135	N/K	No	No	14-Jun-67
3136	N/K	No	No	28-Dec-67
3137	Apr-64	No	No	c.Jun-67
3138	24-Nov-65	No	No	3-Jul-68
3139	N/K	No	No	14-Jun-68
3140	N/K	No	No	10-Mar-67
3141	5-Dec-66	No	No	13-Jan-70
3142	1-Apr-65	18-May-67	No	13-Jul-70
3143	N/K	No	No	9-May-68
3144	17-Aug-65	No	No	29-Feb-68
3145	7-Jul-65	No	No	27-Feb-68
3146	18-Nov-66	No	No	14-Apr-69
3147	N/K	No	1-Nov-66	2-Feb-70
3148	7-Dec-65	No	No	3-Dec-68
3149	N/K	c.24-Mar-67	No	Nov-69
3150	26-Jan-67	No	No	Aug-69
3151	N/K	No	No	By Oct-69
3152	N/K	No	18-Aug-66	30-Sep-69
3153	N/K	No	No	16-Jun-67
3154	N/K	No	No	8-Nov-67
3155	23-Dec-66	No	No	4-Aug-69
3156	12-Aug-66	No	No	12-Mar-68
3157	4-Nov-65	No	No	1-Apr-68
3158	19-Dec-66	No	No	29-May-69
3159	N/K	No	No	28-Feb-69
3160	N/K	No	No	30-Apr-68
3161	N/K	No	No	30-Jul-69
3162	N/K	No	No	9-Apr-69
3163	N/K	No	No	28-Mar-69
3164	N/K	No	No	10-Jan-69
3165	N/K	No	No	6-Nov-68
3166	N/K	No	No	6-Nov-68
3167	N/K	No	No	7-May-69
3168	N/K	No	No	12-May-69

SOUTHERN RAILWAY PORTSMOUTH LINE CORRIDOR STOCK

4 RES Units 3054 - 3072

Numbered 3054 – 3072, the nineteen 4-RES units were delivered in 1937 between April and July when they were introduced into service. These units comprised two motor brake thirds, a dining first and a kitchen third. All the third class accommodation was subsequently reclassified as second. The motor coaches were built at Eastleigh works on Lancing frames, the dining firsts were built by Metro-Cammell and the kitchen thirds by BRCW.

Overall length of the 4-RES units was 264' 6" and the weight was 161 tons 7cwt. They seated 30 first and 104 third, with a further 12 first and 36 third in the dining areas.

Motor Coach Third

These motor coaches weighed 46½ tons and were to diagram No. 2114. Originally designated as motor brake thirds these consisted of a motorman's compartment accessed by inward opening doors on each side of the coach. Each unit had a corridor connection at the front to enable passengers from the adjacent unit access to the restaurant car. As a consequence the motorman's driving position could be internally closed off from the passenger gangway by a swing door.

The headcode frame was located on the offside of the corridor connection giving the units a rather one-eyed appearance, which in view of their association with routes to Portsmouth led to the nickname of 'Nelsons' for all the 4-COR, 4-BUF and 4-RES stock.

Behind the driving cab was the guard's brake. This was 10' 7" long and had a pair of outward opening doors to each side of the coach; these doors being located at the cab end of the van. From the guard's brake there was a door opening forwards into the driving cab and another into the passenger vestibule to enable through passenger access between coupled units; both these doors being on the offside of the van when the driving cab was leading.

Then came an entrance vestibule with outward opening doors each side of the coach and a central internal sliding door leading into a six-and-a-half bay saloon with seating for 52, seating being two aside each side of the central gangway. There was a partition at the centre of the saloon with sliding door dividing it into 3 and 3½ bays and finally another entrance vestibule and with central sliding door access. The odd half-bay in the saloon was adjacent to the vestibule at the guard's end of the coach. Smoking was permitted in this larger saloon.

Large sidelight windows topped by a two-piece sliding ventilator were provided in the passenger saloon; that at the coupe end being smaller than the remainder.

Two 250hp English Electric 163 motors were fitted to the motor bogie which was located beneath the guard's brake. The unit's electrical equipment was also by English Electric. These units were able to be coupled to the earlier 6-PUL, 6-PAN, 6-CITY and 5-BEL units but were not compatible with the 2-BIL, 2-HAL, 2-NOL, 4-LAV and suburban units.

Dining First

The dining firsts consisted of a lavatory, five first-class compartments (each seating six joined by a side corridor), another lavatory and a dining saloon with twelve first-class seats and an entrance vestibule. Each compartment had an access door whilst there were three doors located on the corridor side opposite the partition of the first /second, the sliding door of the third and the partition of the fourth/fifth compartments. Beyond the intermediate lavatory a full-width partition (with sliding door) gave access to the two-bay dining saloon. This saloon had tables with loose chairs arranged with two aside seats on the compartment side and a single seat on the corridor side. As a consequence the central gangway was off-centre (towards the same side as the corridor). A further sliding door gave access to the entrance vestibule at the end of the coach, which had access doors on each side.

The dining saloon area had large sidelight windows with sliding ventilators above, these contrasting with ¼ light /droplight arrangement of the compartment section on the non-corridor side of the coach. Smoking was permitted in all the compartments except that adjacent to the centre lavatory.

The dining first coaches weighed 33 tons and were marshalled with the compartment end against the motor coach. They were built to diagram No. 2505 by Metro-Cammell at Washwood Heath.

Kitchen Third

The kitchen third had a pantry, kitchen and servery as well as a five-bay dining saloon with 36 seats, a lavatory and an entrance vestibule. The dining saloon featured tables with loose chairs, the central gangway allowing two aside seating each side so there were four chairs at each table. The bay at the vestibule end had the lavatory compartment to one side with a single table for four opposite. Large sidelight windows were again fitted.

The kitchen equipment was all-electric with boilers and ovens using line voltage whilst grills, hotplates and refrigerators operated at 220 volts supplied by a dynamotor mounted below the underframe. This coach weighed 35 tons 7cwt and was to diagram No. 2571 being constructed by BRCW at Saltley. It was marshalled with the kitchen end at the centre of the unit.

4 RES in service

The units were put to work as intended on the Waterloo - Portsmouth via Guildford route from 1937, a few 4-RES MBTs being run-in coupled to 4-COR trailers prior to the commencement of the full electric service. Three units were withdrawn during the war after enemy action damage and another was converted to 4-BUF in 1956. The remaining fifteen units continued in service until January 1964, although three units had their restaurant cars converted to griddle cars in 1962. From about 1963, electrical codes were allocated to each vehicle, these are shown below.

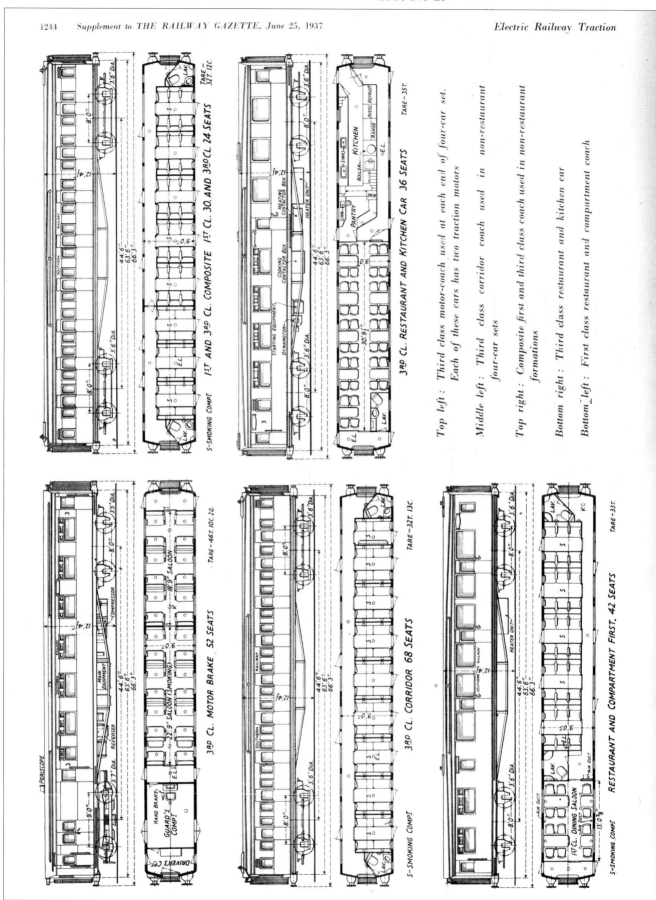

From 4th January 1964, a stock reshuffle brought nine 4-BUF units to the Waterloo - Portsmouth route to replace the surviving 4-RES units, although the three griddle car units, now reclassified 4-GRI, remained on this route. The twelve remaining 4-RES units were sent for short-term storage (three at Ford, three at Peckham Rye and six at Haywards Heath) before working to Lovers Walk where their kitchen cars were removed and withdrawn; being replaced by a former 6-PUL Pullman car (5 units) or a former 6-PAN trailer second (7 units). These units were then reclassified as 4-PUL or 4-COR(N) and were used on Victoria - Littlehampton services. They only had short lives in this form and from 1965 they were further reformed to standard 4-COR formations using further ex 6 PUL and 6-PAN vehicles, and were reclassified as 4-COR and renumbered as units 3159 - 3168. The withdrawn kitchen cars were worked to Strawberry Hill where their motor generator sets were recovered for subsequent use in new 4-BIG buffet cars, prior to disposal.

4 RES Demise and Withdrawal

Following withdrawal from 25th January 1964 at Lovers Walk, all the kitchen cars were worked to Strawberry Hill for stripping and the motor generator sets were required for the new buffet cars being built for 4-BIG units. They were then stored; some at Micheldever (12603/07/11/12/14/18), the others remaining at Strawberry Hill (12601/04/08/10/16/19).

All were subsequently moved to Newhaven during July and August 1964 for scrapping, but as breaking was about to cease there the Micheldever train was later moved to Hassocks during November 1964. Final disposal to South Wales scrap dealers was from Micheldever. The body of 12607 was broken-up (probably also at Newhaven) although the underframe returned to Micheldever.

Portsmouth Electric stock at Waterloo in June 1938.

R F Roberts

Unit no. *Diag no.*	MBT *2114*	TRT *2571*	TFK *2505*	MBT *2114*	Reclassified as	See unit	Notes
Code	A-1A	BC	BD	A			
3054	11139 11177	12619 Clara	12248	11140	4-PUL	3054	
3055	11142	12610 Gwladys	12246	11141	4-PUL	3055	
3056	11143 12605	12609	12245 11828 [1] 11245	11144	4-GRI	3086	[1] *Diagram 2309, Code BA (4-COR TCK).*
3057	11145	12611 Elinor	12247	11146	4-PUL	3057	
3058	11147	12606	12234	11148	Withdrawn		*War damage*
3059	11149	12612 Enid	12250 12242	11172	4-PUL	3059	
3060	11151	12615	12249	11152	Withdrawn		*War damage*
3061	11153	12607 Ethel	12233	11154	4-PUL	3056	
3062	11155	12616 10034	12235	11156	4-COR(N)	3065	
3063	11157	12617	12232	11158	Withdrawn		*War damage*
3064	11159	12601 10045	12236	11160	4-COR(N)	3066	
3065	11161 11202	12605 12602	12237	11163	4-GRI	3087	
3066	11163	12604 10033	12238	11164	4-COR(N)	3066	
3067	11165	12608 10046	12239	11166	4-COR(N)	3067	
3068	11167	12602 12609	12240	11168	4-GRI	3088	
3069	11169	12603 12602 12603 10042	12241	11170	4-COR(N)	3069	
3070	11171	12614 10041	12242 12250	11172 11229	4-COR(N)	3070	
3071	11173	12618 10044	12243	11174 11175 11174	4-COR(N)	3071	
3072	11175	12613	12244	11176	4-BUF		*See 4 BUF notes*

Individual Unit Notes 3054 - 3072

3054	MBT 11139 exchanged with 11177 (ex 3130) Dec-45 after war damage repairs, *(details, date and location unknown)*. TRS 12619 withdrawn 25-Jan-64 and to Strawberry Hill for stripping and scrapped at Newhaven Aug-64. 12619 replaced by Pullman car Clara (ex 3020) and unit reclassified as 4-PUL.
3055	TRS 12610 withdrawn 25-Jan-64 and to Strawberry Hill for stripping and scrapped at Newhaven Aug-64. 12610 replaced by Pullman car Gwladys (ex 3017) and unit reclassified as 4-PUL.
3056	TRS 12609 to Eastleigh Apr-61 and extensively modified as a prototype Griddle Car and to 3068 when released Jan-62. Remainder of unit stored out of use as three-car at Gatwick from 11-May-61, although used in traffic as a six-car train with similarly reduced 3068 from Oct-61. TFK 12245 slightly damaged c.Jan-62 and replaced by TCK 11828 (ex 3138), unit still running as 3-car coupled to 3138 (now also a three-car). Griddle 12605 (ex 3065) completed Nov-62 and TCK 11828 returned to 3138 and replaced by 'own' 12245 (ex repairs); unit back to traffic as 4-RES. Unit reclassified as 4-GRI from 4-Jan-64 and renumbered 3086.

3057	TRS 12611 withdrawn 25-Jan-64 and after stripping at Strawberry Hill, to Micheldever for store and scrapped by G Cohen Ltd, Morriston c.Aug-66. 12611 replaced by Pullman car Elinor (ex 3004) and unit reclassified as 4-PUL.
3058	Unit damaged by fire due to enemy action at Hampton Court 8-Dec-40 and withdrawn 25-Dec-40 and TFK 12234 and TRT 12606 both withdrawn and bodies scrapped. Both MBTs damaged but repaired by Sep-41 and 11147 to 3116, 11148 to 3073 and unit deleted. Underframe of TRT 12606 used as basis of Viaduct Inspection vehicle DS3188 from 11-50. Underframe of TFK 12234 used as basis of ship's gangway carrying vehicle 080335 at Southampton Docks from May-54.
3059	Unit damaged by fire due to enemy action at Hampton Court 8-Dec-40. MBT 11150 to 3116 from May-41. TFK 12250 to 3070. Replaced by 11172 and 12242 (both ex 3070). TRS 12612 withdrawn 25-Jan-64 and after stripping at Strawberry Hill, to Micheldever for store and scrapped by G Cohen Ltd, Morriston c.Aug-66. 12612 replaced by Pullman car Enid (ex 3014) and unit reclassified as 4-PUL.
3060	Unit destroyed by enemy incendiaries at Portsmouth Harbour 10-Jan-41 and all coaches withdrawn 26-Mar-41 when remains scrapped. The underframes of 11152 and 12249 were salvaged and taken to Lancing but later cut-up there. Both MBTs replaced by new construction Oct-46, 11151 and 11152 both to 'new' unit 3157.
3061	TRS 12607 withdrawn 25-Jan-64 and after stripping at Strawberry Hill, bodywork scrapped by Aug-65 (*probably at Newhaven?*) and underframe stored for possible departmental use at Micheldever though not so used, (*eventual disposal unknown, coach deleted from records 12-Jul-68, possibly cut-up at Micheldever or to Bird Group, Long Marston?*). Replaced by Pullman car Ethel (ex 3018) and unit reclassified as 4-PUL and renumbered 3056.
3062	TRS 12616 withdrawn 25-Jan-64 and stripped at Strawberry Hill and scrapped at Newhaven Aug-64. 12616 replaced by 6 PAN TSK 10034 (ex 3027) and unit reclassified as 4-COR(N) and renumbered 3065.
3063	Unit badly damaged by V1 blast at Wimbledon Park 29-June-44 and deleted 5-Aug-44. MBT 11157 and body of TRT 12617 scrapped, MBT 11158 repaired Jan-46 also TFK 12232 rebuilt as composite and renumbered 11861 May-45, both these vehicles to 'new' unit 3158. MBT 11157 replaced by new construction Sep-46 and to unit 3144. Underframe of TRT 12617 used as basis of Viaduct Inspection vehicle DS3187 from Nov-50.
3064	TRS 12601 withdrawn 25-Jan-64 and stripped at Strawberry Hill and scrapped at Newhaven Aug-64. Replaced by 6 PAN TSK 10045 (ex 3033) from 19-Jan-64 and unit reclassified as 4-COR(N) and renumbered 3068.
3065	Unit new to traffic 9-Jun-37. MBT 11161 damaged in collision with 3142 at Wimbledon Park Jan-45 and to 3142 after repairs at Eastleigh. Replaced by 11202 (ex 3142). TRS 12605 to Eastleigh about Jun-61 and extensively modified as Griddle Car and to 3056 when released Nov-62. 12605 replaced by similarly modified 12602 (ex 3068 via 3069) Apr-62. Unit reclassified as 4-GRI from 4-Jan-64 and renumbered 3087.
3066	TRS 12604 withdrawn 25-Jan-64 and stripped at Strawberry Hill and scrapped at Newhaven Aug-64. Replaced by 6-PAN TSK 10033 (ex 3027) and unit reclassified as 4-COR(N).
3067	TRS 12608 withdrawn 25-Jan-64 and stripped at Strawberry Hill and scrapped at Newhaven Aug-64. Replaced by 6-PAN TSK 10046 (ex 3033) and unit reclassified as 4-COR(N).
3068	Unit to Lancing for overhaul about May-61 and TRS 12602 removed and to Eastleigh and extensively modified as Griddle Car and to 3069 briefly when released c.Feb-62 though then to intended unit 3065 Apr-62. Remaining three cars of 3068 stored at Gatwick from 23-Jul-61, though used briefly in traffic with similarly reduced 3056 in Oct-61. 12602 replaced by similarly modified 12609 (ex 3056) from Jan-62. Unit reclassified as 4-GRI from 4-Jan-64 and renumbered 3088.
3069	TRS 12603 temporarily replaced by newly converted Griddle car 12602 (ex 3068) from c.Feb-62 until Apr-62 when 12602 to intended unit 3065 and 12603 back to formation. TRS 12603 withdrawn 25-Jan-64 and after stripping at Strawberry Hill, stored at Micheldever before moving to Newhaven Aug-64 and taken to Hassocks by Nov-64. Coach then moved to Andover but spent a period back at Micheldever c.Aug-65 before returning to Andover by Jul-66. Moved to Salisbury 21-Jul-66 and taken for scrapping to G Cohen Ltd, Morriston from there 28-Jul-66. 12603 replaced by 6-PAN TSK 10042 (ex 3031) and unit reclassified as 4-COR(N).
3070	MBT 11171 and TRT 12614 both damaged in buffer stop collision at Waterloo 26-Aug-39. Unit damaged by fire due to enemy action at Hampton Court 8-Dec-40 and MBT 11172 and TFK 12242 both to 3059 after repairs. Replaced by MBT 11229 (ex 3073) and TFK 12250 (ex 3059). TRS 12614 withdrawn 25-Jan-64 and after stripping at Strawberry Hill, stored at Micheldever and scrapped by G Cohen Ltd, Morriston c.Aug-66. 12614 replaced by 6-PAN TSK 10041 (ex 3031) and unit reclassified as 4-COR(N).

3071	MBT 11174 damaged (*where?*) Jul-55 and temporarily replaced by 11175 (ex 3072) until Oct-55. TRS 12618 withdrawn 25-Jan-64 and after stripping at Strawberry Hill, stored at Hassocks and Micheldever thence Internal User as an office at Hither Green MPD May-65, eventually cut-up on site about 16-Sep-66. 12618 replaced by 6-PUL TSK 10044 (ex 3014). This was an original 6-PAN vehicle ex 3032. Unit reclassified as 4-COR(N).
3072	TRT 12613 damaged by fire Jun-54 and unit reduced to a three car until 12613 repaired and replaced in unit from 14-Jan-56. Unit out of use Jul-54 to Aug-54 and TFK 12244 used in 6-PUL 3007 at this time, and again out of use from Jul-55 to Oct-55 when MBT 11175 used in unit 3071. TRT 12613 now converted to a 36 seat cafeteria car with the former kitchen end unchanged and the dining saloon altered to a 5½ bay area with loose chairs at tables arranged two-aside each side of the central gangway with the odd ½ bay at the inner end of the coach, and unit reclassified as 4-BUF from 3-56 although it was non-standard in layout and seating capacity. The diagram No. of 12613 was amended to 2602 following rebuilding. [*See also 4-BUF section*].

PART 2 of this piece is already scheduled for Issue No 30 in April.

Portsmouth - Waterloo express approaching Raynes Park having been diverted due to engineering work, 29 October 1959.
J N Faulkner